Unfulfilled Union

To my parents

Unfulfilled Union

*Canadian Federalism and
National Unity*

Garth Stevenson

Canadian Controversies Series

Macmillan of Canada

110733R

Canadian Cataloguing in Publication Data

Stevenson, Garth, 1943–
    Unfulfilled union

(Canadian controversies series)

Includes index.
ISBN 0–7705–1787–0

1. Federal government–Canada.   2. Federal-provincial relations
(Canada).*   I. Title.   II. Series.

JL27.S72   321′.02′0971   C79–094503–7

Printed in Canada for
The Macmillan Company of Canada Limited
70 Bond Street
Toronto, Ontario
M5B 1X3

Contents

Books
in the
Series

Canadian Controversies Series

Canadian political commentators have adopted the full range of political styles, from cold detachment to partisan advocacy. The Canadian Controversies Series is disciplined by the idea that while political analysis must be based on sound descriptive and explanatory modes of thought, social scientists should not abnegate the role of evaluating political systems. Such evaluations require a conscious approach to the interrelationships between facts and values, empirical and normative considerations in politics.

Each theme in the series has been chosen to illustrate some basic principles of Canadian political life and to allow the respective authors freedom to develop normative positions on the related problems. It is hoped that the volumes will stimulate debate and advance public understanding of some of the major questions which confront the Canadian political system. By treating the enduring themes and problems in Canada, the authors will also illustrate the important contribution that social science can offer to politics in terms of facts, ideas, theories, and comparative frameworks within which meaningful controversy can take place. Creative political thought must not be divorced from the political fabric of a country but form an integral part of it.

ROBERT J. JACKSON
General Editor

Preface

A distinguished American political scientist once described Canada as the only country where one could buy a book about federalism at an airport, a remark that perhaps reveals more about the inadequate standard of airport services in his own country than it does about the state of Canadian political science. Yet despite, or perhaps because of, the volume of writing and commentary on the subject, the current Canadian debate about federalism strikes me as remarkably ill-informed. Moreover, the balance of articulate opinion has in the last decade shifted excessively in a direction that I can only regard as disastrous. Hence the present book.

Among those who contributed to the completion of the project, special mention must be made of Robert J. Jackson, the general editor of the series. I am afraid that I repaid him for his support rather badly by deserting the department of which he was chairman, but I trust he will regard the accelerated completion of the book as at least partial compensation.

Some of the ideas in the present volume were presented initially in a paper entitled "Federalism and the Political Economy of the Canadian State". Several persons contributed to my understanding of Canadian federalism by their comments on that paper, including Janine Brodie, Peter Leslie, Mary Beth Montcalm, Michael Oliver, Leo Panitch, Richard Simeon, Valerie Summers, Mel Watkins, and Reg Whitaker. Not all of them will agree with everything in this book, but their insights are gratefully acknowledged.

Margaret Woollard and Virgil Duff of Macmillan of Canada were continuously helpful, and I can recommend them to aspiring authors without reservation. Last but certainly not least, I would like to thank Monika Porritt for typing the manuscript on very short notice but with astonishing accuracy and speed.

GARTH STEVENSON
Edmonton, Alberta
November 1978

Unfulfilled Union

1   The Meaning of Federalism

I cannot think it would be statesmanlike ... to yield up the solid advantages obtained by the present union of the two Canadas. I could fancy if a dissolution were accomplished today, that ten years hence we would look back with astonishment at the utter imbecility of 1,300,000 Anglo-Saxons in Upper Canada and 300,000 in Lower Canada, frightened by some 700,000 Frenchmen into surrendering forever the noble St. Lawrence and all the fertile land it traverses. For one, Sir, I will never be a party to such a transaction — until every other remedy has failed.

GEORGE BROWN[1]

The optimal strategy for a neo-colonial transnational economy is precisely one in which the number of officially sovereign states is maximized and their average size and strength — i.e., their power effectively to impose the conditions under which foreign powers and foreign capital will have to operate — is minimized. Even in the 1920s, the real banana republics were small — say, Nicaragua rather than Colombia. And today it is pretty evident that the USA or Japan and their corporations would prefer to deal with Alberta rather than with Canada, Western Australia rather than the Australian Commonwealth, when it came to making economic terms.

ERIC HOBSBAWM[2]

During Canada's centennial celebrations in 1967, a national magazine invited its readers to participate in selecting the most typically Canadian joke. The winning entry proved to be a local version of the ancient elephant joke, which recounts how persons of various nationalities responded in different ways to the task of writing an essay on some aspect of the elephant. While the German wrote on the elephant as a military weapon, the Frenchman on the elephant's love life, and so forth, the punch line in the Canadian version records that the Canadian essayist's title was "The elephant: Does it fall under federal or provincial jurisdiction?"

Not only the outcome but the occasion of this contest testifies to the pervasiveness of federalism in Canadian life. The centennial which we celebrated in 1967, after all, was not really the centennial of Canada, not even the centennial of the Canadian state (which was founded in 1841), but only the centennial of Canadian federalism. In geo-political terms it was also the centennial of the date at which New Brunswick and Nova Scotia became part of Canada, but that event was not the first, the last, nor even the most important step in Canada's territorial expansion, although it may have paved the way for the greater expansion that followed.

Federalism, clearly, is for most Canadians inseparable from their image of their country, and this has probably never been more true than it is at present. Except among Quebec separatists, belief in the desirability of some kind of "federalism", however defined, seems to be virtually universal. If political-science students observed by the author over several years are in any way representative it appears that Canadians are completely unable to imagine their country as being other than federal, or as having any existence apart from federalism. If pressed to consider alternatives, they invariably assume that this must mean the dissolution of the federal tie and independence for each of the ten provinces.

While unusual and perhaps even unique by world standards, this obsession with federalism is by no means misguided. Federalism is undoubtedly, for better or for worse, a fundamental attribute of the way in which Canada conducts its public business, although the consequences of this fact, perhaps because it is taken so completely for granted, have received little systematic investigation. Interest groups and political parties are structured along federal lines, corresponding with the structures of government itself, as are educational institutions, the professions, and even the private sector of the economy. Statistical data are collected and organized in such a way as to highlight the boundaries between the provinces. Intergovernmental conferences have become a basic part of the political process, arguably more important than Parliament or the provincial legislatures.

These facts are not in dispute, although judgments as to their desirability may vary. They cannot be explained away, even by those who agree with John Porter that the obsession with federalism is an obstacle to creative politics and who dismiss the reputed socio-cultural differences between the various provinces as "hallowed nonsense".[3] Porter's point, however, is well taken when he argues that the attention given to federalism distracts attention from other types of issue, and may even be deliberately designed to do so. If politics is about who gets what, when, and how, Canadians are subtly but constantly encouraged to view these fundamental questions in jurisdictional or interprovincial terms. What does Quebec want? What does Alberta stand to lose? What is "Ottawa" taking from "the provinces" and what will they seek in return? Are we becoming more centralized or more decentralized? A few lonely critics, like Porter, have argued that these are completely meaningless questions, designed only to mystify the masses. In contrast, politicians, the media, and an increasing number of academics often go to the other extreme and give the impression that these are the only significant questions in Canadian political life. The reality lies somewhere between the two extremes. Questions about federalism are real and important, even if they may sometimes be posed in mystifying language, but they are not the only questions in our political life. So pervasive is federalism in our political life, however, that the more fundamental questions to which Porter and others have drawn attention cannot easily be considered or resolved outside of the federal context in which they occur.

DEFINING FEDERALISM

Despite their constant use by Canadians, and their frequent use in other countries, the word "federal" and its various derivatives are not lacking in ambiguity. Their history has been long and complex, and their polemical use, to prove a point or to lend respectability to a position, is neither a recent nor a uniquely Canadian phenomenon. Even those who are professionally concerned with the study of federalism have failed to agree on what it means, what is included, and what should be excluded. As we shall see almost any possible definition presents problems.

Certain words used in political discourse, words like "legislature", or "bureaucracy", or "election", are quite easily defined, for the fairly narrow and concrete phenomena to which they refer are easily recognized, whether or not one approves of them. Other words, such as "democracy", or "liberalism", or "socialism", pose greater problems because they are broader in scope and too intimately associated with past and present ideological controversies to be defined in a manner that satisfies everyone. Some would go so far as to argue that these words are no more than ideological symbols, devoid of real content and substance. Certainly their repeated use as ideological symbols has left them vulnerable to such accusations, however real and concrete they may seem to their respective devotees.

The word "federalism" perhaps belongs at least partially in this category, as the suffix "ism" would suggest. This fact might explain the difficulty of defining it. On the other hand only a few political thinkers — Pierre Elliott Trudeau would probably be one of them — have endowed the concept of federalism with the heavy load of symbolic attributes more normally attached to such words as democracy, liberalism, and socialism. It has thus seemed more plausible to treat federalism as a concrete, easily defined, and value-free concept like bureaucracy or legislative institutions. Yet somehow the effort to treat it this way never entirely succeeds. The concept of federalism seems to be a hybrid which shares some qualities of both categories of political concept.

In searching for definitions there are worse places to begin than the *Oxford English Dictionary*. The reader thereof will find "federal" defined as "of or pertaining to a covenant, compact or treaty" but with the cautionary note that this definition is obsolete. Persevering, one finds a further definition: "of or pertaining to or of the nature of that form of government in which two or more states constitute a political unity while remaining more or less independent with regard to their internal affairs." Apart from the question-begging "more or less", which neatly evades the essence of the problem, this definition is notable chiefly for the fact that the word "state" is applied to the "two or more" units which constitute the federal entity. This seems to distinguish federalism from other forms of decentralized government, since no one would confer the word "state" on a mere administrative district or municipality. Even this apparent precision, however, vanishes when one seeks in the same dictionary the meaning of "federation", for this is said to mean: "the formation of a political unity out of a number of separate states, provinces or colonies, so that each retains the management of its internal affairs." It appears that provinces or colonies, both of which may be something less than states, may suffice after all. How then to draw the line between federalism/federation and other forms of decentralized government? In this second definition a new and different basis of distinction has made its appearance, for it is clearly implied, if not explicitly stated, that the components of the federation, whether states, provinces, or colonies, must have previously enjoyed a separate existence.

Defining federalism in this way would seem to have the advantage that federal countries could be easily identified, but there are ambiguities here as well. The three Prairie provinces in Canada and a majority of the fifty states in the U.S.A. had no separate existence prior to the federal union; they were formed subsequently out of territories which the central government had acquired by purchase or conquest. Since it would be absurd to exclude Canada or the U.S.A. from any definition of federalism, the definition must be modified to specify that only some of the sub-national units need to have enjoyed a previously separate existence. A more serious difficulty arises in the case of India, which reorganized its internal boundaries several years after independence so as to abolish all the existing states and replace them with new ones. Some students of federalism refuse to consider India as a federation, but the majority would probably argue that it is one. One seems to be back at the point of departure. The states of India are "more or less" internally independent, and therefore India is federal, more or less. But how much more or less should the definition allow?

So far we have been preoccupied with distinguishing a federation from a non-federal or unitary state. However, a definition of federalism must also serve the purpose, which is even more essential in Canada's present circumstances, of distinguishing federalism from arrangements that should be disqualified for the opposite reason, because they are too decentralized. The European Community, for example, is not a federation, because the powers of the Commission at Brussels, and of the other Community institutions, are too insignificant in relation to the governments of the member countries. As was noted earlier, the use of the term "federal" with reference to a "covenant, compact or treaty" is now considered obsolete, although at one time the word was so used. The "sovereignty-association" proposed by the Parti Québécois, as well as other hypothetical arrangements that would drastically reduce the powers of the central government in Canada, must be excluded from any useful definition of federalism. They must be excluded not because they are undesirable (although the author happens to be of this opinion) but because to include them in a category that also includes the United States and the Federal Republic of Germany would make the category too heterogeneous to have any analytical usefulness.

This brings us to another problem of semantics, namely the distinction between a federation and a confederation. These closely related words were not at first clearly distinguished, and in Canada are still not, but in the rest of the world they have gradually acquired distinct meanings. Outside of Canada, "confederation" is a word used mainly by historians, and is most often used with reference to various arrangements among sovereign states, usually for purposes of mutual defence, that fall short of establishing a new state or a central government with meaningful power and authority. Perhaps the European Community, the North Atlantic Treaty Organization (NATO), and other such institutions are the closest contemporary equivalent of these early "confederations".

This conventional distinction between "federation" and "confederation" admittedly makes little etymological sense, but the distinction is clearly a meaningful one, however much Canadians might wish that different words had been employed.

In any event the distinction has been sanctified by long usage, particularly in the United States. The earliest "confederation" in the English-speaking world was the New England Confederation, which lasted from 1643 to 1648, a period for much of which England was too distracted by its own bourgeois revolution to provide much protection for its North American colonies. Threatened by the Indian tribes and the nearby colonies of other European powers, the New Englanders formed an alliance and established a commission of eight delegates, two from each colonial government, to decide collectively on questions of defence and external relations. Since these delegates had no authority apart from that of the colonial governments that appointed them, and since in practice it soon appeared that any one government could veto a decision by the commissioners, this confederation was more like a modern international organization than a modern federal state.[4]

In 1778, two years after the Declaration of Independence, the thirteen colonies formed a military alliance with rudimentary common institutions somewhat similar to those of the earlier New England Confederation. The agreement which brought this new arrangement into force was known as the Articles of Confederation, a circumstance that would lead subsequent generations of Americans to associate the word "confederation" with loose alliances of this type, while reserving the word "federal" for their present, more centralized, constitution. However, the Americans of the eighteenth century did not yet make this distinction. Instead, the word "federal" seems to have been used in the sense which the *Oxford English Dictionary* now regards as obsolete, to refer to the Articles of Confederation themselves. At the Philadelphia Convention of 1787, which drafted the present constitution of the United States, supporters of the "Virginia plan" on which that constitution is based used the term "federal" in that sense, and argued that a "merely federal" union, such as then existed, was inadequate to secure the objectives of "common defence, security of liberty, and general welfare". In its place they proposed to establish what they called a "national" government, with authority to impose its will on the states.[5]

A delegate from New York, where opposition to this idea seems to have been exceptionally strong, protested that the Virginia plan was unacceptable for precisely this reason:

> He was decidedly of opinion that the power of the Convention was restrained to amendments of a Federal nature, and having for their basis the Confederacy in being. . . . New York would never have concurred in sending Deputies to the Convention, if she had supposed the deliberations were to turn on a consolidation of the States, and a National Government.[6]

In response to such sentiments, the nationalists who wanted "a consolidation of the States" began to use the reassuring and familiar word "federal" with reference to their own plans, although they did not abandon its use with reference to the Articles of Confederation. This deliberate attempt to blur what was in fact a fundamental distinction can best be seen in the series of anonymous essays by which Alexander Hamilton, John Jay, and James Madison attempted to persuade the voters of New York to ratify the proposed new constitution. These essays, which still rank among the classics of political science, are themselves known as the Federalist Papers, although their purpose was to argue the inadequacy of "federalism" in its original sense. Once the union was achieved, the word "Federalist" was adopted as the name of the political party representing the mercantile and financial interests who wanted a strong central government and subordinate states. In fact Hamilton, the first leader of the Federalist party, had presented at the Philadelphia Convention a plan for a constitution even more centralized than the one that was finally adopted.[7] Some of Hamilton's ideas, although rejected by his own countrymen, were later to be incorporated in the British North America (BNA) Act of 1867.

As a result of these developments, the word "federal" and its derivatives became associated with a considerable degree of centralization, at least in the United States. The Swiss Confederation, which until 1848 was little more than a loose alliance of sovereign states, and the German Confederation, an even more nebulous organization established by the Congress of Vienna in 1815, helped to perpetuate the view that "confederation" referred to a compact that fell short of establishing a new central government. The Swiss, however, somewhat confused the issue by continuing to use the word "confederation" even after they had adopted a constitution that was "federal" in the American sense.

As far as Canada is concerned, one constitutional historian has speculated that the use of the term "confederation" to describe the proposed union of the British North American colonies had exactly the same purpose as the adoption of the word "federal" by proponents of the Virginia plan after 1787. In both cases, according to this view, a word normally associated with the absence of a strong central government was deliberately misused by those who in fact intended to create one in an effort to confuse those who might find such a project alarming.[8] John A. Macdonald was certainly using an idiosyncratic definition in 1861, when he stated that "the true principle of a Confederation" meant a system in which all the powers not specifically assigned to the provinces were given to the central government, unlike the American constitution whose tenth amendment, adopted in 1791, said precisely the reverse.[9] A. A. Dorion, the leading French Canadian opponent of "Confederation", was more correct, or at least more conventional, a few years later when he defined "a real confederation" as "giving the largest powers to the local governments and merely a delegated authority to the general government".[10] However, Macdonald won and Dorion lost, so that Macdonald's usage of the term has acquired semi-official status in Canada, however bizarre it may seem to Americans. Dorion's definition, recently revived by René Lévesque, may be historically justified but has become somewhat irrelevant, since none of the "confederations" that Dorion had in mind are still in existence, nor have any new ones under that name been established. Both Canada and Switzerland, however, use the word "confederation" for what is actually a federal union in the modern American sense.

The terminological confusion perpetuated by the originators of modern federalism in both Canada and the United States continues to blur the distinction between real federalism, as represented by the actual constitutions of both countries, and the more primitive types of arrangement of which the New

England Confederation is one example. True federalism, which by definition requires a powerful central government independent of the governments of the units which comprise it, is a relatively recent historical phenomenon, and a relatively unusual one. The United States was the first country to adopt federalism in this sense, and the delegates to the Philadelphia Convention deserve the credit for inventing it. On the other hand loose alliances of sovereign entities, which can vaguely be described as "federal" in the older sense, have existed on countless occasions in different cultural and historical contexts.

Unfortunately the distinction is not always made, and general discussions of federalism frequently wander far afield in search of its reputed progenitors. Since compacts, leagues, and alliances of various kinds are a ubiquitous phenomenon in human history, the scope for imaginative histories of "the federal idea" is almost unlimited. At a time when classical civilization was much admired, the various alliances of city-states in ancient Greece were often cited as examples of early federalism. Later, at a time when English-speaking people referred to themselves without irony as "Anglo-Saxons", it was declared that "federalism" had been invented by the primitive Germanic tribes, a conclusion that appeared plausible since modern federalism existed both in the English-speaking world and in central Europe. More recently Daniel Elazar, an American political scientist of Jewish descent, has attributed the invention of federalism to the twelve tribes of Israel at the time of Moses.[11] An equally strong candidate for the honour of having invented "federalism" — since they were presumably unaware that the Jews had invented it already — would be the Five Nations of the Iroquois Indians, whose defensive alliance flourished in what is now the northern part of New York State long before the arrival of European settlers. A much more durable but similar alliance was the original Swiss Confederation, which dates from 1291, even though its importance was dismissed by Madison and Hamilton in Federalist Paper number nineteen on the grounds that it "scarcely amounts to a confederacy".[12] As noted previously, the modern Swiss federal state, although retaining the same name, was not founded until 1848.

All of these examples, and countless others that could be

cited, are basically irrelevant to the study of federalism in the modern sense of the term. If one confines the term "federation" to unions of previously separate states, colonies, or provinces which created a new state, even though they retained some degree of local autonomy for the pre-existing entities, the list becomes much shorter. The United States was the first, and for a long time the unique, example of such a federal union. Other federations have proliferated only since the middle of the nineteenth century, as will be seen later in this chapter, a period that corresponds with the emergence of the modern liberal "nation-state" as an almost universal phenomenon.

Although it is relatively easy to determine what federalism is not, the many writers on the subject have failed to agree on a satisfactory definition of what it is, even though almost every one of them has attempted to produce a definition. The most frequently used definitions, such as those used by K. C. Wheare, Daniel Elazar, W. H. Riker and Geoffrey Sawer, emphasize institutional and legal criteria: two levels of government, each independent of the other; a written constitution specifying the jurisdiction of each; judicial review of legislation as a means of maintaining the jurisdictional boundaries; the requirement that each level of government have a direct relationship with the people; and so forth. Political scientists like Elazar and Riker tend to interpret these criteria rather broadly, while lawyers like Wheare and Sawer are more inclined to exclude doubtful cases. Wheare, although born in Australia and teaching in England, included as federal constitutions only those which closely resembled the constitution of the United States, with the result that only Australia and Switzerland passed the test. He admitted, however, that Canada was a federal state in practice, even though certain features of the British North America Act departed from the federal norm.[13]

Apart from the fact that they tell us little about how political systems really operate, these formal criteria are so restrictive that their applicability to even the most federal of states can be questioned. Federal legislation in Switzerland is not subject to judicial review, provincial statutes in Canada can be disallowed, and the West German federal government is not completely independent of the *land* governments since the *länder* control the upper house of the federal parliament. One political scientist, Michael Reagan, has even questioned whether the United States qualifies as a federation by these criteria, since he considers that in practice there is no field reserved to the states in which Congress is unable to legislate.[14]

In reaction against the rigidity and formality of these traditional criteria, writers on federalism began in the 1950s to explore alternative approaches to its definition. W. S. Livingston abandoned institutional criteria almost entirely and developed the concept of a "federal society", which he defined as any society in which economic, religious, racial, or historical diversities are territorially grouped. A formally unitary state in which political practices and conventions protected such diversities, such as the United Kingdom, should be considered to have some federal characteristics. Rufus Davis went a step further, questioning whether any "federal principle" could really be discovered to distinguish federal from non-federal states; the difference was merely one of degree. Carl Friedrich defined federalism not as a static situation but as a process, the process by which a number of separate political communities were gradually integrated.[15]

While political scientists shifted their attention from formal institutions to political processes and behaviour, economists took an entirely different approach to defining federalism. Wallace Oates, in his book entitled *Fiscal Federalism,* wrote that federalism existed in any state where the public sector was decentralized, so that some decisions about taxing and spending were made by smaller territorial subdivisions in response to demands originating within themselves.[16] From an economist's perspective it matters little whether such decentralization is protected by constitutional guarantees or whether it can be unilaterally revoked by the central government. At least in the short term, the economic consequences are the same in either case. While useful for its own purpose, this definition is so broad that hardly any state, at least in the industrialized world, could avoid being classified as federal.

It is probably rash to attempt yet another definition of federalism when so many authorities have failed to agree on one that is totally satisfactory. Possibly no single definition of so elusive and controversial a concept could be satisfactory for all purposes. Nonetheless, the definition below is offered in the belief that it meets three essential criteria for a definition of federalism: (1) the definition should not be unduly restrictive; (2) it should serve to distinguish a federal state both from a unitary state and from looser forms of association; and (3) it should emphasize the political aspects of federalism.

With these criteria in mind, federalism will be defined as follows. It is a political system in which most or all of the structural elements of the state (executive, legislature, bureaucracy, judiciary, army or police, and machinery for levying taxation) are duplicated at two levels, with both sets of structures exercising effective control over the same territory and population. Furthermore, neither set of structures (or level of government) should be able to abolish the other's jurisdiction over the territory and population which both have in common. As a corollary of this, relations between the two levels of government will tend to be characterized by bargaining, since neither level can fully impose its will on the other.

The condition that neither level of government should be able to abolish the other's jurisdiction effectively distinguishes federalism both from a unitary state and from looser forms of association. In a unitary state there may be some decentralization for administrative and even legislative purposes, but the central government can take back the power it has delegated to the lower levels of government or can even abolish them, as the British Parliament abolished the Parliament of Northern Ireland. In an alliance, league, or common market, on the other hand, the member states can withdraw or secede, an action which clearly prevents the central institutions, such as they are, from exercising any jurisdiction over their territories or populations. If the definition is a valid one, it follows that in a true federation the provinces or states have no right to secede and (to adopt one of Canada's contemporary buzzwords) no right of self-determination. If such a right existed before, they surrendered it when they entered the federal union.

A somewhat legalistic way of expressing these characteristics of federalism is to say that the provinces or states are not sovereign entities, but at the same time that the central government does not possess full and complete sovereignty either, since it lacks the power to abolish the other level of government. These facts may be represented symbolically by a written constitution, judicial review, elaborate procedures for amendment, and statements to the effect that sovereignty resides in "the people" (as in the United States) or "the Crown" (as in Canada). These symbolic aspects of federalism are not unimportant, but their importance exists only because they metaphorically represent, and may provide ideological justification for, real facts concerning the distribution of political power.

As to which countries are federal by this (or any other) definition, opinions will vary. Any effort to classify a particular country should be based on observation of how its political institutions actually operate. In some countries military *coups* and other changes of regime have occurred so frequently that one cannot say what is their "normal" or usual pattern of political activity. Others have simply not been studied enough for reliable data to be available. There is no doubt however that the few countries which are invariably included on any list of federations — and Canada is unquestionably one of these — would qualify as federations under this definition. On the other hand, countries such as the United Kingdom, which may have characteristics in common with at least some of the federations, would not.

WHY FEDERALISM OCCURS

The origins of American federalism have been discussed above, while those of Canadian federalism will be considered in more detail in the next chapter. It would be unduly parochial, however, not to make a few comments about the origins of Swiss and German federalism. Although they differ in many respects, an important similarity is the fact that in both cases a looser, non-federal, association between sovereign states was transformed into a true federation as a result of war. In Switzerland the conservative Catholic cantons launched the Sonderbund war of 1847 to protect themselves against the emerging threat of bourgeois liberalism. Their defeat enabled the more progressive cantons to impose a federal constitution on the American model and establish a modern liberal state in place of the outmoded "confederation". In the German case the defeat of Austria by Prussia in the war of 1866 led to the dissolution of the loose "confederation" which had been established in 1815 as the successor to the old Holy Roman Empire. With Austria now excluded from further involvement in German affairs, a Prussian-dominated federation was established in northern Germany in 1867. The southern states entered it voluntarily in 1870, at the end of which year it adopted the title of "German Empire".[17] Some form of German federalism has existed ever since, except during Hitler's dictatorship and for a few years after his defeat.

In the twentieth century federal unions took place in Australia (1901), the U.S.S.R. (1924), Malaya (1948), Rhodesia and Nyasaland (1953), the West Indies (1958), and Cameroun (1961). In four of these six cases the federating units were colonies of the British Empire, although in the Australian case the initiative for federation was taken entirely by the Australians themselves. Soviet federalism permitted the new Russian republic to reunite with most of the outlying territories of the old empire, which had been temporarily detached from Russia during the civil war. The Federal Republic of Cameroun united two territories which had been held under United Nations trusteeship by Britain and France respectively. In the early 1960s Malaya changed its name to Malaysia when it absorbed a number of other British colonies. The Rhodesia and Nyasaland and West Indian federations disintegrated at about the same time, with some of their components becoming independent and others remaining under British rule.

A number of other countries are frequently referred to as federal, although it cannot be said, at least without serious qualification, that they resulted from a union of previously separate entities. Argentina, Brazil, Mexico, and Venezuela all adopted "federal" constitutions in the nineteenth century, possibly in imitation of the United States. Most external observers, however, are sceptical about Latin American federalism, on the grounds that the component states do not retain any meaningful degree of autonomy. This is possibly unfair to Brazil, at least prior to the military *coup* of 1964, but seems to be an accurate judgment of the others.

The case of India has already been mentioned in passing. The British ruled most of that country, including the present Pakistan and Bangladesh, as a unitary colony from 1857 until 1935. In the latter year the Government of India Act established provincial legislatures, and thus a sort of quasi-federalism somewhat similar to the Latin American type. In 1947 the British handed over their authority to two new states, India and Pakistan, which between them soon absorbed the various princely states that had never been under direct British rule. Both successor states have adopted constitutions that divide legislative powers between two levels of government, and the sub-national governments, at least in India, enjoy considerable autonomy. As noted previously, however, the central government in India was able to "reorganize" the boundaries of the component states soon after independence, an event that would surely be unthinkable in such genuinely federal countries as Canada, Switzerland, or the United States. It is also interesting that the Supreme Court of India, in an important case upholding the central government's power to expropriate mineral resources belonging to the states, declared flatly that India was a decentralized unitary state rather than a federal one.[18]

The case of Nigeria is very similar. Although they had previously ruled it as a unitary state, the British endowed it with the dubious blessing of a "federal" constitution in 1954. It remained a federation after gaining its independence in 1960, but the federal constitution was suspended by the military regime during the ultimately successful civil war against the separatists in the south-eastern province, who attempted with some foreign assistance to establish an independent "Biafra". Post-war Nigeria, however, has re-established sub-national state governments, even though the boundaries of the new states bear no relation to the old.

Three European cases remain to be considered. Austria adopted a federal constitution in 1922, Yugoslavia in 1946, and Czechoslovakia in 1968. The Yugoslavian constitution of 1946 has since been replaced by a new one of almost unbelievable complexity, but its federal features have if anything been enhanced. All three countries are in a sense the successors of the Habsburg Empire which dissolved in 1918, and they share the common characteristic that their internal boundaries and component units have a longer history as distinct entities than the countries themselves. On these grounds, and in terms of the real autonomy enjoyed by the sub-national governments, Austria and Yugoslavia have at least as good a claim to be considered "federal" as India and Pakistan, even though they are not really unions of previously independent entities. The case of Czechoslovakia is more dubious.

Many students of federalism, however, refuse to recognize as a federation any state that did not result from a union of previously separate entities which retained their identities after union. As a result, efforts to generalize about the reasons why federations come into existence tend to ignore the ambiguous cases or those in which the sub-national governments were established by devolution of power from the centre. K. C. Wheare lists the conditions leading to federal union as follows: the need for common defence, desire for independence from foreign powers, desire to gain economic benefits, some previous political association, similar political institutions, geographical closeness, similar social conditions, and the existence of political elites interested in unification.[19] No previous or subsequent writer on federalism has really added anything to this list.

Despite its completeness, or perhaps because of it, Wheare's list of conditions is not very informative. The first two conditions are almost indistinguishable, the last would seem to be present by definition, and several of the others are so vague as to be almost useless. Wheare does not present anything that can be called a theory of federal unification.

The most interesting theoretical question about the origins of federal unions is whether military insecurity or anticipated economic benefits is the more important motive, or whether in fact both must be present. It is also conceivable that a security motive might be more important in some cases and an economic motive in others.

The case for the pre-eminence of economic motives was made most memorably by Charles Beard in his classic study: *An Economic Interpretation of the Constitution of the United States*.[20] Beard suggested that the move to adopt the present constitution was led by merchant capitalists and that the constitution itself was carefully drafted to protect their economic interests. For Beard, American politics after the revolutionary war were dominated by the conflict between this class and the more numerous but less influential farmers who, in his view, mainly opposed the constitution. The merchants wanted a strong central government to repress further revolutionary outbreaks by agrarian radicals (such as Massachusetts had experienced in 1786–87), to prevent the repudiation of debts and the printing of paper money, and to protect their commerce on the high seas. The adoption of the constitution marked the swing of the revolutionary pendulum back to the right and the restoration of "order".

Not all economic interpretations of federalism emphasize class conflict, as Beard does. The kind of economic motives that Wheare seems to have in mind are those emphasized by more conventional American historians, as well as their Canadian and Australian counterparts: larger markets, the removal of tariff barriers, penetration of the western hinterlands, and so forth. Marxist historians of course would view even these types of motive as reflecting the interests of ruling classes, and perhaps as leading to conflict with other classes that opposed them. Even where there was such opposition, however, the establishment of a federal state might not in some circumstances be necessary to achieve these objectives. Western European capitalists seem to be achieving quite similar objectives through the very limited integrative arrangements represented by the European Community, which falls far short of establishing federalism.

Security motives for federal union are emphasized by William H. Riker, who views federalism as a "bargain" by which political elites in the states or provinces agree to sacrifice some but not all of their autonomy in return for protection against an external threat or, more rarely, a share in the benefits of military expansion and conquest. The bargain is usually initiated by a relatively large and powerful entity (Virginia, the Province of Canada, or Bismarck's Prussia) and accepted by smaller states or provinces, which have more to lose because they will have relatively little influence within a larger union, but more to gain because they could not hope to attain security, let alone expansion, by themselves.[21]

Obvious external threats to security were certainly present at the time of union in some federations, such as Switzerland, Bismarck's Germany, the U.S.S.R., and Pakistan. The importance of a security motive in the Canadian case will be discussed in the next chapter. Security motives are somewhat harder to discern in some other cases, such as Australia, postwar West Germany, and Cameroun, but may not have been entirely absent.

It may be that no single factor can explain every instance of the formation of a federal union, and even in a particular case a variety of factors may have contributed. The author of a recent book on federalism, R. D. Dikshit, adopts both of these assumptions. Dikshit's purpose is to explain not only why federal unions take place, but also why they differ in the extent of the powers conferred on the central government, and why some federal unions are more durable and successful than others. Dikshit distinguishes factors leading to union from factors leading to the retention of some degree of regional autonomy. A preponderance of the first will lead to the formation of a unitary state, while a preponderance of the second will prevent any union at all from taking place. Only a balance between the two will lead to federalism, and only if the balance is maintained will federalism survive.[22]

Dikshit's factors leading to union are essentially the same as K. C. Wheare's, although he differs from Wheare in including a common language, culture, and religion as one of his conditions. His factors conducive to the maintenance of regional autonomy are essentially the reverse of the factors leading to union, for example regionally grouped cultural diversity rather than cultural homogeneity, competitive economies with conflicting interests rather than the expectation of economic benefits from union, and so forth. Federal union does not demand that all of the factors in either category be present, for there are several possible combinations that will bring it about, although the precise nature of the new federal state will vary accordingly. West Germany is a very centralized federation, according to Dikshit, because most of the factors leading to union were present in 1949, while the factors conducive to maintaining regional autonomy were virtually absent. Only the absence of a military threat (since the country was effectively protected by the United States) prevented a centralized unitary state from emerging instead of a federation. On the other hand, Pakistan at the time of its formation had practically all of the conditions which lead to the maintenance of regional autonomy, while the military threat from India was the only factor that contributed to union. The result was a weak federation that could not prevent the secession of its largest unit in the civil war of 1971.

EVALUATING FEDERALISM

It was mentioned earlier that federalism is not a value-free concept. Like other "isms", it inspires strong sentiments both favourable and unfavourable, although most Canadians have found it so difficult to imagine alternatives to federalism that, except recently in Quebec, they have not considered it worthwhile to evaluate something that seems to be their inevitable fate. Since a unitary Canadian state has seemed beyond the realm of possibility, Canadian concepts of federalism have differed in many respects, but have resembled one another in taking federalism itself for granted.

Elsewhere this has been less true, and different views have been expressed concerning the desirability of a federal, as opposed to a unitary, state. Among the more strikingly unfavourable assessments was that of former Nigerian Prime Minister Sir Abubaker Balewa, who at his last meeting with Harold Wilson said to the latter: "You are fortunate. One thing only I wish for you, that you never have to become Prime Minister of a federal and divided country."[23]

Since he was assassinated four days after making this remark, and since his death proved to be the opening event in the Nigerian civil war, Balewa's pessimism was possibly justified. Others have expressed, although in less memorable circumstances, his view that federations are characterized by disorder, conflict, and political bickering, which may be the less attractive side of the intergovernmental bargaining that is, by our definition, an almost inevitable aspect of federal politics. Defenders of federalism, on the other hand, would argue that regional and cultural conflicts are obviously not caused by federalism, since they exist in unitary states like Ethiopia, Spain, or the United Kingdom.

Another widely used argument against federalism was presented almost a century ago by A.V. Dicey, an English writer on constitutional law. Dicey believed that federal regimes were characteristically weak, legalistic, and conservative. A federal constitution subjected the state to legal restraints that prevented it from acting effectively, in contrast to the British system under which Parliament was free to adopt any legislation that seemed appropriate.[24] Governments in federations tended to be cautious and relatively inactive, with little capacity for innovation. Federalism also tended to increase the influence of judges, who defined the boundaries of each government's jurisdiction, and of lawyers, whose arcane skills were needed to operate effectively in such a political environment.

Radicals and conservatives both would tend to agree today that Dicey's preference for a "strong" state was based on a rather naive confidence that the unrestrained state would act benignly. On the other hand, only an anarchist would argue that states have never done so, and Dicey's view of federalism finds some apparent support in the experience of both Canada and the United States. Both countries have lagged behind the rest of the industrialized world in implementing economic and social reforms, including those that have ceased to be controversial elsewhere. In both countries the political arena is dominated by lawyers to a remarkable and unwholesome extent. On the other hand, one need not attribute these faults to federalism. Other factors, such as the political weakness of the working class, probably offer more convincing explanations.

The admirers of federalism have not lacked arguments of their own since the middle of the eighteenth century, when Montesquieu published his *De l'esprit des lois*. It is not entirely clear what Montesquieu meant by federalism, and no state that we would call federal existed in his lifetime, but his views greatly influenced the authors of the American constitution. As well as having originated the notion of "the separation of powers", Montesquieu argued that a federal republic was a means of combining the freedom possible in a small state with the security against external threats that was only possible in a large one.[25]

Since in the thermonuclear era it is doubtful whether any state can guarantee security, a modern variation on Montesquieu's view might be that federalism combines the economic advantages of large size with the possibilities for self-government that exist in a smaller political community. A non-federalist could argue that neither part of this proposition is fully supported by experience. The prosperity of Norway, Switzerland, Singapore, and Kuwait suggests that size is not always an economic advantage. On the other hand the reputed benefits of grass-roots democracy and freedom in a "small" sub-national political system may really exist in the Swiss canton of Appenzell-Inner-Rhodes but bear no discernible relation to the facts of political life in Quebec, Ontario, New York, or California, all of which are larger than many nation-states.

Another argument sometimes heard in support of federalism is really the converse of Dicey's argument against it. According to this view, a "weak" state whose power is divided between two sets of authorities and restrained by legal restrictions is safer than a "strong" and vigorous state, because it is less likely to be oppressive. Dispersed and divided power is less dangerous than concentrated power, and the cumbersome decision-making procedures in a federal state make it less likely that unpredictable eruptions of popular sentiment will be reflected in public policy. Even if government at one level tries to be oppressive, government at the other level, as well as the judiciary, will prevent it from doing too much harm. This is essentially Madison's argument in the celebrated number ten of the Federalist Papers, and it recurs in several of the other papers as well. It was also a favourite argument of American conservatives during Franklin Roosevelt's New Deal and of Australian conservatives during the Labor government of Gough Whitlam. When subjected to critical examination, this argument for federalism looks remarkably like an ideological facade for vested economic interests.

A somewhat different but related argument for federalism is that it protects minorities and enables cultural, linguistic, religious, and ideological diversity to flourish. A prominent supporter of this perspective is Pierre Elliott Trudeau, whose well-known but often-misunderstood hostility to "nationalism" is really no more than the view that the state should not be intolerant of diversity and should not be identified with any ethnic or cultural group. In a federal state, he would argue, this is less likely to happen.

Several examples can certainly be cited of diversities protected by federalism. Multilingualism in Switzerland provides an obvious example. West German states and Canadian provinces have adopted a variety of solutions to the difficult problem of the relationship between Roman Catholic and public education. Socialists in pre-war Vienna and the CCF-NDP in Saskatchewan achieved important reforms that would not have been possible at the national level. The more progressive American and Australian states extended the vote to women and abolished capital punishment long before there was nation-wide support for these innovations.

None the less, in certain respects this optimistic view of federalism is not fully supported by experience. Federalism may protect those minorities which happen to comprise a majority within one of the provinces or states, but it protects them precisely by allowing them to act as majorities, which means that they in turn can oppress the sub-minorities under their jurisdiction. Federalism has ensured the survival of the French language in Canada, but it has been of no benefit to Chinese in British Columbia, Hutterites in Alberta, or Jehovah's Witnesses in Quebec. All of these groups were unpopular at various times, and the provincial governments were more responsive to the hostile sentiments directed against these minorities than was the more remote central government. Had Canada been a unitary state, these groups might have benefited. The history of blacks in the American South and of Australian aborigines in the state of Queensland supports a similar conclusion.

One is tempted to conclude that both the arguments against federalism and the arguments in its favour can be as easily refuted as supported. Franz Neumann, in his essay "On the Theory of the Federal State", concluded that federalism might be good, bad, or indifferent, depending on the circumstances, and that it was impossible to evaluate federalism in general.[26] W. H. Riker, in his book on federalism, stated that each particular case of federalism had to be examined separately to determine the balance sheet of costs and benefits. Attempting to perform this exercise himself, although in a rather superficial manner, he decided that federalism had benefited francophones in Canada, white racists in the United States, and business interests in Australia.[27] In a later essay, however, he concluded rather inconsistently that federalism really made no difference in terms of policy outcomes, a statement which he attempted to support by arguing that federal Australia was little different from unitary New Zealand.[28] From this he reached the further conclusion, which readers of this volume may be unhappy to hear, that the study of federalism was a waste of time!

While it is hoped that Riker was incorrect in reaching this conclusion, his earlier view that each case of federalism should be examined individually on its own merits is one with which the present writer would concur. In succeeding chapters of this volume attention will be focused exclusively on Canadian federalism, beginning in the next chapter with an account of its origins and purposes, and of the constitutional document in which those purposes were expressed. Chapter 3 discusses how Canadians (or at least the articulate minority of them) have viewed their federal system over the years. Chapter 4 seeks to explain why the provincial level of government has become so much more powerful and important than the Fathers of Confederation intended. Chapter 5 looks at some of the consequences of this fact for Canadian unity; Chapter 6 considers the distribution of revenues between the two levels of government; and Chapter 7 deals with conditional grants and the spending power of Parliament. Chapter 8 discusses methods of resolving intergovernmental conflicts and Chapter 9 is devoted to constitutional amendment, including proposals for amendment that have not been carried out. Chapter 10 concludes the book by examining the current problems and prospects of the Canadian federal system.

NOTES

1. Speech at Brampton in 1855, quoted in J. M. S. Careless, *Brown of the Globe,* Vol. I: *The Voice of Upper Canada 1818–1859* (Toronto: Macmillan, 1959), pp. 206–07.
2. "Some reflections on 'The Break-up of Britain'", *New Left Review,* no. 105 (September–October 1977), p. 8.
3. John Porter, *The Vertical Mosaic: An Analysis of Social Class and Power in Canada* (Toronto: University of Toronto Press, 1965), p. 382.
4. W. H. Bennett, *American Theories of Federalism* (University of Alabama Press, 1964), pp. 179–95.
5. James Madison, *Journal of the Federal Convention* (Freeport, New York: Books for Libraries Press, 1970), pp. 73–74.
6. Ibid., pp. 167–68.
7. Ibid., pp. 185–87.
8. W. P. M. Kennedy, *The Constitution of Canada* (London: Oxford University Press, 1922), pp. 400–05.
9. Joseph Pope, *Correspondence of Sir John Macdonald* (Toronto: Oxford University Press, 1921), p. 11.
10. Canada, Legislature, *Parliamentary Debates on the Subject of the Confederation of the British North American Provinces* (Quebec, 1865), p. 250.
11. Daniel Elazar, *The Principles and Practices of Federalism: A Comparative Historical Approach,* Working paper no. 8 (Philadelphia: Center for the Study of Federalism, n.d.).
12. Clinton Rossiter, ed., *The Federalist Papers* (New York: Mentor Books, 1961) pp. 132–33.
13. K. C. Wheare, *Federal Government,* 4th ed. (New York: Oxford University Press, 1964), pp. 18–20.
14. Michael Reagan, *The New Federalism* (New York: Oxford University Press, 1972), pp. 10–11.
15. W. S. Livingston, "A Note on the Nature of Federalism", and Rufus Davis, "The Federal Principle Reconsidered", both reprinted in A. Wildavsky, ed., *American Federalism in Perspective* (Boston: Little, Brown, 1967); Carl Friedrich, *Trends of Federalism in Theory and Practice* (New York: Praeger, 1968).
16. Wallace E. Oates, *Fiscal Federalism* (New York: Harcourt, Brace, Jovanovich, 1972), p. 17.
17. For a fuller account, see Burt Estes Howard, *The German Empire* (New York: Macmillan, 1913), pp. 1–18.
18. Asok Chanda, *Federalism in India: A Study of Union-State Relations* (London: Allen and Unwin, 1965), pp. 111–18.
19. Wheare, *Federal Government,* p. 37.
20. Charles Beard, *An Economic Interpretation of the Constitution of the United States,* 3rd ed. (New York: Free Press, 1965). The book was first published in 1913.

21. W. H. Riker, *Federalism: Origin, Operation, Significance* (Boston: Little, Brown, 1964), pp. 12–13.
22. R. D. Dikshit, *The Political Geography of Federalism* (New Delhi: Macmillan, 1975), pp. 226–33.
23. Harold Wilson, *The Labour Government, 1964–70* (Harmondsworth, Middlesex: Penguin Books, 1974), p. 256.
24. A. V. Dicey, *Introduction to the Study of the Law of the Constitution,* 10th ed. (London: Macmillan, 1961), pp. 138–80.
25. Montesquieu, *De l'esprit des lois,* Vol. I (Paris: Garnier, 1973), pp. 141–44.
26. "On the Theory of the Federal State", in Franz Neumann, *The Democratic and the Authoritarian State* (Glencoe: Free Press, 1957).
27. Riker, *Federalism,* pp. 151–55.
28. W. H. Riker, "Six Books in search of a subject, or does federalism exist and does it matter?" *Comparative Politics,* II (1968-69): 135–46.

2   Origins and Objectives of Confederation

The unification of the British North American colonies in 1867 was part of a general pattern of events that saw the reconstruction of existing states and the establishment of new ones in many parts of the world. The unification of Italy had begun a few years earlier and was completed by the end of the decade. Bismarck's North German Confederation came into existence on the very same day as the new British Dominion, and in the same year that the Austrian Habsburg Empire was reorganized into an Austro-Hungarian Dual Monarchy. In the following year the Meiji restoration began the transformation of Japan into a modern industrial state. While these events occurred overseas, the most important and the most painful of the decade's upheavals took place in immediate proximity to British North America, and had a direct impact upon it. The American Civil War established, at a cost of 700,000 lives, the domination of industrial capital in the United States. In the process it permanently resolved the ambiguity that had persisted in American federalism by indicating clearly that the states were not sovereign entities in a loose alliance but parts of a single nation. Although this view had been eloquently stated by the great Federalist John Marshall, who was Chief Justice of the United States from 1801 until 1835, it was only after the civil war that it became universally accepted.

All of these events reflected the impact of the industrial revolution and of the enhanced international competition for markets and raw materials that it produced. Their effect was further to stimulate the forces of industrialization and economic growth by removing barriers to the flow of commodities and capital at the same time as they enhanced the ability of the various states to promote the accumulation of capital and to defend themselves against one another. In part the events took place simultaneously because similar circumstances were at work in each of the countries concerned, while in part they directly affected one another. As the reorganization of Austria was in part a response to that of Germany, so the reorganization of British North America was in part a response to that of the United States, while Japan was inspired to modernize itself largely by the growing threat which it faced from the major Western powers.

The event we call "Confederation" arose from a convergence of internal and external circumstances, so that probably no single-factor explanation can account for it. Its complexity is enhanced by the fact that it simultaneously did three things, none of which would have been possible without the others. It reorganized the internal government of "Canada" in the pre-confederation sense of Ontario and Quebec, it united this entity with New Brunswick and Nova Scotia, and it provided for the expansion of the federalized state westwards to the Pacific. In the process of doing so it paved the way for economic development and ended a potentially dangerous power vacuum in the northern part of North America. Those who argue today that Confederation can be undone without reversing all of its consequences should perhaps be required to put forward more impressive arguments than they have managed to produce so far.

The internal difficulties of the Province of Canada were among the proximate causes of Confederation. That province had been established in 1841, on the recommendation of Lord Durham's report, by uniting the two colonies of Lower and Upper Canada. The distinction between the civil law of the lower province and the common law of the upper one had been retained after union. When a brief attempt to impose unilingualism, another of Durham's recommendations, had proved unworkable, the status of the French language had been recognized after a few years. At about the same time the principle had been established that the government was dependent on the confidence and support of the elected lower house of the legislature.

In spite of these developments, the effort to govern both

English-speaking and French-speaking Canadians within a unitary, or at least quasi-unitary, state proved difficult, and discontent increased on both sides, despite repeated efforts to make the arrangement workable. From about 1849 onwards a rather distinctive system of inter-cultural elite accommodation had developed. Cabinets were constructed to include representatives of both cultural communities, although there was never a requirement that the cabinet be supported by a "double majority" including majorities of the parliamentarians from each section. Governments were headed by two party leaders from the two sections, rather than a single Prime Minister, and there were separate attorneys general for the two sections in consequence of the different legal systems. Some of the legislation adopted by the provincial Parliament applied only to one of the sections, with parallel but distinct legislation applying to the other. Thus matters such as education and municipal affairs could be dealt with differently in the two halves of the province. This system was quite unique, and it is somewhat misleading to describe it as embodying "the federal concept", a position that has been taken by one historian.[1] It did bear some resemblance to arrangements, then and later, between England and Scotland, an analogy which John A. Macdonald pointed out on at least one occasion.[2]

While this was an ingenious solution, it seems that it did not work particularly well. Each section of the province harboured the belief that it was being constrained and dictated to by the other. Since they were of roughly equal size and had equal representation in the Parliament, such a belief was equally plausible on both sides. Legislation could be adopted pertaining to either section without the support of a majority of its representatives. The equal representation of the two sections was discovered by residents of the western half to be an intolerable affront to liberal principles once the western half became the more populous, although the injustice of it had somehow managed to escape their notice when they were a minority of the total population. Ethnic and religious antagonisms were exacerbated by many of the issues which came before the legislature, and were reinforced by divergences of economic interest between the sections. Farmers and manufacturers in the western part of the province, like their counterparts in the larger western hinterland of a later date, resented the commercial hegemony of Montreal and the measures that were taken with the aim of funnelling their commerce through that city.

For all of these reasons it became increasingly difficult to construct governments that could retain for long the confidence of the lower house. By about 1857 things were widely believed to be approaching an *impasse,* and a variety of changes in the existing constitution began to be proposed as possible solutions. These included the establishment of representation by population, the transformation of the unitary state into a federal union of the two sections, complete separation between the two, as had existed for half a century before 1841, and even a formal requirement that the government be supported by a double majority. Each of these solutions had a fatal flaw: "rep by pop" would leave the mainly French-speaking lower section at the mercy of the more populous upper one; a federation with only two parts would make each of the two provincial governments in practice more powerful than the central one; separation would destroy the economic and commercial unity of the St. Lawrence system; and the double majority requirement might make the formation of any government impossible.

Since neither the status quo nor any of these alternatives was widely acceptable, the territorial expansion of Canada began to be viewed as a possible means of escape from its difficulties, although this would probably not have been considered had not economic motives, which will be considered subsequently, pointed in the same direction. Expansion might be either eastwards, to include the other British colonies on the Atlantic seaboard, or westwards, to absorb the inland fur-trading empire of the Hudson's Bay Company, with each half of the province of Canada tending to prefer the alternative that corresponded to its own point of the compass. Expansion in both directions at once might satisfy both sections, might permit federalism (a separate government for each section with a central government over both) while avoiding the dangers of a double-headed monstrosity, and might enable French-speaking Canadians to accept representation by population in the lower house at the same time as the more onerous conventions of the existing system could be safely eliminated.

In 1858 the Cartier–Macdonald ministry in the Province of Canada committed itself to seek a federal union of British North America, and Canada, New Brunswick, and Nova Scotia sent delegations to London to discuss the project. This initiative failed because it came too soon. The internal problems of the Province of Canada were already insoluble by any other means, and the various economic interests that led to Confederation were already becoming apparent. However, the external conditions outlined at the beginning of this chapter did not yet exist. The 1860s were to be the decade of state-building, in Canada as elsewhere.

The change that took place in the new decade was the emergence of an external threat to the security of British North America. It will be recalled that W. H. Riker considered this a necessary condition for any federal union, and that other writers on federalism, such as Dikshit and Wheare, considered it important although not essential. In the Canadian case it probably was essential, both to secure the necessary amount of support for unification in the colonies themselves and, equally important if not more so, to win the support of the British government. Although internally self-governing, the colonies were exposed to direct Imperial influence through their governors, and this influence was now brought to bear in favour of a federal union. In addition, any change in the status of the colonies required legislation by the Parliament in Westminster.

The threat, of course, came from the United States. British relations with the government in Washington had deteriorated during the civil war, a situation for which the British were more to blame than the Americans (and for which the Canadians bore little if any responsibility), but which exposed Canada to the threat of an American invasion in the event of war. By 1864 it was apparent that the industrial North would win the civil war and incorporate the southern states back into the union, presenting the British empire with a very powerful and unfriendly opponent. Another source of danger inherent in the outcome of the civil war was the removal of the controversy over slavery from the agenda of American politics. Previously that controversy had prevented the United States from expanding northwards, since to do so would have upset the delicate balance between slavery states and free states. This obstacle to the annexation of Canada had now disappeared. Although the British government had discouraged efforts towards Confederation until 1864, it reversed itself in that year for reasons of military defence and security.[3] A united British North America, especially one tied together by railways, would be more defensible and could bear a larger share of the costs of its own defence. In particular, the port of Halifax with its British naval base could be used to send British troops to Canada even when the St. Lawrence was frozen, and without the necessity of crossing American soil.

The American threat also made the need for Confederation more apparent to the colonists themselves, or at least to those who were exposed to it. Not surprisingly, enthusiasm was minimal in Nova Scotia, which had no boundary with the United States and was defended by the Royal Navy. There was no enthusiasm at all in Newfoundland, which was hundreds of miles away from U.S. territory. New Brunswick and Canada felt more exposed. The Confederation debates in the Canadian Parliament, which took place a few weeks before the end of the civil war, contain many references to the American danger, particularly vehement on the part of the two members for Montreal, George Etienne Cartier and D'Arcy McGee.[4] John A. Macdonald and George Brown, who both had somewhat ambivalent attitudes towards the United States, were more restrained in their comments, but they also emphasized the defensive advantages of Confederation. Soon after the civil war ended, the effect of such arguments was reinforced by the activities of the Fenians, Irish guerrillas who had learned their military skills while serving in the U.S. army.

ECONOMIC MOTIVES FOR CONFEDERATION

The greatest controversy over Confederation, among historians and even to some extent at the time it occurred, concerns the economic motives that lay behind it. These motives were as varied and complex as the socio-economic structures of the colonies themselves. Everyone agrees that they were important, and some argue that they were the only motives that really mattered. Whether they were or not, they cannot be reduced to a single narrow explanation, such as A. A. Dorion's assertion that Confederation was no more than a scheme to enrich the Grand Trunk railway by creating traffic between Canada and the Maritimes. Obviously the Grand Trunk was a part of the coalition of economic interests that supported Confederation, but it could hardly have carried the project by itself.

The most important class interests at the time of Confederation were those of the capitalists and the farmers. The wage-earning workers were still quite few in number, and many of them were disenfranchised. The white-collar *petite bourgeoisie,* so vast in numbers and influence today, then scarcely existed.

Some debate has recently taken place among historians concerning the relative importance of mercantile and industrial capitalists at the time of Confederation. The significance of this apparently arcane controversy lies in the view of some Marxists that the two types of capitalists are quite distinct and have conflicting interests, with the domination of the former variety allegedly an obstacle to healthy economic development. As one participant in the controversy has pointed out, Marx included railway builders and operators in the industrial category while some of his Canadian disciples do not, a matter of some consequence in the Canadian case. It also seems that the two groups cannot be clearly distinguished, at least in nineteenth-century Canada.[5]

Among historians of Confederation, J. M. S. Careless, the biographer of George Brown, emphasized the role of the rising industrialists, as did the Marxist Stanley Ryerson. Donald Creighton, the biographer of John A. Macdonald, emphasized the commercial capitalists or merchants, whose earlier adventures he chronicled in his first book, *The Commercial Empire of the St. Lawrence.* The neo-Marxist R. T. Naylor has done so to an even greater extent and from a different perspective. treating Confederation and the National Policy as reactionary and sterile policies that stunted Canada's economic and political development.[6] In fact there seem to have been a variety of capitalist interests behind Confederation: some general and some more specific, some concerned with commerce and some with industry, some centred in Toronto and some in Montreal (and possibly some in London).

Canada enjoyed a period of industrial expansion beginning

about 1859, partly through the impetus of railway-building. By the 1860s it had a relatively advanced economy by the standards of the time, and was certainly far more industrialized than the United States had been in 1787. The American civil war gave some impetus to industrialization in Canada, as well as in the United States. Industry was scattered through a number of locations in the Province of Canada, although the west end of Lake Ontario, later to be termed "the golden horseshoe", was already important. The industrialists sold their products to the farmers and other primary producers, but they needed larger markets. In the decade that preceded Confederation their attention turned increasingly to the Hudson's Bay Company territories west of the Great Lakes, which they hoped to annex and turn into a larger hinterland, a vast extension of Upper Canada. Commercial and financial interests in Toronto also stood to gain from westward expansion. Since Toronto was farther west than its traditional rival, Montreal, it could expect to become the metropolitan centre for the new hinterland.

In Montreal itself, which was then much larger than Toronto, and about one-half English-speaking, the major financial institutions were located; these included the Bank of Montreal which counted the government of the province among its customers. Toronto interests, including George Brown, had recently organized the Bank of Commerce as a counterweight, but it was still smaller than the Bank of Montreal. Montreal capitalists were more interested in expanding towards the Atlantic than towards the West. This partly reflected the interest of the Grand Trunk, whose costly bridge across the St. Lawrence at Montreal might otherwise become a white elephant, but more generally reflected the desire to give Montreal a larger hinterland in relation to that of Toronto.

These different interests of capitalists in the two halves of the province corresponded with more widely held sentiments in their respective sections, in part of course because the dominant economic interests had the means to propagate their own viewpoints. In Canada West the farmers, partly because of George Brown and his *Globe,* supported westward expansion which would ease the pressure of growing population on the limited supply of land and end the necessity of migrating to the

United States in search of new agricultural opportunities. In Canada East French-speaking Canadians, most of whom were farmers, feared the growing economic, demographic, and political power of Canada West and feared even more the consequences of annexing a western hinterland that would be merely an extension of it. Some French Canadians, George Cartier and his followers, later accepted westward expansion, but only as part of a package that included federalism (a province of Quebec with its own legislature) and absorption of the Maritimes (as a counterweight to Ontario and the West).

This complex of interests was tied together by the Great Coalition of 1864. George Brown, the spokesman for Toronto business, joined forces with John A. Macdonald, whose political allies included Cartier and Galt, the spokesmen for Montreal business. Macdonald's genius, symbolized by the location of his Kingston constituency midway between the two major cities, lay in his ability to represent the interests of the whole ruling class, or at least the lowest common denominator of such interests. Brown accepted expansion to the east, Cartier accepted expansion to the west, and Macdonald accepted federalism, about which he had serious reservations even though he had been a long-time supporter of uniting the colonies. Macdonald's preference for a unitary state, which he called a legislative union, was consistent with his relative detachment from specifically regional interests, part of the secret of his political success. However, a federal union was the only kind that could possibly be acceptable to French Canadians or Maritimers, and Brown shrewdly understood that a federal state would be "capable of gradual and efficient expansion in future years".[7] The United States had convincingly demonstrated that federalism was ideally suited to facilitate the westward course of empire.

Economic motives for Confederation were perhaps weaker in the Maritime colonies than in the Province of Canada, but were by no means completely absent. The promised Intercolonial Railway would benefit New Brunswick's North Shore and the central part of Nova Scotia; the south-western portions of both provinces, which would not benefit directly, were predictably the centres of opposition to Confederation. Nova Scotia's coal industry, whose political spokesman was Charles

Tupper, had a particularly strong interest in the projected railway, both as a means of transportation and as a market for its product.

An additional motive for Confederation, which the Maritimes shared with the Province of Canada, was provided by the expectation that the United States would terminate its reciprocal trade agreement with the colonies, as it actually did in 1866. This forced all the colonies to re-orient their trade on an east-west rather than a north-south basis. It threatened to end the arrangements by which Canada had used American seaports for its trade with Britain during the winter months. It also meant that Maritime fishermen could no longer fish in American waters, and would need help to defend their own waters from American encroachments.

> The change in the Quebec resolutions at the London Conference in December 1866 which gave the federal government control over seacoast and inland fisheries reflected the importance of the new instrument of Confederation as a means of resisting New England. With the ending of reciprocity, Nova Scotia, New Brunswick and Quebec took refuge behind an organization more efficient for the checking of encroachments on British fishing grounds, the prevention of smuggling, and bargaining for a new treaty.[8]

The opponents of Confederation, like its supporters, represented a diversity of interests. Unlike the supporters, the opponents had little contact across provincial boundaries, little support from the United Kingdom, and no agreement among themselves as to what alternative should be proposed. In Canada West (Ontario) most of the opponents were agrarian radicals or "Grits" who refused to follow George Brown into the coalition government. They were interested in westward expansion but not in a link with the Maritimes, which they expected to reinforce the power of commercial interests, particularly in Montreal. Some of them wanted to break the link between the two halves of the Province of Canada, but on this issue they were not unanimous.

In Canada East (Quebec) a few anglophones looked forward with dismay to the revival of the political boundary between the two halves of the province, even under a federal union. Most of the opposition, however, came from francophone *petit-bourgeois* nationalists, the *Rouges,* who were less optimistic than Cartier about the chances of cultural survival in a multi-province federation. Their preferred solution was a federal arrangement between the two halves of the Province of Canada, with the other colonies excluded and westward expansion indefinitely delayed.

In the Maritimes opposition came from business interests, both commercial and industrial, that feared Canadian competition. They were reinforced by other interests that desired closer contacts with the United States, especially in the area around the Bay of Fundy where ties with New England were traditionally close. Especially in Nova Scotia (and in Newfoundland, which resisted the lure of Confederation for more than eighty years) the anti-Confederationists were able to exploit a widespread popular feeling of attachment to the province as an autonomous community. Some supported Maritime union and others the status quo.

THE TERMS OF UNION

The terms of what became Canada's constitution reflected both the diversity of interests and motives behind Confederation and the ideological preferences of the colonial politicians who attended the conferences at Quebec in 1864 and at London in 1866. Prominent among the latter were enthusiasm for "a Constitution similar in Principle to that of the United Kingdom", a phrase which appears in the preamble to the British North America Act, and a desire to avoid what were considered the undesirable aspects of the American constitution. John A. Macdonald in particular was obsessed with the belief, a somewhat superficial one for a man so shrewd in other respects, that the American civil war might have been avoided if the American constitution had granted only limited and specified powers to the individual states, rather than leaving them with all powers not granted to the federal government.[9] He acknowledged that the political circumstances in 1787 had probably left the Americans with no alternative, but he was determined to avoid the same mistake himself.

Fortunately for Macdonald, circumstances were more propitious for him than they had been for Alexander Hamilton, whose views on federalism and on other political subjects were very similar to his own. The forces of agrarian radicalism were much weaker in British North America than they had been in the thirteen colonies, and their political representatives, being on the opposition benches, were excluded from the conferences that drafted Canada's constitution. Canada also lacked any equivalent of the southern plantation owners, who had opposed the centralization desired by the Federalist merchants. In addition there were no vested interests attached to provincial autonomy in what became Ontario and Quebec, since the governments of those provinces did not exist between 1841 and 1867. It was both easy and logical to give specifically defined powers to those governments which were to be established, while leaving the general, unspecified, or "residual" power with the government that already existed, that of Canada.

Only in the Maritimes did Macdonald have to deal with already-existing governments that would have to be enticed into accepting a completely new level of government superior to themselves, and even there he was aided by discreet pressure from London and the fact that some of the Maritimers, like Charles Tupper, shared his preference for a centralized regime. The chief concerns of the Maritime delegates at the conferences were provincial revenues and representation in the Senate, rather than the division of legislative powers. The demands for provincial legislative powers came mainly from the French Canadians, for whom the establishment of a Quebec legislature was the major attraction of Confederation. The powers which they demanded for that legislature were mainly related to social institutions, education, the family, and the legal system. Even the celebrated provincial jurisdiction over "property and civil rights", expressly designed to protect Quebec's legal system by repeating a phrase first used in the Quebec Act of 1774, at first included the qualifying phrase "excepting portions thereof assigned to the General Parliament". These words were removed at the last moment by the British Colonial Office.[10]

The stated preference for "a Constitution similar in Principle to that of the United Kingdom'' combined a widely shared sentiment with more pragmatic and mundane considerations. Access to British capital and markets was essential to the economic objectives of Confederation, and British assistance would be essential to defend Canada against the United States. A firm assertion of loyalty to British principles might increase pro-Canadian sentiments in the United Kingdom, where they were not particularly strong. Many influential people in the United Kingdom believed that the colonies were economically worthless and a source of friction with the United States, and that they should be encouraged to sever the British connection.

British principles also had certain implications for the constitution itself. Since everyone knew, more or less, how British government operated, certain matters, such as the principle that the government was responsible to the lower house of Parliament, did not have to be specified or described. Monarchy, which is based on the principle that political authority flows from the top downwards, had never before been combined with federalism, and in a sense was logically incompatible with it. However, it suited the kind of union that Macdonald and most of his colleagues wanted to create. Ottawa would be subordinate to London and the provinces would be subordinate to Ottawa, with a British Governor General in Ottawa and a federally appointed Lieutenant-Governor in each province, each of whom would have the power to "reserve" legislation for the final decision of the government that had appointed him. Both London and Ottawa could disallow the acts of the level of government immediately below them, even though such acts had received the assent of the Governor General or Lieutenant-Governor. The judicial system revealed similarly hierarchical notions. Ottawa would appoint the judges of the provincial courts, and it was understood, although not stated, that the final court of appeal would be the Judicial Committee of the (Imperial) Privy Council, which already exercised that function for all of the colonies.

These provisions of the BNA Act have offended constitutional purists, and led K. C. Wheare to deny that Canada really had a federal constitution, although he admitted that it functioned as a federal system in practice.[11] Their effect, however, should not be overstated. Reservation of acts by a

Lieutenant-Governor soon became unusual, although the power was unexpectedly used in Saskatchewan as late as 1961. Disallowances of provincial legislation have been more frequent (although there have been none since 1943) but they could not prevent a determined provincial government from repeatedly adopting the same legislation, nor could the federal Parliament itself legislate in provincial areas of jurisdiction. Furthermore, an American authority stated in the 1920s that "virtually every provincial law which has been disallowed by the Dominion government during the past fifty years would probably have been declared unconstitutional if passed by an American state legislature".[12] The states in the prototype of modern federalism, at least after the fourteenth amendment in 1869, enjoyed no more real autonomy than the Canadian provinces.

Insofar as specification was required, the BNA Act established the framework of a central government closely resembling both its British prototype and its immediate predecessor, the government of the Province of Canada. Although the latter had experimented with the rather un-British innovation of an elected upper house, an appointed Senate was provided. The newly established (or re-established) provincial governments of Ontario and Quebec would be organized along similar lines, although Ontario was given a unicameral legislature, setting a precedent which all the other provinces eventually followed. All provinces were given freedom to modify their own institutions, apart from the office of Lieutenant-Governor.

The heart of any federal constitution is the division of legislative powers. In the Quebec and London resolutions, and in the BNA Act (which followed their provisions quite closely), powers were allocated so that the central government could carry out the major objectives of Confederation. For reasons already referred to, Parliament was given all legislative powers not specifically assigned to the provincial legislatures. The Quebec resolutions described this as a power to make laws for "the peace, welfare, and good government of Canada", consciously or unconsciously recalling the "general welfare" clause of the United States constitution. Regrettably, the Colonial Office later changed this to "Peace, Order, and good

Government", contributing to a lasting myth that the Fathers of Confederation were less "liberal", whatever that may mean, than their American counterparts.

The federal government was given unlimited power to tax and borrow, the latter being particularly important at a time when colonial governments depended on the London bond market. Tariff and commercial policy would also be under its control, as would the banking system and the currency, the postal service, weights and measures, and patents and copyrights. Jurisdiction over agriculture (and immigration) was shared with the provinces, while, at the London conference, fisheries were placed under federal jurisdiction, for reasons already discussed. For the sake of uniformity the criminal law was placed under federal control, a departure from American practice that perhaps reflected Macdonald's experience as a defence counsel in criminal cases.

The provisions for transportation, an essential part of the economics of Confederation, were complex. The federal government was given jurisdiction over navigation and shipping, and was also required to begin building the Intercolonial Railway within six months of the union, and to complete it as quickly as possible. Macdonald originally proposed to list all the means of interprovincial communication that were placed under federal authority, but roads and bridges were excluded at the suggestion of Leonard Tilley, the Premier of New Brunswick.[13] This still left the federal government with steamships, railways, canals, telegraphs, and other works and undertakings connecting two or more provinces, and with steamships connecting Canada with other countries. It could also assume jurisdiction over "works" entirely within one province by declaring them to be for the general advantage of Canada. In the legislative debates on the Quebec resolutions Macdonald cited the Welland Canal between Lake Erie and Lake Ontario as an example of the "works" that would fall under this provision.[14]

The enumerated provincial powers included those "cultural" matters of particular concern to the French Canadians, such as education, social institutions, the family, and the law relating to "property and civil rights". They also included municipal institutions, which were well developed in

Canada West but less so in Canada East, and which hardly existed in the Maritime colonies. The administration of justice was an important area of provincial responsibility. The provincial control over education was qualified by safeguards to protect religious minorities. This covered both the Protestants of Quebec, who included a large part of Canada's ruling class, and also the Roman Catholics of the Maritimes, whose Archbishop was a strong supporter of Confederation.[15]

The provincial governments were given certain powers over economic matters, which proved important later on. They shared jurisdiction over agriculture with the federal government, could borrow on their own credit, could incorporate companies "for provincial objects", and controlled roads, bridges, and whatever other "works" were not under federal jurisdiction. They received the public lands, including timber, and the mineral resources, of which Nova Scotia's coal was then the most important, including the power to impose royalties. At the Quebec conference a strangely prophetic discussion concerning the division of energy resource rents between the two levels of government took place. Tupper and McCully of Nova Scotia objected that the federal government might impose an export duty on coal, thus cutting into provincial royalty revenues. A. T. Galt, the Canadian Minister of Finance, replied that Ottawa would not want to impose export duties, but only to prevent the provinces from doing so. The Attorney General of Nova Scotia pointed out that Nova Scotia's royalty was not an export duty since it affected the price to all consumers, domestic and foreign.[16] The issues raised in this discussion have not yet been resolved.

Resource revenues, however, were a relatively minor aspect of public finance in 1867. All of the provinces had depended mainly on customs tariffs and excise taxes for their revenues prior to Confederation, and these sources of revenue were assigned exclusively to the federal government. The provincial power to impose direct taxes was of little immediate value, since such taxes would have been politically unacceptable. In fact the fear of direct taxation probably contributed significantly to anti-Confederation sentiment in the Maritimes. The only available solution was to make the provincial governments largely dependent on federal grants or subsidies.

The Quebec resolutions provided for grants of eighty cents *per capita,* based on 1861 levels of population. Since this formula did not satisfy the Maritimes, the London conference modified it by providing that grants to New Brunswick and Nova Scotia would be based on their actual populations until each province reached a ceiling of 400,000 inhabitants. Additional grants were also provided to all provinces, ostensibly for the support of their legislatures.[17]

A careful reading of the British North America Act suggests that the Fathers of Confederation had a good grasp of political economy, as it was then understood, and that they produced a constitution well suited to achieve the purposes for which it was designed. Railway-building and westward expansion did in fact take place. The cultural conflicts that had paralysed the Province of Canada were made more manageable. The United States was forced to accept, although not to welcome, the existence of a neighbouring British Dominion, as it tacitly recognized by negotiating the Treaty of Washington in 1871. In all of these respects the British North America Act was a success.

It was less of a success, however, in serving the symbolic and ideological purposes of a constitution. "A Constitution similar in Principle to that of the United Kingdom" may have seemed an adequate statement of ideological purpose at the time, but it had little capacity to stir the masses, and as Imperial ties grew weaker it became simply unintelligible. The fact that the Act was an Imperial statute, while unavoidable, had the serious consequence, among others, that there was and is no official text in the French language. Thus it could hardly acquire any symbolic significance for between one quarter and one third of the new Dominion's population.

By the standards of today the position accorded to French Canada in the Act was inadequate and, from the viewpoint of national unity, counterproductive. However, it reflected the economic and demographic realities of the time. There were few francophones outside of Quebec and little expectation, in an age of limited personal mobility, that there would ever be many more. Even in New Brunswick the Acadians were only 15 per cent of the population, as compared to more than one third a century later; the ethnic composition of the province was only subsequently to be altered by the lower birth rate of the anglophones and their greater tendency to migrate to the United States. In the Province of Quebec also the anglophones were a higher proportion of the population than they are today. In several rural counties of Quebec they were a majority and in Montreal about half the population. Moreover industry and commerce were almost entirely controlled by anglophones, in Quebec as elsewhere. Canadians of French ethnic origin were actually a smaller proportion of the population in every one of the original provinces than they are now, but they were a larger proportion than now of the total Canadian population; a paradox explained by the fact that the western provinces and Newfoundland, which have few French Canadians, are included in the total today but were not at the time of Confederation.

For these reasons all French-Canadian politicians took it for granted that Quebec would be bilingual, and none seems to have expressed any interest in extending bilingualism to the other provinces of the original Confederation. Institutional bilingualism at the federal level, corresponding to that which the anglophone minority enjoyed in Quebec, seemed a reasonable tradeoff. A Quebec government and legislature, even with limited powers, was an improvement over the Act of Union. Moreover Quebec was one province out of four, not one out of ten, and had approximately one third of the seats in both houses of Parliament. Thus it was easy to be optimistic, as Cartier was, about French Canada's future under the BNA Act, and even easier to conclude that no better bargain was realistically available. Disillusionment would come later with the ungenerous response of other provinces to the growth of their francophone minorities, the development of the prairie West after its annexation into an overwhelmingly anglophone region, and the slow but steady erosion of Quebec's influence in federal politics.

DEMOCRACY AND CONFEDERATION

Before leaving the subject of Confederation, it is appropriate to make some observations concerning the procedures by which the terms of the federal bargain were worked out and then brought into force. These procedures restricted effective participation to a very small number of persons, and even symbolic participation by the voters was virtually excluded. The effect was to deprive the constitution, and the federation itself, of democratic legitimacy, a problem that has become more rather than less acute over the years. Another unfortunate effect has been to reinforce an ideological notion that is very intimately associated with the denial of popular participation then and later: the so-called compact theory of Confederation.

The Fathers of Confederation, both Conservatives and Liberals, were not supporters of democracy. Universal suffrage had few supporters in the nineteenth century; John Stuart Mill, later to be considered a founder of modern liberal-democratic theory, was one of those who argued against it. Even the word "democracy" did not become respectable before the First World War, when it was adopted as a slogan of wartime propaganda, and it is arguable that the word was accepted then by political and economic elites only because it had been emptied of most of its content. One should not be surprised, therefore, that political elites in the 1860s saw no reason to consult the people about Confederation. Moreover, as Stanley Ryerson has argued, the series of difficult compromises which it involved could have made consultation hazardous:

> With all its intricately balanced commitments to the Grand Trunk directors, the Colonial office, and the governments of the Maritimes, it needed to be put through with an absolute minimum of popular involvement or debate.[18]

Ryerson is referring here to the plan for Confederation that emerged from the Quebec conference, but the "intricately balanced commitments" had begun even earlier with the formation of the coalition government in the Province of Canada. It was in the unrecorded negotiations at that time that agreement was reached between the political representatives of what became "Quebec" and "Ontario", and that agreement was embodied in the proposals that the Canadian politicians made to their Maritime counterparts. At the Quebec conference Canada functioned as a single province, although it had two votes in recognition of its duality. The Canadians unveiled a plan which the Maritimers were able to modify only slightly, and which became the Quebec resolutions. Yet many important questions, particularly those pertaining to relations between the two linguistic communities in the Province of Canada, were hardly discussed at the Quebec conference because they had been decided earlier, and because the Maritimers were not particularly interested in them. The rather placid proceedings of the Quebec conference bore little resemblance to the Philadelphia Convention of 1787, which had had to confront both the issues that divided the thirteen colonies from one another and the issues that divided them internally.

The participants at Quebec were members of governments responsible to elected legislatures, but this did not mean that they were totally subject to those legislatures. Then as now, party discipline permitted governments to play the legislature off against the electorate, and vice versa. Charles Tupper's government in Nova Scotia, elected in 1863, did not have to face the electorate again until after Confederation had been achieved, and it also managed to avoid submitting the terms of the federal bargain to the Nova Scotia legislature, where to do so might have exposed fissures in the governing majority. Retribution came at the provincial election in 1867, when the supporters of Confederation were swept out of office, but this was too late to affect the outcome.

In New Brunswick the pro-Confederation government of Leonard Tilley had less control over the legislature, although Confederation itself was probably more popular in New Brunswick than in Nova Scotia. Unable either to risk submitting the Quebec resolutions to the legislature or to control his caucus if he avoided doing so, Tilley requested a dissolution and was defeated at the polls. The anti-Confederation government in turn was forced to seek a dissolution and Tilley was returned to office in 1866, an event which suggests that the electorate had probably accepted Confederation. (The corruption and external interference in this election was about equally divided between government and opposition.) However, the legislature never had the opportunity to vote on the terms of Confederation in New Brunswick.

In the Province of Canada the Quebec resolutions were submitted to the legislature, which debated them in the winter of 1865. They were approved by majorities in both houses, and in both linguistic communities, although the latter was not of course a formal requirement for any kind of action by the legislature. In both houses agrarian radicals from Canada West, where American ideas of popular sovereignty had some support, moved that approval be deferred until the people had been given a chance to express their views, presumably in an election. Both motions were easily defeated by the government's supporters, as was a motion in the upper house that called for a referendum.[19] What the result of either an election or a referendum at that time would have been is a question that cannot now be answered; for both practical and ideological reasons the government was in no hurry to find out.

The government of the Province of Canada also refused to allow the legislature to amend the Quebec resolutions, maintaining that they must either be accepted completely or rejected. To justify this position, Macdonald and other government spokesmen referred to "the implied obligation to deal with it as a treaty", by which they meant that to allow amendments would be to break faith with their counterparts in the Maritimes who had accepted the original terms, and would require a re-opening of interprovincial negotiations.[20] This was the origin of the celebrated "compact theory", or the view that Confederation was a contractual arrangement among provincial governments and can only be revised in any particular by their unanimous consent. Ironically, this theory was later to be exploited by autonomy-minded provincial governments, some of which represented the very parties and interests that had opposed Confederation in the 1860s. Yet a deeper strain of consistency underlies the compact theory, in both its earlier and later versions. Its later adherents, like its originators, have wished to restrict popular participation in the making of important political decisions. In both cases a respectable justification for this objective has been sought by emphasizing the right of "provinces" (meaning provincial politicians) to be consulted, rather than the rights of the people. In thus distracting attention from the real issue, successive generations of politicians have hindered the development of a fully realized sense of political community from sea to sea. The ultimate effect in our own time has been to threaten the survival of the federal state so laboriously patched together between 1864 and 1867.

The process by which Confederation was accomplished seems in some respects to fit a conceptual framework which has recently become fashionable among Canadian political scientists, the so-called theory of consociational democracy.[21] Originally developed in the Netherlands, but transplanted to Canada soon afterwards, this concept purports to explain how some liberal democracies are able to survive without a widely accepted set of ideological symbols and common values that would define the political community and distinguish it from others. The explanation offered is that in such countries the population is segmented into sub-groups, each with its own symbols and values, each represented by political elites who are trusted to bargain with other elites on behalf of the group's interests. A sense of community among the masses is not required and may even be dysfunctional.

British North America in the 1860s certainly seems to have had some of the attributes that political scientists associate with consociationalism. There were few common symbols or values, and little contact among the populations of the different provinces, or between the two linguistic groups even where they coexisted on the same territory. Deals were certainly made among elites who, willy-nilly, had virtual freedom to negotiate without much regard for popular sentiments. Yet all of this had its dangers, as suggested by the continuing fragility of the whole arrangement (although this has other causes as well), and by the fact that the concept of consociationalism has itself become a rather sophisticated ideological tool to justify the continuing elitism of Canadian politics. Elitism in political decision-making is closely associated with the maintenance of cultural and provincial barriers, real or imaginary, among the people of Canada, so that each serves to reinforce the other. By celebrating both, or at least failing to question them, the theorists of "consociational democracy" are playing an ideological role. The consociational concept is the compact theory in a new guise.

NOTES

1. William Ormsby, *The Emergence of the Federal Concept in Canada; 1839–1845* (Toronto: University of Toronto Press, 1969).
2. Canada, Legislature, *Parliamentary Debates on the Subject of the Confederation of the British North American Provinces* (Quebec, 1865), p. 30.
3. Chester Martin, "British Policy in Canada Confederation", *Canadian Historical Review,* XIII (1932): 3–19.
4. *Confederation Debates,* pp. 53–62 and 125–46.
5. L. R. Macdonald, "Merchants Against Industry: An Idea and its Origins", *Canadian Historical Review,* LVI (1975): 263–81.
6. J. M. S. Careless, *Brown of the Globe,* 2 vols. (Toronto: Macmillan, 1959 and 1963); Stanley Ryerson, *Unequal Union: Confederation and the Roots of Conflict in the Canadas 1815–1873* (Toronto: Progress Books, 1968); Donald Creighton, *John A. Macdonald,* 2 vols. (Toronto: Macmillan, 1952 and 1955); R. T. Naylor, *The History of Canadian Business,* 2 vols. (Toronto: Lorimer, 1975).
7. *Confederation Debates,* p. 86.
8. Harold Innis, *The Cod Fisheries: The History of an International Economy* (New Haven: Yale University Press, 1940), p. 364.
9. Joseph Pope, *Memoirs of Sir John A. Macdonald* (Toronto: Oxford University Press, 1930), pp. 242–43.
10. W. R. Lederman, "Unity and Diversity in Canadian Federalism", *Canadian Bar Review,* LIII (1975): 597–620.
11. K. C. Wheare, *Federal Government,* 4th ed. (New York: Oxford University Press, 1964), pp. 18–20.
12. W. B. Munro, *American Influences on Canadian Government* (Toronto: Macmillan, 1929), p. 37.
13. Joseph Pope, *Confederation: Being a series of hitherto unpublished documents bearing on The British North America Act* (Toronto: Carswell, 1895), pp. 22–30.
14. *Confederation Debates,* p. 40.
15. W. L. Morton, *The Critical Years: The Union of British North America, 1857-1873* (Toronto: McClelland and Stewart, 1964), pp. 191–92.
16. Pope, *Confederation,* pp. 79–80.
17. J. A. Maxwell, "Better Terms", *Queen's Quarterly,* XL (1933): 125–39.
18. Ryerson, *Unequal Union,* p. 369.
19. *Confederation Debates,* pp. 269–316, 327–33, 962–1020.
20. *Confederation Debates,* p. 31.
21. For a useful introduction to the concept, see K. D. McRae, ed., *Consociational Democracy: Political Accommodation in Segmented Societies* (Toronto: McClelland and Stewart, 1974).

3   Two Concepts of Canadian Federalism

Although Confederation had not been achieved without controversy, it was soon tacitly accepted, even by its erstwhile opponents. Nova Scotia's anti-Confederation government, elected in September 1867, had to recognize that Confederation was irreversible. Joseph Howe, the leading opponent of Confederation in the province, accepted a seat in the federal cabinet. His example was followed a few years later by A. A. Dorion, who had been the leading French-Canadian opponent of Confederation, but who ended his political career as federal Minister of Justice, in which capacity he recommended the disallowance of several provincial statutes. John Sandfield Macdonald, another prominent opponent of Confederation, became Ontario's first Premier, and was attacked by George Brown's *Globe* for alleged subservience to his federal namesake, Prime Minister John A. Macdonald.

In short, the conduct of politics within the framework of a federal constitution came to be accepted as an irreversible fact of life, even by those who would have preferred a different outcome. Yet the conflicting interests and sentiments that had been reflected in the debates over Confederation persisted, and were supplemented by new conflicts that arose from the federal structure of government itself: competition for money, power, patronage, and prestige between the two levels of government. The difference was that old and new conflicts were now expressed in divergent interpretations of Confederation, the existence of which was accepted by all parties. Arguments over concepts of federalism became, as they have remained, a characteristically Canadian form of political controversy, or a language in which controversy was expressed. Federalism has proved a broad enough concept to accommodate a wide variety of perspectives.

Two recent writers on Canadian federalism have both managed to discover as many as five distinct types or concepts of federalism to which different Canadians have adhered at different times. J. R. Mallory, in a paper written in 1964, referred to quasi-federalism, classic federalism, emergency federalism, co-operative federalism, and double-image federalism.[1] The first he identifies with John A. Macdonald, whose original preference for a unitary state was expressed after 1867 in efforts to subordinate the provincial governments to the federal one which he headed. Classic federalism is the view that each level of government should be independent and supreme within a clearly defined area of jurisdiction, with minimal interaction between the two levels. Emergency federalism is the view that the central government can and should assume broadly defined powers in wartime and in other unusual circumstances. Co-operative federalism is associated with the blurring of jurisdictional boundaries between the two levels of government, so that each becomes inextricably involved in the other's affairs. Double-image federalism perceives Canada as fundamentally a union of two cultural and linguistic communities, and argues that federal institutions and practices must be interpreted or adapted to reflect this.

A very similar list of concepts is discussed at much greater length by Edwin Black in his book, *Divided Loyalties.*[2] Black includes both Macdonald's quasi-federalism and the emergency federalism of the twentieth century under the heading of what he calls the centralist concept. He includes the compact theory, not mentioned by Mallory, as a concept in its own right. His other three concepts of federalism are the same as Mallory's, although he calls them by different names. Mallory's classic federalism is referred to by Black as the co-ordinate concept. Instead of co-operative federalism, Black uses the term administrative federalism. Instead of double-image federalism, Black refers to the concept of Confederation as a dual alliance.

Each of these concepts, as Black demonstrates in his book, can be used to represent an aspect of Canadian federalism, either as it is or was or was believed to be by some group of Canadians at some period of time. Yet the concepts are not strictly comparable to one another. The compact theory, for example, was more of an ideological notion or a statement of principle than a description of how federalism operated in practice. On the other hand administrative federalism is a useful term to describe the actual pattern of intergovernmental relations in the generation that followed the Second World War, but it hardly represents an ideal, a principle, or an ideological concept. It simply resulted willy-nilly from the inability of either centralizers or decentralizers to impose their own version of federalism on one another.

The concept of the dual alliance also poses certain difficulties, since it is arguably not a concept of federalism but rather a concept of Canadian society, which might be compatible with a variety of institutional arrangements. The Royal Commission on Bilingualism and Biculturalism, appointed by the government of Lester Pearson, was among the leading promoters of the dual alliance but could not agree as to what, if any, version of federalism was compatible with it, so that it never produced the volume of its report that would have dealt with constitutional changes. Other proponents of dualism have espoused the co-ordinate concept or the compact theory. For that matter the dualist concept is logically quite compatible with centralized quasi-federalism or even a unitary state, assuming that the central government gave adequate expression to the objectives and interests of both linguistic communities. On the other hand the recently fashionable version of dualism which equates French Canada with one province and uses the term "English Canada" as a collective description of the other provinces is logically not compatible with the survival of the Canadian state, a fact recognized by its more honest and logical adherents.

In a fundamental sense there are really only two concepts of federalism, which may be viewed as opposite ends of a continuum. The concepts and the continuum are possible because federalism itself is a compromise between unity and diversity, symbolized by two levels of government which ostensibly represent these two aspects of the federal polity. Federalism has been admired by some because it promotes unity and by others because it protects diversity; conceivably it does both. However in practice most adherents of federalism, and most citizens of federal states, are more deeply committed to one of these goals than to the other, so the two goals correspond with two concepts of federalism, depending on which is emphasized. In the absence of more suitable terms we may call them centripetal federalism (emphasizing unity) and centrifugal federalism (emphasizing diversity). Centripetal federalists prefer to strengthen the federal government's power at the expense of the provincial governments; centrifugal federalists prefer to do the reverse. Federalism itself requires that neither tendency be carried to extremes, since one could result in a unitary state and the other in the dissolution of the union. In Canada, at least to date, both centripetalists and centrifugalists have always been faced with effective counter-vailing forces.

Canadian concepts of federalism have received their most articulate expression from three groups of people. Politicians, not surprisingly, head the list. A second source of expressions of the federal concepts has been the judiciary, insofar as it has been called upon to interpret the federal constitution. The third group consists of historians, political scientists, economists, and other academic writers on federalism and related subjects.

Some would argue, like John Porter, that these are the only groups of people who really have any interest in federalism.[3] This is probably an overstatement. Polling data suggest that most Canadians have an opinion concerning the distribution of power between the two levels of government, and that the vast majority are federalists in the sense that they do not wish either level to be abolished. One study done in Alberta also suggests that people are reasonably well-informed about the actual powers and functions of the two levels.[4]

Nonetheless, it seems reasonable to confine the discussion of concepts to politicians, judges, and academics, since these are the only groups that have really articulated them to any great extent. The needs and interests of the corporate elite have been closely related to the federal structure of the state, and may well have been decisive in the long run, but they have not often been articulately expressed and can only be inferred from that elite's behaviour. Canadian journalism, apart from a few overtly political individuals like George Brown, Henri Bourassa, and Claude Ryan, has not been of such a standard as to deserve consideration in a discussion of the history of political ideas. In practice, therefore, the three groups mentioned at the outset seem to have had the field to themselves.

Politicians have had the most obvious interest in articulating concepts of federalism, and the most frequent occasion to do so. Soon after Confederation (immediately, in the case of Nova Scotia) it was made illegal for anyone to sit concurrently in Parliament and a provincial legislature, forcing all prospective politicians to opt for one or the other. The investment of time and effort in a career at one level makes it difficult to switch to the other level without cost, and the provincial level of government has become too important to be merely the stepping-stone to the federal level that state-government office in the United States often is. Thus there are in a sense eleven distinct political elites in Canada. This in itself is not unusual among federations, but it is reinforced in Canada by the more unusual fact that some parties and party organizations operate only at one level. In certain provinces the effectively competing parties in federal and provincial elections do not even have the same names, and even where the names are identical the organizational ties between them are often very tenuous. While the reasons for this will be explored in a subsequent chapter, it is mentioned here only to suggest that the unusual fragmentation of the political elite is associated with a diversity of views on federalism.

The role of the judiciary in expounding concepts of federalism has been an almost inevitable corollary of its role in defining the jurisdictional boundaries laid down by the federal constitution. The opportunity to perform both roles has arisen not only in the process of actual litigation, such as arises when an individual or corporation challenges the legality of some action by a government, but through reference cases, by which in effect a government asks the judiciary for legal advice. Although reference cases are not permitted in most other federations, and have been criticized in Canada, they have accounted for a large proportion of the major judicial opinions on federalism.

An equally unusual, and more important, peculiarity of the judicial role in relation to Canadian federalism has been the decisive impact of an external tribunal, the Judicial Committee of the Privy Council. Until appeals to this body from Canada were abolished in 1949 (and indeed for a few years after because of cases that had originated previously), the Judicial Committee was the major interpreter of the Canadian constitution and the major expounder of explicit views on the nature of Canadian federalism. The Supreme Court of Canada, which was not even established until eight years after Confederation, remained in the shadow of the superior tribunal and indeed tended to adopt the latter's concepts and points of view.

This peculiar situation, which even the Australians had the foresight largely to avoid, had the effect that for almost a century the most influential concepts of Canadian federalism were largely defined by outsiders, men who had no practical knowledge of Canada, or of federalism, and who were not even required to live in the society that to a large degree was shaped by their opinions. The consequences were a disaster for the cause of centripetal federalism, and one which has been only partially repaired since the belated abolition of appeals finally made the Supreme Court of Canada supreme in fact, as well as in name.

The third group, the academic writers on federalism, has probably been the least important, although it has become more conspicuous, and perhaps more influential, with the recent expansion and proliferation of universities. For much of Canada's history the intellectual elite was very small and its output of publications even smaller, since there was little time to write and scant opportunity to publish. The universities were under the thumb of the church, the state, or big business. Science, technology, and the professions were emphasized, as they were considered both more useful as means to economic growth and less likely to subvert established values than the humanities and social sciences. Political science in particular was distrusted as an American heresy. None of these circumstances was conducive to much expression of ideas about federalism, or about anything else. Despite the obstacles, however, some important contributions were made, and in a quantitative sense, at least, recent years have seen a great improvement.

CENTRIPETAL FEDERALISM

A centripetal concept of federalism was clearly embodied in the British North America Act, and was perpetuated after 1867 by the fact that the politicians who had drafted the terms of that Act dominated the political life of the new Dominion. Chief among them, of course, was John A. Macdonald, the principal author of the Quebec resolutions which had served as the basis for the BNA Act. As Prime Minister from 1867 until 1873, and again from 1878 until his death in 1891, Macdonald continued to expound the views that had inspired his constitutional draftsmanship, while at the same time he attempted to put them into practice. The centripetal concept of federalism, although increasingly challenged in the last years of Macdonald's life, thus enjoyed a semi-official status at the outset.

Macdonald was well aware, as was every other observer of Canadian life, that the new Dominion was a fragile and artificial creation whose impressive constitutional facade contrasted with a very limited degree of social and economic integration. He did not however consider the diversity of Canadian society and the persistence of local attachments to be an argument in favour of political decentralization. On the contrary, it was precisely these circumstances that made a strong central government essential. As a Hamiltonian conservative Macdonald believed that the state could and should play an autonomous and creative role, rather than merely reflecting the social diversity that lay beneath it. A weakly integrated society needed a strong central government just as a broken leg needs a plaster cast to bind it together. With an optimism that now seems rather naive, Macdonald was convinced that the "gristle" of Confederation would "harden into bone" if the centralized constitution were given a chance to operate for several years. In a letter written in 1868 he expressed his confidence that the centripetal forces would prevail:

> I fully concur with you as to the apprehension that a conflict may, ere long, arise between the Dominion and the "States' Rights" people. We must meet it, however, as best we may. By a firm yet patient course, I think the Dominion must win in the long run. The powers of the General Government are so much greater than those of the United States, in its relations with the local Governments, that the central power must win.[5]

Although the passage of time did not confirm the validity of this forecast, one can perhaps understand the confidence with which it was made in 1868. It must be remembered that Macdonald, Cartier, and other federal politicians had been members of a Canadian government before as well as after Confederation. The new Dominion had inherited from the old Province of Canada a sense of continuity and a functioning administrative machine, not to mention the recently completed buildings on Parliament Hill in Ottawa. It must have been easy to overlook how much had changed with the coming of federalism and the launching of the new provincial govern- ments at Quebec City and Toronto. In the first few years those provincial governments were in any event almost subservient to the federal one, with which they were linked by personal and party ties. Cartier through his personal followers and clients practically ran the government at Quebec City, while Ontario's first Premier actually occupied a seat on the government benches in Ottawa at the same time as he governed the province. Even if they had wanted to resist federal leadership these governments would not have been able to do so, since the provinces over which they presided were newly established entities with meagre administrative and political resources. Macdonald's use of the terms "General Government" and "local governments" rather than "federal" and "provincial" had some basis in fact.

These circumstances proved to be of short duration, and, in his second and longer period of office as Prime Minister, after 1878, Macdonald faced far more serious competition from the provincial governments. Yet he continued to believe that with enough persistence, the centripetal forces would triumph in the end. Inherent in his concept of federalism was the view that Canada was a nation, with national interests, whatever sources of disunity it contained. In 1865, during the parliamentary debates on the Quebec resolutions, he had referred to "a new nationality" and had described the Maritimers as "people who are as much Canadians, I may say, as we are".[6] If there was a nation there must be national interests, and only a powerful "General Government" could express and represent them. These presumed national interests were expressed, after 1878, as the so-called "National Policy", whose three elements were a protective tariff to promote industrialization, immigration to populate the West, and a transcontinental railway.

In order to pursue what were defined as national interests, the federal government had been given extensive powers under the BNA Act, reinforced after 1869 by its control of the lands and resources in the vast territories acquired from the Hudson's Bay Company. The powers of provincial governments had been kept at a minimum in the hope that they would thus have little power to obstruct the pursuit of national interests. If they none the less attempted to do so, Macdonald's concept of federalism required that they be firmly dealt with. The powers of the Lieutenant-Governor, in his dual role as a federal officer and as the chief executive of the province, and the power of the federal government itself to disallow provincial legislation, could be used if necessary. The threat of their use might also persuade an uncooperative provincial government to mend its ways.

The existence of the western hinterlands provided a justification for the centripetal concept of federalism, as well as an opportunity for the central government to assert its authority. Although some of the economic interests that supported Confederation were deeply interested in westward expansion, the sense of urgency that led to the acquisition of the Hudson's Bay Company's empire in 1869 and the addition of British Columbia to the Dominion two years later was mainly inspired by the fear that these territories would otherwise be absorbed by the United States. British Columbia joined Confederation as a province, and Louis Riel forced a reluctant federal government to create another new province in Manitoba, but the central government and the economic interests behind it were not inclined to give the West more than a minimal degree of autonomy. It is not accidental that 77 per cent of all provincial statutes disallowed by the federal government, the vast majority of them before 1911, originated in the West.[7] The tight control over frontier settlement by the Mounted Police, and the retention of Prairie lands and resources by the federal government long after provincial governments had been organized, were part of the same pattern. The fear that any relaxation of control would open the gates to American influence was at least a part of the explanation for these policies. Their legacy was an understandable resentment in the West itself, and a deeply rooted anti-western prejudice in central Canada, where many people were persuaded that westerners could not be trusted to resist American blandishments. Recent controversies over energy resources have revealed the persistence of both sets of attitudes.

Macdonald's concept of federalism recognized that in addition to national interests there were provincial, regional, and local interests. These were considered legitimate and genuine, although less important than the national interest, and to some extent the provincial governments represented them. However, they were not represented exclusively by the provincial governments. Instead the task of representing them was shared by both levels of government. Macdonald expressed this view to the Lieutenant-Governor of Nova Scotia in 1886:

> The representatives of Nova Scotia as to all questions respecting the relations between the Dominion and Province sit in the Dominion Parliament, and are the constitutional exponents of the wishes of the people with regard to such relations. The Provincial members have their powers restricted to the subjects mentioned in the BNA Act and can go no further.[8]

In other words, Nova Scotian interests were represented through the House of Commons, the Senate, the cabinet, and other federal institutions, as well as through the provincial government. Nova Scotia's representatives in Ottawa were the proper persons to interpret its interests in regard to the matters placed under federal jurisdiction, or matters not specifically assigned to either level of government. Its representatives in Halifax only represented its interests in regard to matters placed under provincial jurisdiction. In this particular instance Macdonald was advising the Lieutenant-Governor not to grant a dissolution to Nova Scotia's Liberal government, which wanted to fight an election on the issue of secession. A provincial government, in Macdonald's view, had no authority to deal with such questions.

The implications of this theory should be obvious. The

federal government represented the whole of the national interest, and a portion of provincial and local interests as well. Provincial governments could not represent the national interest at all, and represented only the portion of provincial and local interests that was not represented by the federal government. If all this was true, there could be little question of the two levels of government being equal in status.

Unlike the federalists in the early years of the United States, proponents of centripetal federalism in nineteenth-century Canada did not receive much assistance from the courts. To some extent this was their own fault. Although the BNA Act had given the federal government the power to establish a general appeal court for Canada, the Macdonald government did not bother to do so before its resignation over the Pacific Scandal in 1873. The Liberal government of Alexander Mackenzie did establish the Supreme Court of Canada in 1875, but it is possible that the delay contributed to that court's failure to emerge from the shadow of the Judicial Committee of the Privy Council. In its early years the Supreme Court attempted to expound a centripetal view of federalism, but there was no one on it with the eloquence and prestige of a John Marshall, and few cases came before it in the early years that provided much opportunity to exercise the influence of its American counterpart. Federal governments inexplicably did not take the opportunity which was provided them to ''pack'' the court with skilful and articulate proponents of the centripetal position. Admittedly the possibility of appeal to the Judicial Committee of the Privy Council would have severely limited the usefulness of such a strategy. The Judicial Committee itself expressed a moderately centripetal view of federalism in a few early cases, notably *Russell* vs. *the Queen* (1882), but in the year after Macdonald's death it began a process of curtailing federal powers which was to occupy it for almost half a century.

Academics also provided little support for centripetal federalism in the nineteenth century, partly because their influence was minimized by circumstances that have already been discussed. This was in contrast to the United States after the Civil War, where influential academics like Francis Lieber, Elisha Mulford, John W. Burgess, and Woodrow Wilson expounded notions of centripetal federalism borrowed from

Bismarck's Germany and embellished with Hegelian notions of national destiny.[9] In Canada, characteristically enough, the only academic of comparable fame or influence was Goldwin Smith, an imported English liberal who ridiculed the possibility of building a Canadian nation.

Macdonald's last years were clouded by cultural conflict, economic recession, and the emergence of strong provincial governments. At his death the federal Conservative party collapsed into disarray, never fully to be restored in all its nineteenth-century splendour. In 1896 the Liberals took office with a platform of "provincial rights" and under the leadership of Wilfrid Laurier, who, as a young follower of A. A. Dorion, had opposed Confederation in 1867. The effect of these events on the federal system was less than might have been expected. Like the earlier Liberal government headed by Alexander Mackenzie, the Laurier Liberals did not hesitate to use the power of disallowance, and their long unbroken period of office in Ottawa inclined them more and more to espouse a centripetal position. It was the Conservatives, in opposition, who now began to take up the cry of "provincial rights", usually on behalf of their fellow partisans who controlled the government of Ontario from 1905 onwards.

Controversy over federalism became irrelevant with the outbreak of the First World War, and after the war circumstances were not conducive to defence of the centripetal concept. The ill-advised behaviour of the ironically named "Union" government between 1917 and 1921 embittered both Quebec and the West, while post-war transportation policies impoverished the Maritimes. Regional discontent in the 1920s overshadowed any sense of national purpose, a concept which had been discredited by wartime experience in any event. The inheritor of this political situation was William Lyon Mackenzie King, a Prime Minister more famed for political manoeuvring than for eloquence. King had no interest in federalism, and he believed that national unity could best be assured by having the central government do as little as possible. The most dramatic achievement of his first nine years in office was to bring the National Policy to an end by "returning" public lands and resources to the Prairie provinces.

Controversy over federalism was renewed by the Great

Depression after 1929, and centripetal concepts were elo-quently expounded for the first time in more than a generation. While the depression exposed Canadian federalism to great stresses and strains, it also convinced many Canadians that the central government should assert its authority more decisively than it had done in the preceding decade, and that if necessary the constitution should be amended to give it the powers required. The lesson seemed clear that a decentralized regime with semi-autonomous provincial governments was inadequate to alleviate the consequences of the depression or to prevent similar catastrophes in future.

While the revival of the centripetal concept was in some ways reminiscent of the Macdonald version half a century earlier, the circumstances were very different. Macdonald's federalism had emphasized the economic role of the state as an importer of capital and labour, a builder of railways and canals, and a developer of western hinterlands. In doing so it corresponded to the interests of a rising *bourgeoisie* which needed the assistance of a strong state to accumulate capital and which, at a time of limited urbanization, low expectations, and restricted suffrage, had little need to take the demands of other classes into account. In the 1930s the centripetal concept of federalism was again associated with support for "the positive state", but the sources of that support and the tasks which the state was expected to perform had changed. Those who wanted to strengthen the central government now wished to do so in order that it could protect the elderly, the unemployed, and the primary producers unable to sell their products, in order that it could plan the economy for the benefit of the many rather than the few, and in order that it could pursue social and cultural as well as economic objectives. On the other hand, business was now decidedly more ambivalent in its attitude towards the state than it had been in the nineteenth century, since universal suffrage had made the positive state a double-edged sword from its point of view. In fact Canadian as well as American capitalists had discovered and welcomed the characteristic of federalism identified long before by A. V. Dicey: that is, its ability to frustrate and impede the actions of governments by imposing judicially defined legal restraints on their freedom and authority.[10] Since the major federal political parties continued as in the past to be closely allied with big business, one paradoxical result of this situation was that the federal government itself was no longer a firm or consistent exponent of centripetal federalism. That exceptions could be made, however, was shown by the unexpected revival of the practice of disallowance when Alberta's Social Credit government adopted legislation that threatened the mortgage companies and the chartered banks.

As in the past, the judiciary gave little encouragement to supporters of the centripetal concept. Admittedly there was a brief period at the onset of the depression when Ramsay MacDonald's Labour government in Britain had affected the composition of the Judicial Committee of the Privy Council, and when that body appeared to be embarking on a new course of support for centripetal federalism. The scope of the federal "trade and commerce" power was broadened at the expense of "property and civil rights" in a decision that upheld the Combines Investigation Act. Aeronautics and radio broadcasting were placed under federal jurisdiction in decisions that cited the general power "to make Laws for the Peace, Order, and good Government of Canada".[11] However, this promising trend of judicial interpretation ended abruptly a few years later, at the very moment when the circumstances of the depression most required that it continue.

Instead, it was left to political radicals and academics to perpetuate the tradition of centripetal federalism, albeit in a new guise. Like much else in the 1930s, this was something of a novelty. Until the depression the strongest current of political radicalism had been of an agrarian character, and from the *Rouges* and Clear Grits to the United Farmers of Alberta its adherents had distrusted the central government as the tool of Montreal merchants and bankers, at the same time as they expounded the virtues of local autonomy. The new Co-operative Commonwealth Federation (CCF), however, was of a different character. While it sought to incorporate the old tradition of agrarian radicalism, and held its founding meetings in Calgary and Regina, its political philosophy came from central-Canadian intellectuals who were strongly influenced by the Fabian Society and the British Labour Party. Like the Fabians, they had a rather naive faith in the positive state that separated them sharply from Marxism. In a Canadian context they placed their faith in the central government, which seemed to be the only one even potentially capable of creative action, and they deplored the constraints that provincial ambition and judicial interpretation had placed on its authority.

Perhaps the most important academic exponent of centripetal federalism, in this or any other period, was F. R. Scott, a founder of the CCF and a professor of law at McGill University. In numerous articles, not to mention some satiric poems, he attacked the Judicial Committee of the Privy Council for distorting and misinterpreting what had been intended as a highly centralized constitution. At the same time he argued that a return to Macdonald's assumptions concerning the constitution was essential to the cause of economic and social reform in Canada. Social planning and the welfare state were the modern equivalent of "Peace, Order, and good government".[12]

Not only Fabian reformers, but also Marxist revolutionaries, demanded the strengthening of Ottawa at the expense of the provincial governments to deal with the depression, and perhaps also to confront the rising threat of fascism overseas. The Communist party's brief to the Royal Commission on Dominion-Provincial Relations looked forward, as Macdonald had done, to the virtual disappearance of the provincial governments. The fact that provincial governments had been retained after Confederation was attributed to "semi-feudal influences, seeking to preserve the powers of landlordism and feudalism in the provinces". After listing a number of necessary reforms that had been blocked by the courts and the provincial governments, the brief continued:

> ... all forces desiring economic progress demand the completion of Canadian national unification to enable the Dominion government to meet these burning needs. ... Every Canadian who truly loves his country and is devoted to the welfare of its people is against the blocking of national progress by the provincial dismemberment of the nation at the hands of reaction.[13]

Tim Buck's pleas, and those of the Royal Commission itself, fell largely on deaf ears. It was the imperatives of war, not the miseries of depression, that converted the federal government and the ruling class, at least temporarily, to the cause of centripetal federalism. The federal government's conversion was, however, prolonged far into the post-war period by the transformation of the Liberals into a "government party" seemingly entrenched in power, dependent on the expanded federal bureaucracy for ideas and personnel, and curiously detached from their affiliated parties in the provinces.[14] In the process they abandoned the last vestiges of their traditional position, more symbolic than real in any event, as the party of "provincial rights". Prime Minister Louis St. Laurent (1948-57) was the most convinced centripetal federalist to occupy the office since Macdonald, as suggested by the most celebrated, if not most accurate, of his aphorisms, "Le Québec est une province comme les autres." Under his leadership the federal government abolished appeals to the Judicial Committee of the Privy Council and affirmed the right to amend the BNA Act without consulting the provinces.

The St. Laurent decade was a period of prosperity, similar in some ways to the era of Laurier. An avuncular French Canadian presided over a central government that seemed to solve problems without effort, and few noticed the storm clouds brewing on the horizon. English-speaking academic writers on federalism in the 1950s almost unanimously took a centripetal view, and were even supported by some of their French-speaking counterparts. Donald Creighton's two-volume biography of Macdonald was an impassioned defence of the National Policy. Maurice Lamontagne brought Keynesian economics to the defence of centripetal federalism in *Le Fédéralisme Canadien,* and urged his fellow-Quebecers to abandon the sterile policy of obstructing federal initiatives.[15] F. R. Scott soldiered on in the pages of the law journals, and was joined by younger scholars like Bora Laskin. With the abolition of appeals to the Judicial Committee of the Privy Council the trend of judicial interpretation seemed at least to be flowing in their direction, as suggested by a number of opinions extending the federal power over trade and commerce, as well as other opinions which curtailed the power of the Quebec provincial government to interfere with civil liberties. A book of essays co-edited by Scott and published in 1958 actually suggested that the battle for centripetal federalism had been won and that pressures were tending irresistibly towards centralization.[16] The optimism proved unwarranted, to say the least. A decade later the federal system was in disarray, and by the 1970s the surviving academic and political advocates of centripetal federalism were outnumbered and ideologically on the defensive. The alternative concept of centrifugal federalism, which had been temporarily eclipsed, re-emerged in full force. Its advocates, like their opponents, could draw sustenance from a deep reservoir of tradition.

CENTRIFUGAL FEDERALISM

The concept of centrifugal federalism was first articulated by provincial politicians, particularly in Ontario. The latter fact, unlike the first, may seem surprising, since Canada West had shown the greatest enthusiasm for Confederation of any province before 1867, but the government of the largest and richest province was in one sense the natural leader of a movement for provincial autonomy. Contributing factors were the Macdonald government's tendency to take Ontario for granted and the fact that Toronto capitalists gained less than they had expected from the annexation of the West. The contract to build the Pacific railway went to a group closely associated with the Bank of Montreal.

The man who did more than any other to advance the cause and to propagate the doctrine of centrifugal federalism was Oliver Mowat, the Liberal Premier of Ontario from 1872 until 1896.[17] Mowat had been a supporter of the Macdonald–Brown coalition and a Father of Confederation, in which capacity he moved the resolution dealing with provincial legislative powers at the Quebec conference. After a brief period as a judge, he resigned to become Premier of Ontario when Edward Blake opted to pursue his career in federal politics. Although John A. Macdonald had hoped to perpetuate coalition governments at both levels, his own government had increasingly taken on a Conservative hue, with the result that Liberals became supporters of provincial autonomy and supporters of provincial autonomy became Liberals. One consequence was that the Liberal party, while remaining true to George Brown's ideals, was able to incorporate (and incidentally make harmless) the remnants of anti-Confederation sentiment in all of the provinces. Expounding the centrifugal concept of federalism was in part a means to this end.

No one played this game more skilfully than Oliver Mowat, but he had imitators elsewhere, such as his Quebec ally and counterpart Honoré Mercier. The Nova Scotia Liberal party, incorporating most of the anti-Confederation forces, was able by mobilizing anti-federal sentiment to monopolize political power at the provincial level for an unbelievably long time, from 1882 until 1925 without interruption. In the process it permanently degraded the politics of the province. Nova Scotia remains unique among the provinces in its total lack of any meaningful distinction between the government and the official opposition.[18]

In its original, most durable, and most successful version, the centrifugal concept of federalism took the form of the compact theory, whose rather ironic origins have already been described. In his monograph on the compact theory, Ramsay Cook states that there were two versions of it, the compact between two cultural groups and the compact between provinces, but he correctly points out that the latter interpretation was by far the more widespread and influential.[19] Quebec provincial politicians were in the fortunate situation of not having to distinguish clearly between the two versions. In the other provinces, where the compact theory was at least equally popular, the second version was the only one to appear, for fairly obvious reasons.

The main substantive point of the compact theory is the assertion that no change in the constitution can be made except with the consent of all "the provinces". By "the provinces" is meant, of course, the provincial governments. The first occasion on which this argument was presented after Confederation occurred when the Macdonald government increased its grant to Nova Scotia in an effort to head off the secessionist movement in that province. Other provincial governments argued that this was in effect a revision of that section of the BNA Act which dealt with federal-provincial grants, and that the federal government had no right to improve the terms offered to one provincial government without consulting the others. Eighty years later, and in a somewhat similar vein, the Quebec and Ontario governments argued that the federal government had no right to admit Newfoundland as a Canadian province without consent of the governments of the existing provinces. In both cases the federal government in effect brushed aside these objections by arguing that it was not in fact amending the constitution as it affected the interests of existing provinces. In certain other cases, however, it has tacitly accepted the assumptions of the compact theory.

Although the compact theory itself might be fairly innocuous, apart from its highly elitist connotations, it has another far-reaching implication as well. In order to equate "the provinces" with the provincial governments it is necessary to assume that only the provincial governments are capable of representing provincial interests. It will be recalled that Macdonald explicitly denied this and argued that provincial interests are represented at both levels of government. In contrast, Premier Honoré Mercier's opening statement at the Interprovincial Conference of 1887, which had been called at his initiative, described the conference as a successor and counterpart to the conferences on Confederation in 1864, ignoring the rather fundamental distinction that, in 1887, a federal level of government also existed which was not represented at the conference. The conference then proceeded to recommend a number of basic changes in the existing constitution, which recommendations it chose to interpret as evidence that "the provinces" had expressed their views, and that these were the only views worth considering.[20] If one begins from the compact theory, it does not take much of a conceptual leap virtually to define the federal government out of existence, an implication of the theory that the Canadian Fathers of Confederation presumably did not anticipate in 1865.

The Interprovincial Conference of 1887 has generally been considered a significant victory for the centrifugal concept of federalism, in spite of the fact that only five of the seven provincial governments attended. It came at a time when the controversy over Louis Riel's execution and the failure of the National Policy to stimulate the economy had placed the federal government on the defensive. Although the recommendations of the conference were not implemented (and some of them are still under discussion almost a century later) historians have suggested that the federal government was in fact forced to make concessions to the centrifugal point of view, for example by ceasing to disallow provincial acts on purely political rather than legal grounds.

In any event provincial politicians were no longer entirely alone in expounding a centrifugal concept of federalism. From about this period onwards powerful reinforcement was to be forthcoming from two directions: French-Canadian nationalist intellectuals and the Judicial Committee of the Privy Council.

The execution of Louis Riel in 1885, apart from its effect on the fortunes of the Conservative party, had the far more significant consequence of altering French-Canadian attitudes towards the federal state itself. Riel was regarded by French Canadians as the defender of French-Canadian rights in the West, a role which he had certainly played in 1869–70, although it is more difficult to discern any relevance or rational purpose in his activities of 1884–85. Whatever the merits of his case, his death made him a convenient symbol and rallying point for those who wished to stimulate provincially oriented nationalism in Quebec. His failure, as well as subsequent events in Manitoba and the territories, also underlined what many were beginning to suspect, that the West would inevitably become an English-speaking extension of Ontario and that only in Quebec would a French-speaking majority ever exist. This realization greatly stimulated the tendency, which had always been at least latent, to identify the province of Quebec with French Canada, and thus to emphasize the preservation and enlargement of provincial autonomy as a French-Canadian goal.[21] This was a gradual process, which only reached its culmination in very recent times, but Riel's death, and the victory of Mercier's significantly named Parti National at the provincial election a year later, were important milestones. Among French-speaking Quebec intellectuals the notion that federalism was valid only insofar as it protected provincial and cultural autonomy was henceforth almost universal. That provincial and cultural autonomy were not necessarily synonymous was still at times admitted, but with diminishing force and conviction as the prospects of the French-speaking minorities outside of Quebec deteriorated.

Of more immediate significance in reinforcing the centrifugal concept of federalism was the way in which the Judicial Committee of the Privy Council, under the leadership of Lord Watson, began to interpret the BNA Act. In 1892 it was called upon to determine whether the provincial government in New Brunswick possessed the Crown's traditional prerogative of priority over ordinary creditors in the collection of debts. In giving an affirmative answer to this seemingly technical question, it based its reasoning on the highly questionable assumption that the BNA Act had not altered the relationship between the Crown and the provincial governments, and that the latter were therefore equal in dignity and status with the federal government. Furthermore, it contended that "The object of the Act was neither to weld the provinces into one, nor to subordinate provincial governments to a central authority, but to create a federal government in which they should all be represented, entrusted with the exclusive administration of affairs in which they had a common interest, each province retaining its independence and autonomy."[22]

This decision, or more precisely the reasoning on which it was based, fundamentally altered the whole nature of Canada's federal constitution. It appeared to lend credence to the argument that the purpose of Confederation had been to protect and promote provincial interests, rather than to create a new nation, and it did so just as the generation that had direct memories of the Confederation negotiations and debates was passing from the scene. Henceforth the ideological weight of Imperial authority was placed on the side of those who espoused provincial autonomy, and the supporters of centripetal federalism were placed on the defensive.

The Judicial Committee continued its work with a series of decisions in which it was called upon to define the legislative jurisdictions of the two levels of government. The scope of the expression "Laws for the Peace, Order, and good Government of Canada" was gradually whittled away until, in 1922, Lord Watson's disciple, Viscount Haldane, announced the discovery that the power which it conferred could only be exercised in times of unusual emergency.[23] Federal legislative powers were in practice restricted to the enumerated sub-sections of Section 92 and the most potentially inclusive of these, the sub-section referring to trade and commerce, was given a remarkably narrow definition. Meanwhile the provincial authority over "property and civil rights", originally conferred for the very specific purpose of enabling Quebec to retain its civil code, was elevated into a major obstacle to federal activity, particularly activity which various business interests found disturbing.[24]

Provincial politicians continued to expound the compact theory, or various versions thereof, a task at which Conservatives soon proved as adept as Liberals. In the twentieth century, with the Liberals usually on the government benches in Ottawa and the Conservatives usually controlling the provincial government of Ontario, party positions on federalism became increasingly indistinct; if anything the Conservatives were now the party of "provincial rights" although the increasing dependence of the federal Liberals on Quebec votes meant that they could not openly attack the centrifugal concept even when in office. Conservative premiers of Ontario, particularly Howard Ferguson, who held the office from 1928 until 1932, pursued Oliver Mowat's approach to federalism in both word and deed.

The depression of the 1930s greatly increased the tension and conflict between the two levels of government. While it led increasing numbers of radicals and academics to espouse the centripetal concept, as discussed above, it also led to increasingly strident expressions of the centrifugal concept on the part of provincial politicians. Class conflict increased sharply as a result of the hardship suffered by both workers and farmers. Provincial politicians attempted to neutralize or sublimate it by preaching the doctrine that the province was a community which transcended class distinctions, and which was threatened by sinister external forces of which the federal government was a convenient symbol. In a sense this was the domestic equivalent, although a less harmful one, of the right-wing authoritarianism or fascism that was sweeping across Europe and Japan at the same time. In Quebec and Alberta the phenomenon appeared under the new and ambiguous party labels of Union Nationale and Social Credit respectively. In Ontario and British Columbia the demagogues preferred to style themselves as "Liberals", although their open attacks on the federal party and government bearing the same name would have been unthinkable to an earlier generation.

The economic upswing that followed Canada's mobilization for war dissolved most of the tension, and in the post-war period most English-speaking Canadians appeared to support or at least accept centripetal federalism. Quebec, however, was another story. An uncompromisingly centrifugal position was maintained by Maurice Duplessis' Union Nationale, which returned to office in 1944 after a brief intermission, and by most of the French-speaking academic elite, both clerics and laymen. A particularly eloquent statement of the centrifugal concept was produced in 1956 by the provincial Royal Commission of Inquiry on Constitutional Problems, better known as the Tremblay Commission.[25] Its report defended the compact theory and proposed that the provincial governments take over all direct taxation, all responsibility for social security, and partial responsibility for macro-economic policy. The provinces, and Quebec in particular, were declared to be distinctive cultural communities whose preservation should be the major objective of federalism, with the obvious corollary that the central government should play no role in matters broadly defined as "cultural". Federal-provincial bargaining should be institutionalized and recognized as a normal method of making policy at the national level. Had many English-speaking Canadians read this report at the time, they would probably have considered its recommendations to be bizarre and extreme, but by the twentieth anniversary of its publication they had virtually become the conventional wisdom.

From about 1963 onwards the centrifugal concept of federalism was brought to the attention of English-speaking Canadians as the government of Quebec, spurred on by an increasing host of nationalist intellectuals and by its own insatiable demand for revenue, sought to loosen the ties of Confederation without sacrificing the economic advantages thereof. Other provincial governments were also becoming more powerful, more militant, and more inclined to challenge the federal authority, although W. A. C. Bennett of British Columbia was the only Premier outside of Quebec to abandon all pretence of restraint or moderation and adopt the centrifugal concept without qualification. The Ontario government of John Robarts was characteristically more moderate in its language but far more effective in its actions. The federal government, which had begun to retreat from the centripetal concept even in St. Laurent's last years as Prime Minister, virtually ceased to resist the provincial offensive under Lester Pearson. In response to relentless prodding by Robarts it launched an ill-advised Constitutional Conference in 1968, thus implicitly conceding that it was no longer prepared to uphold the BNA Act. Only the Supreme Court continued to defend Canada's constitution, and to interpret it in something approaching its original spirit, particularly after Bora Laskin became the Chief Justice in 1973.

French-speaking academics and intellectuals who expressed views on federalism almost universally applauded the centrifugal tendency, and in many cases championed the cause of political independence for the province of Quebec. The few who dissented from the prevailing trend included Maurice Lamontagne, Jean-Luc Pépin, and Pierre Elliott Trudeau (all of whom abandoned academic life for federal politics), and Maurice Pinard and Albert Breton (who sought refuge at English-speaking universities). In French-speaking Quebec the ideological hegemony of ethnic nationalism was even firmer by 1970 than it had been a generation earlier, although it differed from the earlier nationalism in its totally secular emphasis and its indifference to the francophone minorities outside of Quebec.

English-speaking academics at first continued their traditional preference for a strong central government, although in the 1960s there were efforts to reinterpret this position in ways that more explicitly recognized Canada's linguistic duality, while retaining a central government strong enough to pursue social reforms and protect Canada from the cultural and economic domination of the United States. Efforts to harmonize these objectives ranged from Donald Smiley's call for an updating of the Macdonald–Cartier tradition to the advocacy of "special status for Quebec" (and a reduction of provincial autonomy elsewhere) by Gad Horowitz and Cy Gonick.[26] Meanwhile the New Democratic party, successor to the CCF, had been persuaded by its intellectual advisors to adopt the concept of Canada as "two nations". The implications of this for federalism were not specified, and the only apparent consequence was to forfeit the allegiance of Eugene Forsey, who eventually became a Liberal senator. Pierre Elliott Trudeau's leadership of the Liberal party after 1968 was welcomed by many centripetal federalists, including Forsey, but others distrusted Trudeau for his hostility to nationalism and his ambivalence towards the positive state.[27] Ironically he was soon to be distrusted even more when he mobilized the power of the federal state against the Front de Libération de Québec (FLQ) in October 1970.

After 1970 there was a remarkable shift of English-speaking academic opinion towards the centrifugal position. Personal hostility towards Trudeau after the October crisis undoubtedly played a part in this evolution, as did an increasing sympathy towards the separatist Parti Québécois.[28] The latter sentiment was not unmixed with envy, since the Parti Québécois was decidedly more successful in nationalist consciousness-raising than were those English-speaking academics who attempted to rally support for anti-American policies. In fact the defeat of Canadian nationalism in both its socialist and liberal variants appeared to convince many academics that the ship of state might founder in a sea of Americanism but that one of its water-tight compartments (to quote from Lord Atkin's opinion in the Labour Conventions reference) could remain afloat with the aid of the French language. The pro-separatist manifesto of the "Committee for a New Constitution" was endorsed in 1977 by an impressive list of prominent Canadian "nationalists."[29]

More surprising even than the sympathy for Quebec nationalism was a growing disposition to emphasize, and to celebrate, the real or imagined diversities of identity and "culture" among the other provinces, which John Porter had dismissed only a few years before as "hallowed nonsense". The celebration of provincial "cultures" and diversities, as well as the harping on regional grievances, had been part of the rhetorical stock-in-trade of provincial politicians for a century. The Constitutional Conference of 1968–71 probably brought it to the attention of a wider audience than ever before, but this did not explain why it should suddenly have been taken seriously by political scientists.[30] One reviewer of Edwin Black's book, *Divided Loyalties,* suggested that academics were adopting pro-provincial positions in recognition of the fact that provincial governments now controlled the budgets of the universities.[31] A similar but more convincing explanation can perhaps be found in the declining geographical mobility that resulted from the slower growth of the universities in the 1970s and the scarcity of new academic positions. Those who for the first time faced the probability of spending a lifetime in a single province were in a similar position to their French-speaking Quebec counterparts, whose mobility had always been limited by language. In both cases the response was to make a virtue of necessity by celebrating the province as a meaningful socio-cultural community, while rejecting the Canadian community as unreal and artificial.

In discussing the progress of the centrifugal concept in recent years it would be remiss to neglect the contribution of the federal Progressive Conservative party from 1967 onwards. Although an adequate analysis of the party's internal controversies remains to be undertaken, it seems reasonable to conclude that John Diefenbaker, a leader who was demonstrably more popular than the party itself, was deposed from the leadership because of his efforts to make the federal party more independent of its powerful provincial affiliates.[32] After Diefenbaker's removal, the provincial affiliates exerted far more influence over the federal party, and the latter's views on federalism became increasingly centrifugal. This tendency was further accentuated by the next change of leadership, when Joseph Clark succeeded Robert Stanfield in 1976. The views on federalism expressed by Clark and his principal lieutenants, in speeches both inside and outside the House of Commons, irresistibly bring to mind a comment made by Chief Justice John Marshall of the United States in one of his major judicial opinions:

> Powerful and ingenious minds, taking, as postulates, that the powers expressly granted to the government of the Union are to be contracted, by construction, into the narrowest possible compass, and that the original powers of the States are retained, if any possible construction will retain them,

may, by a course of well-digested, but refined and meta-physical reasoning, founded on these premises, explain away the constitution of our country, and leave it a magnificent structure indeed, to look at, but totally unfit for use.[33]

NOTES

1. J. R. Mallory, "The Five Faces of Federalism", in P. A. Crépeau and C. B. Macpherson, eds., *The Future of Canadian Federalism* (Toronto: University of Toronto Press, 1965), pp. 3–15.

2. Edwin R. Black, *Divided Loyalties: Canadian Concepts of Federalism* (Montreal: McGill-Queen's University Press, 1975).

3. John Porter, *The Vertical Mosaic: An Analysis of Social Class and Power in Canada* (Toronto: University of Toronto Press, 1965), pp. 379–85.

4. David K. Elton, "Public Opinion and Federal-Provincial Relations: A Case Study in Alberta", in J. Peter Meekison, ed., *Canadian Federalism: Myth or Reality,* 3rd ed. (Toronto: Methuen, 1977), pp. 49-63. The Canadian Institute of Public Opinion's *Gallup Poll Report* frequently includes questions related to federalism. See for example the *Report* of March 19, 1977.

5. Joseph Pope, *Correspondence of Sir John Macdonald* (Toronto: Oxford University Press, 1921), pp. 74–75.

6. Canada, Legislature, *Parliamentary Debates on the Subject of the Confederation of the British North American Provinces* (Quebec, 1865), pp. 27–28.

7. Data compiled from G. V. Laforest, *Disallowance and Reservation of Provincial Legislation* (Ottawa: Queen's Printer, 1955).

8. Pope, *Correspondence of Sir John Macdonald,* p. 379.

9. W. H. Bennett, *American Theories of Federalism* (University of Alabama, 1964).

10. J. R. Mallory, *Social Credit and the Federal Power in Canada* (Toronto: University of Toronto Press, 1954).

11. Proprietary Articles Trade Association *v.* AG for Canada (1931), AC 310; *In Re* Regulation and Control of Aeronautics in Canada (1932), AC 54; *In Re* Regulation and Control of Radio Communication in Canada (1932), AC 394.

12. Frank R. Scott, *Essays on the Constitution: Aspects of Canadian Law and Politics* (Toronto: University of Toronto Press, 1977). This collection includes papers published between 1928 and 1971.

13. Royal Commission on Dominion-Provincial Relations, *Report of Hearings* (Ottawa, 1939), pp. 9718, 9719, 9724.

14. Reginald Whitaker, *The Government Party: Organizing and Financing the Liberal Party of Canada, 1930-1958* (Toronto: University of Toronto Press, 1977).

15. Maurice Lamontagne, *Le Fédéralisme Canadien* (Québec: Les Presses de l'université Laval, 1954).

16. A. R. M. Lower and F. R. Scott, *Evolving Canadian Federalism* (Durham, N.C.: Duke University Press, 1958).

17. Christopher Armstrong, "The Mowat Heritage in Federal-Provincial Relations", in Donald Swainson, ed., *Oliver Mowat's Ontario* (Toronto: Macmillan, 1972).

18. The "paranoid style" of Nova Scotia politics is discussed by George Rawlyk, "The Maritimes and the Canadian Community", in Mason Wade, ed., *Regionalism in the Canadian Community* (Toronto: University of Toronto Press, 1969). On the lack of distinction between Nova Scotian political parties, see Jane Jenson, "Party Systems", in David J. Bellamy *et al., The Provincial Political Systems: Comparative Essays* (Toronto: Methuen, 1976), pp. 118–31.

19. Ramsay Cook, *Provincial Autonomy, Minority Rights, and the Compact Theory, 1867–1921,* Study no. 4 of the Royal Commission on Bilingualism and Biculturalism (Ottawa: Queen's Printer, 1969).

20. Ibid., pp. 41–42.

21. Michel Brunet, *Québec–Canada anglais* (Montréal: Editions HMH, 1969), discusses this evolution from the viewpoint of a Quebec separatist.

22. Maritime Bank *v.* Receiver General of New Brunswick (1892), AC 437.

23. *In Re* Board of Commerce Act (1922), 1 AC 191.

24. For an extended critique of the Judicial Committee, and a defence of centripetal federalism, see Canada, Senate, session of 1939, *Report by the Parliamentary Counsel Relating to the Enactment of the British North America Act, 1867, any lack of consonance between its terms and judicial construction of them and cognate matters.* For a more favourable view see Alan C. Cairns, "The Judicial Committee and its Critics", *Canadian Journal of Political Science,* IV (1971): 301–05.

25. The full report was published simultaneously in French and English by the Quebec Government Printer. For a useful abridgment, see David Kwavnick, ed., *The Tremblay Report: Report of the Royal Commission of Inquiry on Constitutional Problems* (Toronto: McClelland and Stewart, 1973).

26. Donald V. Smiley, *The Canadian Political Nationality* (Toronto: Methuen, 1967); C. W. Gonick, "English Canada and Special Status", and Gad Horowitz, "The Trudeau Doctrine", both in *Canadian Dimension,* V, no. 5 (1968).

27. For a selection of Trudeau's work, see P. E. Trudeau, *Federalism and the French Canadians* (Toronto: Macmillan, 1968).

28. For an expression of this viewpoint see Denis Smith, *Bleeding Hearts, Bleeding Country: Canada and the Quebec Crisis* (Edmonton: Hurtig, 1971).

29. "Canada and Quebec: A proposal for a new constitution", *Canadian Forum,* LVII, no. 672 (June–July 1977): 4–5.
30. See, for example, John Wilson, "The Canadian Political Cultures: Towards a Redefinition of the Nature of the Canadian Political System", in *Canadian Journal of Political Science,* VII (1974):438–83; and S. J. R. Noel, "Political Parties and Elite Accommodation: Interpretations of Canadian Federalism", in Meekison, *Canadian Federalism,* pp. 64–83.
31. Frank Mackinnon, in *Canadian Journal of Political Science,* IX (1976): 499–501.
32. See the interesting memoirs of the party's former national director, James Johnston, *The Party's Over* (Toronto: Longman, 1971).
33. Quoted in Richard E. Johnston, *The Effect of Judicial Review on Federal-State Relations in Canada, Australia, and the United States* (Baton Rouge: Louisiana State University Press, 1969), p. 218.

4   The Political Economy of Decentralization

The preceding chapter has described how two contrasting concepts of Canadian federalism have been expounded throughout the course of Canada's history as a federal state. Yet the history of centripetal and centrifugal federalism as intellectual or political concepts cannot really explain the way in which the structures of Canadian federalism have actually evolved. Even if it were possible to measure precisely the popularity of the two concepts or the eloquence with which they were expounded at different periods in Canadian history, one would not find a particularly close or direct relationship between the centripetal-centrifugal balance at the level of ideas or concepts and the centripetal-centrifugal balance at the level of institutions or political power.

In fact the centripetal and centrifugal concepts have coexisted simultaneously throughout the years of Canada's federal history, and in periods when one was vigorously expressed the other has tended to be also. Political and ideological controversy over federalism is particularly acute during periods when power is shifting from one level of government to the other, and at such times both centripetal and centrifugal concepts will be vigorously and widely expounded. During periods of stability, when the balance of power between the two levels of government is not changing rapidly, controversy over federalism subsides, and there is less need for either of the concepts to be expounded by politicians, judges, or academics. These generalizations seem to correspond with reality to a large degree. The periods of rapid change in Canadian federalism occurred roughly between 1887 and 1914, when power shifted rapidly towards the provincial governments, between 1935 and 1941, when power shifted towards the federal government, and since 1954 (but particularly since 1963), when power again shifted towards the provincial governments. In all of these periods controversy between the proponents of centripetal and centrifugal federalism has been acute, noticeable, and vigorous. Both those who welcomed the prevailing trend and those who opposed it expressed their sentiments in an articulate and vigorous manner. In the more stable periods, on the other hand, there was relatively little discussion about federalism.

If we are correct in arguing that the actual evolution of federalism explains the expression of the concepts, rather than the other way around, we are left with the problem of explaining why that evolution took the course it did. More particularly, we must explain why a federal constitution which was originally so centralized that its principal author, John A. Macdonald, confidently expected the provincial governments to decline or even disappear entirely has instead evolved in such a manner that "among the more or less centralized federations of the modern world, most writers would agree that Canada is about as decentralized as one can get."[1] It is true that for a period of about twenty years, beginning in the early part of the Second World War, Canadian federalism briefly returned to some semblance of the centralization which Macdonald intended. Towards the end of this period academic observers even assumed that the trend was permanent and irreversible. None the less, the reality throughout most of the twentieth century — and at no time more than the present — has been a situation in which the central government exercises less power, and the provincial governments exercise more power, than in any other developed country.

Innumerable efforts have been made to account for this phenomenon, and a variety of factors have been cited as possible contributors to it. Norman Rogers, in a pioneering article, emphasized "changes in political consciousness and sentiment" as the source of centrifugal and centripetal trends in Canadian federalism.[2] Although this theory is impossible to support on the evidence, it seems to be widely popular, perhaps because of its reassuring implication that Canadians always get the kind of federalism they want, and will presumably continue to do so. Rogers also contended, as have a multitude of subsequent writers, that the provincial governments could not be kept in a subordinate position because there was no widespread sense of attachment to Canada as a nation. J. M. S. Careless, following in this tradition, perceived a relationship between the various "limited identities" of Canadians, identities which are ethnic and religious as well as provincial and regional.[3] Many observers have focused on the anglophone-francophone cleavage as the major centrifugal influence on Canadian federalism, even though, as Donald Smiley observes, the government of Ontario has until recently offered more resistance to federal predominance than has the Quebec government. [4]

Another school of thought has attributed the decentralization of Canadian federalism to the interpretation of the BNA Act by the courts, and particularly by the Judicial Committee of the Privy Council. This is the view of centripetal federalists like F. R. Scott and Bora Laskin, who condemn the Judicial Committee for its performance, but it is also shared by those, like Alan Cairns and Pierre Elliott Trudeau, who argue that the Judicial Committee should be commended for transforming an overly centralized constitution into one allegedly more suitable for Canadian circumstances.

There can be little doubt that the Judicial Committee did play a very important role in transforming Canadian federalism, although the reasons why it chose to do so have not been satisfactorily identified. Important as it is, however, judicial interpretation cannot bear the whole responsibility, or even the major part of it, for the evolution of Canadian federalism. If centripetal forces had really been strong, the effects of the Judicial Committee's interpretations could have been largely overcome through constitutional amendments or various devices of constitutional adaptation; this actually happened to some extent during the Second World War and its immediate aftermath. In any event, experience since appeals to the Judicial Committee were abolished in 1949 does not suggest a very strong relationship between judicial interpretation and the evolution of the federal state. During this period the Supreme Court of Canada has largely reversed the Watson–Haldane tradition in its interpretation of the BNA Act; and yet, through most of the same period, power has flowed to the provincial governments at the expense of the central government, at times with the latter's approval or acquiescence, and in apparent disregard of what the Supreme Court was doing. One must seek other factors to explain why the judicial abandonment of the centrifugal concept was not followed by centralization in practice. The fact that it was not distinguishes Canada sharply from the United States, where this did in fact happen from 1937 onwards.

Other possible explanations that have been offered seem equally fruitless. The greater competence of provincial bureaucracies in recent years, for example, is an important fact, but it would seem more likely to be a consequence than a cause of the fact that provincial governments have gained in power and importance. For similar reasons one cannot explain very much by asserting that the subjects enumerated in Section 92 of the BNA Act proved to be unexpectedly more important than those enumerated in Section 91. Many of the tasks performed by the modern state are not explicitly enumerated in either section, and no conceivable reading of the BNA Act would support the illogical distribution of tasks, functions, and powers between the two levels of government that has actually emerged. The important question to answer is why so many matters have in practice been regarded as falling under provincial jurisdiction, in whole or in part, and why the central government has had to share its power with the provincial ones, or to defend it against provincial pressures, to an extent that has few if any parallels elsewhere.

The answer to this riddle seems to lie in certain characteristics of the political economy of Canada, which both produced conflicts between different classes and class fractions and at the same time caused these contending forces to identify their interests with different levels of government, and vice versa. To understand how and why this happened it is important to point out, as Lord Durham did in his report almost a century and a half ago, that the primary function of the state in Canada has been to assist in economic growth, rather than to guarantee internal and external security as was the case with European states. Expressed in Marxist language, this is what the American political economist James O'Connor called the "accumulation" function, meaning that the state directly contributes to the accumulation of profit.[5] Often in Canada it has done this by providing various guarantees and incentives to private enterprise or by intervening directly to supply services such as electric power or transportation without which private profit-making would be impossible. In other words, some of the risks or costs of private enterprise are assumed by the state and paid for by the taxpayer. *Laisser-faire* never existed in Canada. The state has always been a fundamental and essential part of the economic process, and its support has always been of crucial importance to business interests.[6]

Confederation, as we have seen, was largely although by no means exclusively the result of economic motives. Its effect was both to expand the geographical jurisdiction of the Canadian state and to overhaul its machinery so that economic functions both old and new could be performed more effectively. The terms of Confederation, most of which related to economic matters, represented the common denominator of agreement among a variety of economic interests and objectives in the different colonies. Confederation did not, however, end the diversity and conflict among those interests, which soon found expression through a feature of the post-Confederation state which itself was partly the result of that diversity and conflict, namely the existence of two distinct levels of government. In addition, conflict between the dominant class and other classes, particularly the farmers, also had an impact on the dynamics of Canadian federalism.

Under a federal regime conflicting economic interests could theoretically find expression in either or both of two ways: through accommodation and compromise at the level of the central government, assuming that all were represented there to some degree; or through different governments, federal and provincial. Class fractions that perceive the central government as more sympathetic to opposing interests than to their own will tend to seek redress by strengthening the provincial level of government, particularly if they are geographically distributed in such a way that one provincial government represents a geographical area within which one of the frustrated class fractions is particularly important and influential. In such circumstances the provincial government in question will become in a sense the spokesman of the class fraction concerned, as well as carrying out on its behalf the Canadian state's traditional function as the ally and supporter of private enterprise. Efforts will be made to curtail and undermine the power and authority of the unsympathetic and potentially hostile central government, usually by ideological appeals to the virtues of local autonomy, decentralization, and the cultural values allegedly embodied in the province. Any increase in the taxing, spending, and regulatory powers of the provincial level of government will be welcomed, since it will enable that level of government to perform the accumulation function more effectively on behalf of the locally dominant class fraction.

The central government, on the other hand, will be supported by those class fractions which have the most access to it and influence over it, and which can rely upon it to act in support of their economic objectives. Another reason for preferring this level of government may be the fear that overly powerful provincial governments will "balkanize" the country by pursuing policies that restrict the free flow of commodities across provincial boundaries. In addition, classes and class fractions within a province that find the provincial government hostile or unresponsive to their needs will support the strengthening of the central government as a counterweight and may call upon the central government to intervene on their behalf against the provincial government.

Considerations of this kind can lead to fairly long-term alliances between particular class fractions and different levels of government, but changing circumstances may lead to a temporary or even permanent transference of allegiance to the other level. A class fraction which enjoys some influence at both levels of government can also use each one to prevent the other from straying too far out of line, an important consideration in view of the degree of autonomy possessed by modern state apparatuses and the limited but real responsiveness of politicians to subordinate class demands expressed through the electoral process. What Lord Palmerston once said about British foreign policy could be applied to the politics of business in a federal state: its alliances are determined by its interests, not the other way around.

To some degree the extent to which class fractions will rely on the provincial level of government to act on their behalf (and thereby strengthen that level of government in relation to the federal level) depends on how successful the federal level is in accommodating and satisfying all the various fractional interests. Immediately after Confederation a high degree of success in doing so seemed possible. The economies of the different provinces were somewhat similar in character, and severe conflicts of interest among them did not seem likely to arise. Careful efforts were made to represent diverse provincial interests in the cabinet, the Senate, the civil service, and other federal institutions. The apparently most important conflict within the dominant class was the traditional and fierce rivalry between the business interests of Montreal and those of Toronto. The long delay and indecision over the awarding of the Pacific railway contract, as well as the Mackenzie government's policy of having the government itself construct the line, were both the result of not wishing to favour either city at the expense of the other. After 1878, however, this was replaced by the National Policy, under which Montreal received the railway contract although Toronto in the long run reaped greater benefits from its other element, the protective tariff.

For the moment, however, Montreal appeared to be ascendant. Under the skilful leadership of Oliver Mowat the government of Ontario became a rallying point for those who opposed the National Policy: farmers and lumbermen who disliked high tariffs and wanted freer trade with the United States as well as a relief from the financial burden of railway subsidies and incentives. Since Ontario was the largest and richest province and since farming and lumbering were the major industries of central Canada, this was a powerful coalition, as suggested both by Mowat's long tenure in office and by the razor-thin majorities of the federal Conservatives. In 1891 the federal Liberals were persuaded by Mowat to adopt a policy of unrestricted free trade with the United States. The major beneficiary of this would have been the lumber industry of Ontario, which had forged a close alliance with Mowat since the provincial government was the owner of Crown lands and the source of timber licenses.[7] Despite John A. Macdonald's impassioned and probably justified cry that free trade would lead to annexation and the end of the British connection, his party did poorly in Ontario, and he was only saved from electoral defeat by the West (where the CPR was politically influential) and the Maritimes.

Ontario's wealth, power, and size, as well as the contribution of the lumber industry to its provincial treasury, made the government of that province a virtual state within a state; certainly a far cry from the meek and subordinate quasi-municipality that the Fathers of Confederation (including Mowat himself) had expected it to be in 1865. Province-building, as well as nation-building, had begun, with Ontario taking the lead.[8] Provincial powers to manage the public lands and resources, to incorporate companies, and to regulate the vast and nebulous area of "property and civil rights" were used for the benefit of those economic interests that rallied under the provincial banner.

By the turn of the century Ontario had made considerable progress in this direction. At the same time the difficulty of accommodating all economic interests at the federal level had been greatly increased by the growing size and diversity of the Canadian economy and the class and regional conflicts had been exacerbated by the uneven impact of the National Policy itself. Regardless of the BNA Act, the provincial governments had become as important and powerful as the federal one. Disallowance of their legislation virtually ceased, except in the case of British Columbia, which was small and remote enough to be insulated with impunity. Even the B.C. government might have escaped having its legislation disallowed, had not its obsessive dislike of Orientals both embarrassed the British Foreign Office and interfered with the supply of cheap labour for railway-building.

The Canada of the early twentieth century (from Laurier's arrival in office until the beginning of the Second World War) was a country divided along regional lines, largely as a result of the National Policy. The familiar and intractable problem of uneven development (or "regional disparities") had begun to emerge as the industrialization encouraged by the National Policy tariff was increasingly concentrated in Ontario, at the same time as that province also ranked first in agriculture and natural resources. This uneven development not only made it easier for the Ontario government to fight its battle for "provincial rights" but increased its incentive to do so. Since most of the country's wealth appeared to be produced in Ontario, it was plausible to assume, as many Ontarians did and still do, that federal expenditures were taking money out of Ontario's pocket to benefit the undeserving poor in the other provinces. At the same time Ontario was large enough that its government could perform an important accumulation function on behalf of Ontario capitalists, especially those interested in manufacturing or in the development of northern Ontario's mines and forests.

Related to uneven development, and also a consequence of the National Policy, was the emergence of three distinct sectors of the Canadian economy, each with divergent economic interests and class relationships.[9] Of particular importance to the development of federalism was the fact that the three sectors were concentrated in different provinces and regions. Thus each provincial government tended to become the representative and spokesman for a distinct set of interests, rather than a microcosm of the country as a whole.

Secondary manufacturing was one of the three sectors and, as already mentioned, it was heavily concentrated in Ontario. Confederation exposed Maritime manufacturing to Ontario competition, while the National Policy protected Ontario manufacturing from foreign competition and greatly stimulated new industrialization to substitute indigenous products for imports. The seemingly interminable reign of the Ontario provincial Liberals ended in 1905, suggesting that their traces of agrarian populism and their free-trade philosophy were no longer in tune with the character of the province. The new Conservative government was based on an alliance between industrial workers and industrial capitalists, whose solidarity with one another was cemented by the commitment to further industrialization and the need to resist agrarian and anti-tariff interests whose main strength now lay outside of Ontario. Herein lay the source both of the political conservatism of the Ontario working class and of the paradox that the richest and most satisfied province, which also happened to contain the federal capital, remained until very recent times the most militant in resisting the federal government and waving the banner of provincial rights. Even if Ottawa, as viewed from the outlying provinces, seemed partial to the interests of industrial Ontario, the Ontario government was still a far more trustworthy instrument of industrial interests than the federal government. This was shown when Laurier unexpectedly and anachronistically espoused the cause of free trade with the United States and called an election on the issue in 1911. The provincial government of Ontario played a major role in bringing about his crushing defeat.

The second major sector of the economy was export-oriented agriculture. Ontario had originally dominated this sector as well, but after the completion of the CPR main line in 1885 the major growth of this sector occurred in the "Northwest", or the area now occupied by the provinces of Manitoba, Saskatchewan, and Alberta. Prairie wheat became Canada's major export staple and the whole east-west economy was increasingly oriented around it.

Agricultural commodities for export were produced by independent farmers who owned their own land and equipment, in contrast to the wage earners who produced manufactured goods. The antagonism of the farmers was directed against the banks, the mortgage companies, the railways, and the middlemen of the grain trade. The protective tariff was also a source of resentment, since it increased the farmer's expenses while offering him no benefit in return. Thus the farmer's economic interests were contrary to those of the manufacturing sector. An important feature of the agricultural economy was the geographical separation between the farmer and the objects of his antagonism. While the latter were located in Ontario, in Montreal, and to some extent in Winnipeg, the farmers were concentrated on the western prairies, especially in Saskatchewan, where they and their families comprised an actual majority of the population, but also in Alberta, where they were by far the largest occupational group, and in the western part of Manitoba. As a consequence, the conflict between the farmers and their class opponents appeared superficially to be a "regional" rather than a class conflict. A related consequence was that the governments of Saskatchewan and Alberta (Manitoba was a more ambiguous case, at least after the turn of the century) became the representatives and spokesmen of agricultural interests, just as the Ontario government represented and spoke for industrial interests. On the other hand, the farmers viewed the federal government, quite accurately, as the representative of their opponents. Class conflict became federal-provincial conflict.

The third sector of the economy consisted of the export-oriented resource industries: lumbering, mining and smelting, pulp and paper. These resembled the agricultural sector in their dependence on foreign rather than domestic markets, but they resembled the manufacturing sector in that they were based on large-scale enterprises employing wage labour rather than independent commodity production. Class conflict was pronounced, partly because of working conditions and partly because there was no issue that united employees and employers, as the tariff united them in the manufacturing sector. Foreign direct investment, largely American, was important from the outset in this sector. The mining industry was insignificant until about thirty years after Confederation, but grew rapidly thereafter. Forestry had been important since long before Confederation. Pulp and paper expanded rapidly after the United States removed its tariff on newsprint in 1913.

The resource sector was less geographically concentrated than the other two sectors, and was important in every province apart from Alberta, Saskatchewan, and Prince Edward Island. (Alberta already produced coal and oil by 1914, but for domestic consumption only.) However, British Columbia was the only province where the resource sector predominated, producing a distinctive political culture that in many respects makes it more like an Australian state than a Canadian province. Resource-oriented areas in other provinces, such as northern Ontario, Cape Breton Island, and the Abitibi region of Quebec, developed a sense of distinctiveness and an antagonism towards other parts of the province, occasionally expressed in secessionist movements but more frequently in voting for provincial opposition parties.

Only in British Columbia would it be accurate to say that resource capital had virtually exclusive influence over the provincial government, which acted as its representative in the same way that the Ontario government represented the manufacturers and the Saskatchewan government the farmers. In all provinces where it existed, including British Columbia, the resource sector tended to divide the province internally, along class lines and in some cases along regional lines. The antagonism between north and south, for example, is an enduring theme of Ontario politics. However, the resource sector, like the others, reinforced the centrifugal pressures in Canadian federalism. More than either of the other sectors, it was intimately associated with provincial government, because the provinces owned most of the lands and resources. This gave resource capital a weight in provincial politics that was disproportionate to its real importance in provinces like Ontario and Quebec. On the other hand resource capital, unlike the other sectors, was relatively indifferent to the federal level of government, since it required neither protective tariffs nor the elaborate financial and transportation infrastructure of the wheat economy. Thus the rise of the resource sector contributed to the growing importance of provincial governments and the declining relevance of the federal level to the accumulation function of the state. This was particularly true in British Columbia, Quebec, and Ontario. Another consequence of resource development was to revive and strengthen the alliance between the provincial governments of Quebec and Ontario, which had tentatively begun in the time of Mowat and Mercier. Originally based on the common characteristics of large size and political opposition to John A. Macdonald, the alliance was more firmly based in the twentieth century on a common interest in the resources of the Laurentian shield and a desire to minimize the federal government's influence over their development.

These patterns of economic development produced in the early twentieth century a federal system very different from that which the Fathers of Confederation had intended. Manufacturing capital in Ontario (and to some extent in Quebec), resource capital in British Columbia (and to some extent in Ontario and Quebec), farmers in Alberta and Saskatchewan (and to some extent in Manitoba), could all rely on provincial governments to represent their interests and assist in their economic activities. The manufacturers were fortunate enough to exercise influence at two levels of government, sharing power and access with resource capital at the provincial level and with the banks and railways at the federal level. Resource capital and the farmers were weaker at the federal level but contrasted sharply in the extent to which federal policies were relevant to them. Farmer-controlled provincial governments had a very limited ability to protect the farmer against federal policies injurious to his interests, while resource capital was less likely to be affected by federal policies, and, in addition, could usually rely on the two largest and strongest provincial governments as allies. The manufacturers had influence in Ottawa but were not entirely dependent on it. The farmers resented Ottawa but could not be indifferent to it. The resource exploiters had little need of it and could largely ignore it. Only the banks, the life insurance companies, the steamship lines, and the transcontinental railways were almost exclusively oriented towards the central government and dedicated to strengthening its authority in relation to the provinces.[10] As for the wage-earning class, it had little influence anywhere and thus no clear preference for either level of government, although the federal government and those of Ontario and British Columbia made occasional and sporadic responses to its demands.

The behaviour of the various provincial governments followed fairly consistent patterns throughout the period, regardless of which parties were in office. British Columbia was almost constantly in conflict with the federal government, a pattern of behaviour that was partly a genuine reflection of the economic interests it represented and partly a tactic to distract attention from its internal class conflicts. The agricultural provinces of Alberta, Saskatchewan, and Prince Edward Island were also prone to intergovernmental conflict, moderated in the case of Saskatchewan by the fact that it enjoyed great influence in federal politics after 1921. Ontario was truculent when the federal government either flirted with lower tariffs or presented obstacles to Ontario's self-centred strategy of industrialization; in practice this happened when the federal Liberals were in office. Quebec, reflecting the predominant power of railways and finance in Montreal, was relatively passive but sometimes made common cause with Ontario on resource issues. Manitoba ceased to be farmer-dominated by about 1900, and behaved similarly to Quebec, since Winnipeg was a commercial metropolis like Montreal. New Brunswick and Nova Scotia were increasingly docile as they grew more dependent on federal subsidies, federal public works, and the federally owned railway (Intercolonial and later Canadian National), which was the major industry in both. Cape Breton coal, unlike other resource commodities, was mainly and increasingly sold on the domestic market.

The depression of the 1930s produced some changes in this picture. The agricultural sector declined catastrophically, weakening the three Prairie provinces but also weakening the federally oriented banks, railways, grain merchants, and financial institutions. The resource sector also suffered (although to a lesser extent), apart, that is, from gold mining, which was the only industry that actually expanded in this period. Manufacturing suffered least, largely because the Ottawa Agreements of 1932 increased its share of British Empire markets at the expense of its competitors in the United States. The over-all effect was to strengthen Ontario and Quebec, where both gold mining and manufacturing were concentrated, and to weaken the peripheries of the country, especially the Prairie West, where the fiscal structure of provincial and local government collapsed completely. The federal level of government was called upon to rescue the peripheries, but faced increasingly determined and successful obstruction by the governments of the two central provinces.[11]

The Second World War which followed united all classes and class fractions around the common goal of defeating the Germans and their allies, a goal to which provincial governments could make little contribution. The federal level of government assumed unprecedented powers over the economy, while its share of public-sector revenues and expenditures, especially on goods and services, reached unprecedented levels. These developments had some lingering effect after the war, but in fact the political economy of Canada in the post-war period was changing and had changed in fundamental ways that would soon bring a dramatic reversal of the federal-provincial balance.

The transcontinental wheat economy, like the British Empire of which it was part, failed to recover its importance after the war. As it declined, the dominant economic interests that had sustained the federal government in its nation-building role declined with it. The old commercial centres of Montreal and Winnipeg, both of which had been severely battered by the depression, lost their traditional importance. Toronto replaced Montreal as the major Canadian metropolis; Vancouver and later Calgary surpassed Winnipeg as subordinate metropolitan centres in the West. Saskatchewan, the major wheat-producing province, suffered a decline of 100,000 in its population between 1936 and 1951.

Manufacturing was greatly stimulated by the war: enough to produce a false and comforting belief, until Germany and Japan recovered, that Canada had become a major industrial power. Many new industries were established, under the auspices, and in some cases the direct ownership, of the federal state. Yet at the end of the war they were mainly sold or given away to American corporations. Canada's strong position in relation to new technologies like jet aircraft, atomic energy, and synthetic rubber was largely frittered away or sacrificed to cold-war politics and a growing American-inspired prejudice against state enterprise. The British-Empire preferential-trading system was virtually demolished at American insistence. Canadian industry produced American-style consumer goods for Canadian markets or else was integrated into American markets by special arrangements like the Defence Production Sharing Agreement of 1958 (a formalization and extension of the earlier Hyde Park Agreement) and the Auto Pact of 1965. To an increasing extent it was American-owned, American-oriented, and concentrated in southern Ontario, which grew increasingly integrated with, and indistinguishable from, the neighbouring states of New York and Michigan. The uneven development of Canada was thereby exacerbated and the Ontario government's role as the instrument of manufacturing capital was reinforced, with the difference that the manufacturing capital was now for the first time predominantly American. The gradual dismantling of tariff barriers in what was now oddly termed "the free world" made the federal level of government increasingly irrelevant to manufacturing interests.

The greatest expansion occurred in the resource sector of the Canadian economy, mainly in response to the depletion of American raw-material supplies during the war and the preference of the United States for seeking new supplies in a

country that was politically reliable and geographically proximate, rather than overseas. Uranium in the Algoma district of
Ontario, nickel in northern Manitoba, oil in Alberta and
Saskatchewan, natural gas in Alberta and British Columbia,
iron ore in northern Quebec and the newly annexed coast of
Labrador, were all discovered and brought into production in
the post-war years. Except for uranium, the development of all
these resources was dominated by American-controlled corporations. All of them, including uranium, were oriented towards
American markets insofar as they were not consumed within
Canada itself. Hydro-electricity, another provincial resource,
was used to make aluminium for the American market in
Quebec and British Columbia. After 1964 hydro was also
exported directly to the United States from British Columbia,
Manitoba, Quebec, and Labrador. Ironically it was the post-war
government of Louis St. Laurent, the convinced centripetal
federalist, that did the most to orient the Canadian economy in
this direction, thereby contributing to the increasing irrelevance of the central government and the increasing power and
importance of the provincial governments.

The effect of developments in both the manufacturing and
resource sectors was to integrate the Canadian economy into
that of the United States. From Confederation until 1946 the
United States had never taken more than 40 per cent of
Canadian exports. By 1950 it took 65 per cent, a proportion that
was maintained thereafter. With continental integration the
government of the United States in a sense became the central
government for the whole of North America. Whatever
interests the regional fractions of the Canadian ruling class had
in common were interests that to a large degree they shared
with their American counterparts. More and more, however,
they relied on their provincial governments to develop their
northern frontiers, to build roads and supply electricity, and to
represent their divergent interests in federal-provincial
bargaining and even in a variety of quasi-diplomatic external
activities. None of this was really apparent until the 1960s, but
the seeds had been sown somewhat earlier.

A related but distinctive pattern of events was meanwhile
unfolding in the province of Quebec, whose internal balance of
forces was profoundly affected by the changes proceeding at

the national and continental levels. The northern and eastern part of the province was a resource hinterland whose forests and mines had been largely developed, even before the war, by American capital and for American markets. As in other parts of Canada, this pattern of development was intensified after the war. Montreal, on the other hand, had been the financial and commercial metropolis of the Dominion, as well as an important centre of tariff-protected manufacturing. This internal division and complexity, which testified to the economic artificiality of the provincial boundary, had contributed to the failure of pre-war provincial governments in Quebec to articulate any clearly defined set of economic interests, and to their general passivity in dealings with the federal government.

The economic division was complicated and partly reinforced by a cultural one, the effect of which was most apparent in Montreal. The commercial centre of Montreal, where the English language predominated, was bounded by landmarks that aptly symbolized its historic significance: Beaver Hall Hill on the east, the harbour on the south, the CPR station on the west, and the campus of McGill University on the north. French Montreal lay to the east of this area, overlooked by a gigantic illuminated cross on the eastern slope of the mountain, a symbol of traditional values that bears a curious and perhaps more deeply symbolic resemblance to a hydro-electric pylon.

The balance between the two Montreals was drastically altered after the war. English Montreal lost its financial hegemony to Toronto during the depression, while its role as a commercial and transportation centre was weakened with the collapse of both the wheat economy and the British Empire. Its position as a centre of resource capital was undermined by the rise of American and Toronto-based enterprises, as well as by the expropriation in 1943 of the Montreal Light, Heat and Power Company, which became the basis of Hydro-Québec. The decline of English Montreal created a power vacuum in the province that was partly filled by American capital and partly by an expanding francophone *petite bourgeoisie*. Prevented by a language barrier and an obsolescent educational system from participating fully in the private sector of the economy or even in the federal bureaucracy, this element embarked after 1960 on a conscious strategy of using the provincial government, in alliance with American capital, to weaken the role of English-Canadian capital and of the English-speaking minority in the province.

The "Quiet Revolution", as this movement was termed, appeared to perpetuate itself, for every improvement in the francophone educational system, every increase in the powers and functions of the provincial state, every concession extracted from a nervous federal government increased the strength and the numbers of the nationalist *petite bourgeoisie* who had a vested interest in continuing the process. The erosion of federal authority, the decline of English Montreal, and the support which the provincial government received from its counterpart in Ontario and from the New York money market all helped to accelerate these developments. By the 1970s it seemed possible that they would lead to the complete collapse of Canadian federalism.

The Canada of today in its balance of economic interests is thus as drastically different from the Canada of half a century ago as the Canada of half a century ago was different from that of Macdonald and Cartier. Once again the result has been a massive shift of power from the central government to the provincial governments; the ground which the latter lost during the war had been recaptured by the early 1960s, but provincial revenues, powers, and activities have continued to expand at an unprecedented rate since that time. The rapid expansion of federal bureaucracies and programs in areas of marginal significance such as cultural activities, urban affairs, and environmental protection is in large part a symptom of pathetic weakness, as the federal government strives to compensate for the erosion of its power and relevance in the areas of real importance.

If one contrasts the present political economy with the previous one in relation to the three sectors discussed earlier, it is apparent that the resource sector has expanded greatly in the provinces where it was traditionally important, but even more so in Alberta and in the new province of Newfoundland, which now share with British Columbia the position of being the most resource-oriented provinces. The manufacturing sector has held its own, but has become more concentrated in Ontario, more Americanized, and less dependent on protective tariffs.

The agricultural sector has drastically declined, weakening national unity and redistributing power, wealth, and population among the provinces. All of these changes have had an impact on federal-provincial relations.

The Ontario government is more than ever equipped to speak for manufacturing interests, since the formerly influential resource sector of Ontario has declined in relation to the total Ontario economy. In contrast to the pre-war situation, Ontario manufacturing is now predominantly American-owned and continentalist in orientation; the federal level of government is less essential to its purpose than before. On the other hand, Toronto has now replaced Montreal as the financial metropolis and this to some extent has produced a countervailing tendency, since the financial fraction has closer ties to the federal level and a vested interest in national unity. The predominant fraction in the Ontario ruling class, however, is almost certainly the American branch-plant manufacturing sector, which Wallace Clement has described as a "comprador" element.[12] The behaviour of the provincial government in recent years is consistent with this assumption. It has continued, as throughout its history, to lead the fight for provincial autonomy. Its support for continentalism and freer trade, on the other hand, contrasts with its behaviour in the first half of the twentieth century, although in a sense it represents a return to the Mowat tradition. The alliance of Ontario and Quebec against Ottawa was considerably strengthened under John Robarts, who inexplicably acquired thereby an undeserved reputation as a defender of "national unity". In 1967, the same year in which he organized the "Confederation for Tomorrow" Conference, Robarts named Ontario's principal highway after Macdonald and Cartier. The names of Mowat and Mercier would have been far more appropriate to the circumstances.

The Quebec provincial government has been almost exclusively captured by the nationalist *petit-bourgeois* element, or what Hubert Guindon has called the new middle class.[13] American capital, however, is important and influential; in the long term the "new middle class" can only retain its position through a tacit alliance with American corporations and lending institutions, which means that power would have to be shared with them. Significantly, the economic program of the Parti Québécois provides for the provincial state to take over most of the economic sectors now occupied by Canadian capital, while the sectors where American capital is dominant, with the relatively minor exception of asbestos, would remain untouched.[14] Before the Second World War the provincial treasurer was always an anglophone, but American capital apparently does not need this kind of reassurance. Since November 1976 there has not even been a token anglophone in the cabinet, a discourtesy that few other governments in the world would inflict on one fifth of the people under their jurisdiction.

One result of these developments has been the almost complete alienation of the English-speaking *bourgeoisie* resident in Quebec from the provincial level of government, and the strengthening of its ties with the federal level. In 1950, during Quebec's period of transition, J. W. McConnell congratulated his friend Maurice Duplessis for taking a firm stand against Ottawa's tax-rental proposals.[15] It is difficult to imagine a Montreal capitalist of comparable eminence, particularly an anglophone, writing a similar letter to a premier of Quebec in the 1970s.

British Columbia has remained a resource frontier, although Vancouver has gained in importance as a commercial and transportation centre. The province's economy has expanded enormously without changing significantly, and the provincial government's behaviour adheres quite closely to the pre-war pattern. British Columbia has few ties with the federal government or with the rest of the country, and its chief concerns are to minimize any redistribution of its wealth for the benefit of other provinces and to resist federal intrusion into what it regards as its own affairs.

Alberta has been transformed more fundamentally than any province, with the possible exception of Quebec. Before the war it was the least important of the four western provinces, but today it is the most important, although British Columbia still has a larger population. The cause of the transformation, of course, was the rapid development of Alberta's petroleum resources from 1947 onwards. In the process, the farmers inevitably lost their position of dominance within the province. During the period from 1947 until 1973, which coincided approximately with the governments of Ernest Manning and Harry Strom, the dominant class fraction in the province consisted of the mainly American-owned petroleum industry, headed by the multinational giants or their Canadian affiliates: Imperial, Gulf, Texaco, Mobil, and so forth. The sudden rise in oil prices and the capture of most of the proceeds by the provincial treasury, as well as the growth of an indigenous economic elite in Calgary and Edmonton, has made the picture less clear. The present provincial government is dedicated to industrializing and diversifying the provincial economy, goals that are not fully congruent with those of the major oil companies.[16] There is a very striking parallel between this government and the Conservative government of Ontario before the First World War, which had somewhat similar objectives and represented a similar constituency of local businessmen.[17] In both cases, some friction with Ottawa resulted, but the goals pursued in Alberta, as formerly in Ontario, could be much more easily accommodated within a framework of Canadian unity than those of the Quebec nationalists.

Saskatchewan, by contrast, was less fundamentally affected by the discovery of oil. Even before the Second World War, its economy was less diversified and less urbanized than Alberta's, and its post-war growth has been far less spectacular, with the result that Regina and Saskatoon are no larger today than Edmonton and Calgary were in 1947. It would probably be accurate to say that the farmers are still the dominant class within the province, although they are less numerous and their dominance is less absolute than in the past. The unusually extensive role played by the provincial state in resource exploitation seems designed to weaken any challenge to agrarian rule by American or central-Canadian resource capital, but there is always a possibility that it will be reversed by a subsequent provincial government, producing a situation similar to Manning's Alberta. As a province where wheat remains dominant, Saskatchewan recognizes its reliance on the federal state but is often adversely affected by federal policies.

Relations with Ottawa have sometimes been strained, but have generally been better than those of Quebec or British Columbia.

Manitoba in its heyday had been the gateway to the West, and Winnipeg was a link on the imperial chain that stretched back to Montreal and London. The post-depression years were not kind to Manitoba. The western economy shifted from wheat to oil, the grain trade was nationalized by the Wheat Board, export wheat moved west to Vancouver instead of east to Montreal, financial institutions were centralized in Toronto, and even Canadian Pacific Airlines, founded by the Richardson family of Winnipeg, took up residence on the west coast. Manitoba's population actually declined during the war and grew very slowly thereafter. The province has become, along with New Brunswick, Nova Scotia, and Prince Edward Island, a virtual dependency of the federal government. Not even the Maritimes, however, surpass post-war Manitoba in its lack of concern for provincial autonomy. Newfoundland, by contrast, has adopted a much more militant posture under Premier Frank Moores, reflecting the dominant position of American and British resource capital in its economy.

In view of this remarkable diversity of interests, the increasing self-sufficiency of the larger provinces, the Americanization of industry, the rapid development of resources, the decline of agriculture, and the transformation of Quebec, it may be wondered what the federal level of government actually represents and what holds the country together. There are a number of reasons, however, why federalism remains viable. In the first place there are a number of functions, such as providing pensions and unemployment insurance, which it is in the common interest of the principal dominant class fractions to have performed at the federal level. In the second place, there is still an important sector of tariff-protected and predominantly Canadian-owned industry which looks to Ottawa for support, mainly in Quebec, eastern Ontario, Manitoba, and the Maritimes. There is also a more dynamic sector, partly francophone and mainly centred in Montreal, that includes the Power Corporation and a number of enterprises like Bombardier–MLW that depend heavily on federal contracts, Crown corporations, and overseas aid programs. The chartered banks and life-insurance companies, although less influential than in the past, remain a very important part of the federal government's constituency. Finally, business interests in the Atlantic provinces, Quebec, and Manitoba rely on federal equalization payments and regional development programs to prevent their labour forces from migrating elsewhere and to preserve them from what would otherwise have to be prohibitive levels of provincial taxation. It is significant that in recent years the federal government has increasingly relied on this argument to justify its existence, although the argument is naturally expressed in terms of benefits to the people of the poorer provinces rather than in terms of benefits to business.

Moreover, there may be a sense in which a weak federal government is of some benefit to all ruling class interests, at least until such time as the somewhat Utopian prospect of annexation by the United States might become a practical possibility. The corporate elite can easily exploit the jurisdictional controversies that appear endemic in a federal state, and the existence of a Supreme Court with the power of judicial review may provide it with a sort of insurance policy against provincial actions that might be injurious to its interests. This is particularly important in provinces where the NDP is a significant political force, but in no liberal democracy can elected politicians be considered totally reliable from a business point of view.

NOTES

1. W. H. Riker, "Federalism", in F. L. Greenstein and N. W. Polsby, *Handbook of Political Science* (Reading, Mass.: Addison-Wesley, 1975), Vol. 5, pp. 132–33.
2. Norman Rogers, "The Genesis of Provincial Rights", *Canadian Historical Review,* XIV (1933):9–23.
3. J. M. S. Careless, "Limited Identities in Canada", *Canadian Historical Review,* L (1969):1–10.
4. Donald V. Smiley, *Canada in Question, Federalism in the Seventies* 2nd ed. (Toronto: McGraw-Hill, 1976), p. 63.
5. James O'Connor, *The Fiscal Crisis of the State* (New York: Oxford University Press, 1973).
6. H. G. J. Aitken, "Defensive Expansionism: the State and economic growth in Canada", in H. G. J. Aitken, ed., *The State*

and Economic Growth (New York: Social Science Research Council, 1959).

7. H. V. Nelles, *The Politics of Development: Forests, Mines and Hydro-Electric Power in Ontario, 1849-1941* (Toronto: Macmillan, 1974), pp. 335-46.

8. The term "province-building" is taken from E. R. Black and A. C. Cairns, "A Different Perspective on Canadian Federalism", *Canadian Public Administration,* IX (1966): 27-45.

9. Andrew Jackson, "Divided Dominion: Class and the Structure of Canadian Federalism from the National Policy to the Great Depression", Paper presented at the annual conference of the Canadian Political Science Association, 1978.

10. A partial exception was the Canadian Northern Railway, whose construction was heavily subsidized by the four western provinces in an effort to break the monopoly of the CPR See T. D. Regehr, *The Canadian Northern Railway* (Toronto: Macmillan, 1977).

11. Richard Alway, "Hepburn, King, and the Rowell-Sirois Commission", *Canadian Historical Review,* XLVIII (1967):113-41.

12. Wallace Clement, *The Canadian Corporate Elite* (Toronto: McClelland and Stewart, 1975). The term "comprador" referred originally to Chinese merchants in the heyday of Portuguese colonialism. It is used by Marxist scholars to describe those capitalists in a dependent country who profit from their country's relationship with an imperialist power.

13. Hubert Guindon, "Social Unrest, Social Class, and Quebec's Bureaucratic Revolution", *Queen's Quarterly,* LXXXI (1964): 150-62.

14. Pierre Fournier, "The Parti Québécois and the power of business", *Our Generation,* XII, no. 3 (Fall 1977):3-15.

15. Conrad Black, *Duplessis* (Toronto: McClelland and Stewart, 1977), p. 610.

16. Larry Pratt, "The State and Province-Building: Alberta's Development Strategy", in Leo Panitch, ed., *The Canadian State: Political Economy and Political Power* (Toronto: University of Toronto Press, 1977).

17. Nelles, *The Politics of Development,* is a useful source on this government and on its major achievement, the establishment of Ontario Hydro. See also Christopher Armstrong, "The Politics of Federalism: Ontario's Relations with the Federal Government, 1896-1940" (unpublished PhD theis, University of Toronto, 1972).

5 The Consequences of Province-Building

In the preceding chapter it was suggested that the increase in the power and importance of the provincial governments since Confederation, and especially in recent years, was not accidental, but was, rather, a reflection of the needs and preferences of dominant classes and class fractions within the provinces. The powers given to the provincial governments by the BNA Act, and the generous interpretation given to those powers by the Judicial Committee of the Privy Council, made it easier for these dominant interests to pursue their objectives but did not create the interests or the objectives, which existed independently of the constitution. The process that has been called "province-building" represented the fulfilment of these objectives, sometimes in what were viewed as defensive responses to policies of the central government or to external economic circumstances. At the same time the process of province-building has tended to accentuate and reinforce, rather than to overcome, the economic differences among the provinces which provided its original impetus. The result has been a very imperfect realization of Canadian unity, and the triumph in practice of the centrifugal concept of federalism. Indeed, spokesmen for the central government itself now tend to define its role less in terms of nation-building than in terms of protecting cultural minorities or assisting the economically disadvantaged provinces to "catch up" with the richer ones.[1]

Nation-building or economic nationalism, of which the National Policy was one example, is an effort to shape a socio-economic entity which to some degree is self-contained and self-directed, by intensifying internal patterns of interdependence and by restricting or regulating ties with the outside world. Another objective is often to increase the size of the nation's employed labour force and thus of the nation itself, even if this depresses the average *per-capita* income. Province-building or economic provincialism is very similar both in its objectives and its methods, even when it is not carried to its logical conclusion of outright separatism. Both nation-building and province-building invariably are promoted by those class fractions that are dominant within the relevant territorial jurisdiction but are frustrated by having to share their power with external economic interests. In order to achieve their goals, these class fractions must gain some degree of wider popular support (or at least acquiescence) by identifying their own needs with those of the whole society. Depending on the circumstances, they may describe their objectives as "catching up" with a more advanced economic unit (often the same one whose external impact on their own economy is resented), or as protecting some local economic advantage, like Ontario's hydro-electricity or Alberta's oil, from the threat of having to share it with outsiders. The real objectives, and the methods used to achieve them, are in either event much the same.

If economic nationalism and economic provincialism are pursued simultaneously by different class fractions within a federal country, conflict is almost certain to ensue. The economic nationalists want to strengthen interdependence across provincial boundaries and regulate or restrict links with the outside world. The economic provincialists want to regulate or restrict the province's links with the outside world (including other provinces), which conflicts with the first objective of the federal nationalists, and they may want to use external allies (such as multinational corporations or the late General Charles de Gaulle) as part of their province-building strategy, which conflicts with the second objective of the federal nationalists. It is significant that the power of disallowance, which was an important weapon used by federal nationalists against provincialists, ceased to be employed at approximately the time when the National Policy was abandoned. A central government that pursues no nationalist goals of its own can afford to be rather tolerant of province-building, which is why provincialists prefer that kind of central government if they must have a central government at all. However, tolerance has its limits, and even in recent times the federal government and the economic interests which it represents have resisted economic provincialism on a number of occasions, whether by litigation, negotiation, or mere expressions of disapproval. In the latter category could be placed the sponsoring of studies and reports that are critical of economic provincialism, such as A. E. Safarian's monograph, commissioned by the Privy Council Office, and the more extensive studies now being undertaken by the Science Council of Canada on provincial barriers to the movement of factors of production.[2]

It is less certain, but by no means impossible, that economic provincialists will find themselves in conflict with their counterparts in other provinces. If the provincialist policies pursued on both sides are fairly extreme and far-reaching, and if a high degree of interdependence exists, the probability of conflict between two provincial governments is quite high, even though they may wish to avert conflict with one another so that they can present a common front against the federal government. Because Toronto is the commercial and financial centre of Canada, a position which it has only really achieved in the last three or four decades, and because Ontario imports raw materials from and exports finished goods to the other provinces, the provincial government of Ontario and the interests which it represents are quite likely to feel threatened by the provincialist policies pursued in other provinces. The fact that Ontario pioneered in the practice of self-centred province-building, and still pursues it with a degree of skill and success that has been surpassed in no other jurisdiction, in no way lessens this tendency. Thus Ontario has found itself in conflict with Alberta over the prices of fossil fuels in the early 1970s, and with Quebec over some of the measures pursued or threatened by the separatist government after 1976. The Ontario Economic Council has sponsored a critical study of provincial restrictions on the mobility of goods, capital, and labour, although the study had to admit that many of these restrictions were imposed by Ontario itself.[3] It might also be noted that Ontario intervened before the Supreme Court to defend the legality of the federal government's wage and price controls, while the governments of four other provinces intervened to oppose it. However, Ontario is not the only

province that may be threatened by the economic policies of
other provinces, a fact suggested by such episodes as the "egg
war" between Quebec and Manitoba or the conflicts over
hydro-electric resources between Quebec and Newfoundland.

RESOURCE POLICIES

Of all the various means by which Canadian provincial
governments have pursued provincialist goals, the most
frequently used, most successful, and most fully documented
has probably been the exercise of the province's ownership
rights with regard to natural resources. Not coincidentally, this
has been the most difficult strategy for opponents of provincialism, including the federal government, to attack, since it
has been explicitly accorded at least a degree of legitimacy by
the terms of the BNA Act. Section 109 of the Act provided that
"All Lands, Mines, Minerals, and Royalties belonging to the
several Provinces of Canada, Nova Scotia, and New Brunswick
at the Union" would belong henceforth "to the several
Provinces of Ontario, Quebec, Nova Scotia, and New
Brunswick in which the same are situate or arise". British
Columbia, Prince Edward Island, and Newfoundland subsequently entered Confederation on similar terms, qualified in
British Columbia's case by the fact that the federal government
took over certain lands and resources which it intended to use
to subsidize the construction of the Pacific railway. The three
Prairie provinces, on the other hand, were formed out of
territory which already belonged to the federal state, and the
governments of Macdonald and Laurier followed the American
practice of retaining their lands and resources in federal hands
after provincial status was granted. Pressure from the Prairie
provincial governments, and from the federal Progressive party
which represented the same class interests and held the balance
of power in Parliament, led Mackenzie King to promise the
"return" of these lands and resources to provincial hands in
the 1920s. This transaction was finally completed in 1930, and
at the same time British Columbia regained that portion of the
"railway belt" that had not already been handed over to the
CPR.

Section 109 was mainly intended as a means of assuring

revenues to the provincial governments, a fact suggested by its inclusion in the part of the Act headed "Revenues; Debts; Assets; Taxation". Its other implications may not have been appreciated, although Macdonald did complain in 1872 that the Ontario government's control over timber licences enabled it to extract campaign funds from the lumber industry for the Liberal party.[4] The real significance of Section 109, however, lay in its possible use as a means of promoting industrialization and economic diversification, at least in those provinces that were well endowed with resources. Since resources are in practice very unevenly distributed, Section 109 has made a major contribution to the much-discussed phenomenon of regional disparities.

As H. V. Nelles has shown in his outstanding study, Ontario was the first province whose government understood and exploited these possibilities.[5] Beginning with the forests, which were the most important resource industry in the nineteenth century, Ontario originated the "manufacturing condition", by which permits to cut wood on the Crown lands were only granted on condition that the wood be sawed into lumber before being exported from the province. Neither the federal government nor the largely American lumber companies were particularly enamoured of this policy, but they could do little about it since the provincial government owned practically all of the forested land in the province. It would have been difficult to argue that a provincial government should enjoy less freedom than a private citizen in disposing of its own property. Because of the more complex nature of the industry and the technology involved, Ontario had somewhat greater difficulty later on when it tried to extend the manufacturing condition to mineral resources, but even in this area a considerable degree of success was eventually achieved, although by more devious methods.

Ontario was a pioneer in policies of this kind, not so much because its resources were important, but because, in relation to the rest of the provincial economy, they were relatively unimportant. If the resource interests had been the dominant class fraction, as they were in British Columbia, they would probably have been allowed to export with no processing at all, which is in fact what happened in British Columbia and most of the other provinces. Ontario acted differently because it was dominated by industrialists who wanted to improve their competitive position in relation to Quebec and the United States and who sensed the importance of backward and forward linkages from the resource industries in strengthening and diversifying the provincial economy. In strengthening Ontario they strengthened themselves, and vice versa. Only to the extent that other provinces escaped from the control of resource capital could their policies be emulated elsewhere. The creation of an embryonic steel industry by the Lesage government in Quebec, and the Lévesque government's plans to insist on the processing of asbestos, if necessary by "nationalizing" one or more of the firms, suggest that this has happened in Quebec. On the other hand, British Columbia still exports practically all of its copper in raw form, despite some inconclusive talk about building a smelter by the short-lived NDP government of Dave Barrett.

While forests and mines have contributed to industrialization and province-building, the provincial control over energy resources has been even more important. It will be recalled from Chapter 2 that this trendy subject was by no means unknown to the Fathers of Confederation; but the Cape Breton coal which occupied their attention was to prove less important in the twentieth century than hydro-electricity, a resource which was far more abundant in central Canada than in the Maritime provinces. The epoch of provincial dominance in Canada could be symbolized by a hydro-electric pylon, just as the epoch of federal supremacy found its appropriate symbol in the railway steam locomotive.

The Ontario government was the first in Canada, and one of the first in the world, to enter the electric-power business. The establishment of Ontario Hydro, as Nelles has demonstrated, had little to do with any "collectivist" ideology. Rather it represented, like the manufacturing condition, the use of the provincial state to support the objectives of industrial capitalists. The significant fact that this initiative took place at the provincial level reflects the fact that industrial capitalists were concentrated in Ontario, with the result that the Ontario government was the one over which they exerted the greatest influence. In the United States and Australia, by contrast, major hydro-electric projects were undertaken by the federal government. Ontario Hydro was used from the outset, and with considerable success, to provide power at low rates and thereby to improve the competitive position of Ontario industry in relation to that of Quebec and the United States. It also lessened, although it did not completely eliminate, Ontario's reliance on imported sources of energy, chiefly American coal. The alternative strategy of importing Cape Breton coal, which at one point was suggested by the Canadian Manufacturers' Association, was also rejected. Ontario Hydro increased the self-reliance of Ontario and also widened the economic gap between Ontario and the other provinces, reinforcing the uneven development and the concentration of Canadian industry in the one province that had made it possible in the first place. At the same time, it transformed the character of the provincial state, increasing its share of capital investment and its impact on the economy, decisively influencing its relations with the federal government, involving it to some degree in Canadian-American relations, and strengthening its identification with the interests of industrial capital in Canada. Low power rates became as important as high tariffs to Canadian industry. The National Policy became the Provincial Policy.

Partly because manufacturing industry was less influential in the other provinces, they were slower to follow in Ontario's lead, although all except Alberta and Prince Edward Island have eventually done so. Because it was less capital-intensive, thermal generation of electricity remained longer in the hands of private enterprise than hydro, a pattern that has also been visible in the United States, and the relative importance of the two sources of power in each province influenced the chronological order in which provincial governments entered the field. Farmers as well as industrialists learned the virtues of cheap power, a fact that led Saskatchewan to take over not only electricity, but natural-gas distribution as well. Manitoba and New Brunswick moved fairly quickly into hydro. Quebec made a promising start in 1943 but did not complete the process until twenty years later, at about the same time that British Columbia purchased control of its American-owned utility. Nova Scotia and Newfoundland waited until the 1970s.

The eventual outcome, however, was that electricity, which

is the major instrument of industrialization in the twentieth century, as steam was in the nineteenth, ended up in provincial hands and as an instrument of provincial purposes. The federal government was unable or unwilling to assert itself, as shown by its fumbling of the Columbia River Treaty and its failure to influence the outcome of the Churchill Falls affair, by which the poorest of the ten provinces was effectively bullied into submission and robbed of its one competitive advantage by the much larger and stronger province of Quebec. Faced with the refusal of Quebec to permit the transmission of Labrador power across its territory, Newfoundland had no choice but to sell the power to Hydro-Québec at an absurdly low price. Viewed in the light of the persistent refusal of Quebec governments to recognize Newfoundland's jurisdiction over Labrador, the episode has a particularly sinister appearance; but the federal government did nothing. Its inaction was reprehensible but not particularly surprising, given its earlier failure to undertake the national power grid which had been a part of the Progressive Conservative platform in 1957 and 1958. This project would have assisted industrialization in the Atlantic provinces, Manitoba, and Saskatchewan, but it foundered on the rock of provincial autonomy.

Yet another effect of provincially sponsored hydro-electric development has been to strengthen provincial ties with the United States. It has proved politically easier to export power to the south than to redistribute it from the energy-rich to the energy-poor provinces. In 1964 the federal government abandoned its traditional policy of prohibiting long-term power exports. The British Columbia government proceeded to export the Canadian share of the Columbia River power, which it earlier had grabbed for itself by taking over the B.C. Electric Company. Quebec sold the Churchill Falls power to New York, needless to say at a higher price than it had paid to the lawful owner. The grandiose James Bay scheme, also oriented to southern markets, was next on Quebec's agenda. In the meantime the capital-intensive nature of hydro schemes had done more than anything else to tie the provincial governments to the New York money market, whose credit ratings have more impact on provincial policies than anything that occurs in the polling booths on election day.

Alberta and Saskatchewan have played distinctly minor roles in the politics of electricity, but they are far more fortunately situated with respect to petroleum, a source of energy that has recently become of even greater importance. Given their lack of political influence in Ottawa and their long history of subordination to central-Canadian economic and political interests, it was wholly predictable that the federal government would be more vigorous in asserting "the national interest" at their expense than it has been with regard to electricity. The constitutional obstacles to intervention in hydro-electric matters, whatever they are, do not seem to inhibit the federal government from blocking the export of Alberta natural gas for which the United States is the only available market, nor from keeping the domestic price of oil below world levels and imposing an export tax to take a share of the profits from western oil exports, which it then uses to subsidize low prices for consumers in the Atlantic provinces and Quebec.

None the less, both Alberta and Saskatchewan have managed to derive considerable revenues from their petroleum resources, which have benefited their taxpayers and halted the exodus of population from the Prairie region. Alberta's rate of population growth is now the highest of any province. Saskatchewan has used petroleum revenues to buy control of half the potash industry. Alberta has accumulated a massive "Heritage Fund" and has purchased control of Canada's third largest commercial airline. The Alberta government intends to use its petroleum resources as a basis for industrializing and diversifying a provincial economy that remains very vulnerable to external circumstances, both political and economic. A key element in this strategy is the development of a petrochemical industry. Rather than backing this initiative, the federal government has chosen to support a competing project at Sarnia, Ontario, although doubts have been expressed as to whether Canada either requires or can support such duplication.

OTHER ECONOMIC POLICIES

Provinces less well endowed by nature have had to adopt somewhat different strategies in the effort to promote industrialization. The relative decline and increasing capital intensity of agriculture, wartime industrialization in the corridor from Windsor to Sorel, and the concentration of post-war growth around a handful of American-oriented resource projects all contributed to a redistribution of population that endangered a variety of political and economic interests. Albert Breton has argued convincingly that a desire to preserve the existing spatial distribution of population is a rational expression of self-interest for politicians and explains a large part of their activity.[6] It is evident that loss of population could threaten the livelihood of retailers, professionals, building contractors, insurance agents, and other such persons, who tend to serve interchangeably as political and economic elites in the more backward regions of Canada. This fact explains the background to such enterprises as the Manitoba Development Corporation, Industrial Estates Limited in Nova Scotia, and the Société Générale de Financement in Quebec.

Although the efforts which they represented were intensified after the Second World War, these organizations followed in a long tradition of provincial and local incentives to direct investment.[7] The ability of provincial governments to offer incentives was increased in the 1960s by their rapidly increasing tax revenues supplemented by federal equalization payments for all but the three richest. The incentives offered have included loans, tax holidays, guarantees for corporate borrowing in the private sector, and even direct equity participation by the provincial government, which is usually content to act in such cases as a silent partner exercising little or no influence over the management of the enterprise. Where a development corporation or similar entity is formed it is invariably managed mainly by businessmen and given virtual freedom from any control by the provincial cabinet, let alone the legislature.

In addition to direct financial aid, incentives offered to industrial enterprises by provincial governments can include the provision of infrastructure at public expense, unusually favourable terms for the exploitation of Crown timber and other resources, or promises to deal firmly with the labour force. The combination of interprovincial competition to attract industrial investment and provincial jurisdiction over labour-management relations has almost certainly exposed Canadian wage earners to more frequent and obvious intervention by the state on behalf of their employers than they would otherwise have experienced. In both Quebec and Ontario the intervention of the provincial police to support those attempting to cross a picket line is an accepted routine, although in other advanced liberal democracies it would rarely if ever occur except in wartime. It may be significant to note that the unusually harsh reaction (even by Canadian standards) of Premier J. R. Smallwood to the Newfoundland woodworkers' strike of 1959 occurred at a time when he was attempting to negotiate a major deal with the Crown Zellerbach paper company.[8]

How successful provincial industrialization strategies have been in achieving their objectives is a matter on which opinions may differ. The media and the general public probably underestimate the success achieved, since they persist in the erroneous belief that the original intention was to increase *per-capita* incomes in the poorer provinces, a goal quite distinct from and even contrary to the real objective of increasing the population. On the other hand there have been a number of bad effects. Even where the enterprises attracted were legitimate and successful, the effect of ten different industrial strategies has been to fragment even further an industrial sector which is already too fragmented for the size of the Canadian market. Politically inspired locational decisions are unlikely to increase the international competitiveness of Canadian industry, and considerations of comparative advantage have been ignored in the desire of each province to emulate the industrial structure of Ontario on a smaller scale. Moreover, incentives have redistributed income away from provincial taxpayers for the benefit of already-profitable firms, most of which are owned and controlled outside of Canada. The poorer the province's natural advantages, the larger the incentives it must offer, and the greater the regressive effect. Since the size of incentive needed to attract investment can never be estimated precisely, the incentives must be too generous if they are not to be unsuccessful. Finally, one must note the many spectacular disasters. The Come by Chance oil refinery in Newfoundland and the Bricklin automobile factory in New Brunswick suspended operations soon after they were launched, and the Churchill Forest Industries project in

Manitoba disappeared in a thicket of numbered Swiss bank accounts as impenetrable as the northern forest itself. A number of energy-related projects recently proposed in the Atlantic provinces reveal a disquieting tendency to link those provinces more closely with the New England states, while increasing the ability of the latter to compete with Canadian industry. The chief attraction of the Atlantic provinces for the purveyors of such schemes lies in their willingness to accept levels of environmental deterioration that have become politically unacceptable to Americans.

Apart from schemes to attract investment, provincial governments also seek to promote industrialization by their purchasing policies. An important trend in the post-war political economy of Canada has been the shift of government spending on goods and services (a far better indicator of the state's impact on the economy than total government spending) from the federal to the provincial level. Federal spending on goods and services declined from 8.9 per cent of GNP in 1955 to 5.8 per cent in 1976, but that of the provinces increased from 3.2 per cent to 6.9 per cent and that of the local governments (heavily influenced by the provinces) from 5.3 per cent to 8.0 per cent.[9] Hydro-electric utilities, public transit commissions, and the railways, airlines, and telephone systems operated by some of the provincial governments are among the major purchasers of some kinds of industrial goods. Some provinces have exploited this fact in various ways. The Crown-owned British Columbia Railway builds its own freight cars, and Manitoba under the NDP government of Ed Schreyer acquired a major equity stake in a bus-building enterprise, which appears, not surprisingly, to have been given preference as the supplier of buses to Manitoba municipalities. A well-publicized incident in 1977 saw the government of Ontario reject the lowest tender to supply transit vehicles for Toronto, which had been submitted by the Bombardier–MLW firm of Montreal. The excuse was that the unemployment rate was high in Thunder Bay, headquarters of the firm whose bid was accepted, although Montreal's unemployment rate was significantly higher. Perhaps because of its Canadian ownership and federalist sympathies, the unfortunate Bombardier firm received a second blow a few months later, when the Quebec government awarded the contract to supply transit vehicles for Montreal to the Ontario-based and American-owned General Motors. There was some ambiguity as to which tender for this contract was actually lower. As part of the deal, General Motors agreed to transfer part of its production line from Ontario to Quebec, at least for the duration of the contract.

Apart from their own purchasing policies, provincial governments have discriminated in favour of indigenous producers in a number of ways. Provincial liquor control boards prohibit provincial residents from bringing alcoholic beverages across provincial boundaries, although in the Ottawa valley, if not elsewhere, this rule is widely violated and virtually unenforceable. The retail prices of wines and liquors produced outside the province are often set at an unnecessarily high level so as to encourage the purchase of local products, especially in Ontario and British Columbia where wines are produced from locally grown grapes.

A more general but similar phenomenon is the practice, which seems to be gaining in popularity, of encouraging provincial residents to purchase local products. Premier Moores of Newfoundland has publicly lamented the fact that consumers in Atlantic Canada purchase so many products from outside the region, and has urged them to refrain from doing so if possible. The Quebec government of René Lévesque has gone a step further by producing and distributing a book which purportedly enables consumers to identify those products that are actually produced in Quebec or have some "Quebec content". Even at the national level, where appeals to "buy Canadian" have also been heard recently, such practices have an element of absurdity (or worse), recalling the efforts of Dr. Goebbels to promote the virtues of German rhubarb at the expense of imported lemons and oranges. At the provincial level the practice is quite indefensible and incompatible with any notion of federalism. It also ignores the fact that the ties of interdependence run in both directions, a fact of which the Atlantic provinces, in particular, should not need to be reminded. Admittedly there are legitimate grounds for regional discontent in the fact that Canadian industry is so excessively concentrated in the vicinity of Toronto, but provincial versions of economic nationalism are certainly not the answer, and will be counterproductive if they provoke Ontario, which has the largest and richest market, to retaliate in kind.

Another way to favour local enterprises is by manipulating retail sales taxes, which exist in all provinces except Alberta. In 1975 Ontario attempted to stimulate its automobile industry by exempting from the provincial sales tax automobiles "assembled in North America from North American parts". It was revealing of the extent to which the Ontario government had become the servant of American capital that vehicles assembled in the United States were given the benefit of this exemption, although admittedly there was a fairly high probability that such vehicles would contain some Ontario-produced parts. The requirement that the parts be North American, however, was deliberately designed to exclude from the exemption the products of one modest-sized plant in Nova Scotia, a revealing commentary on the sincerity of the Ontario government's oft-expressed concern for the welfare of Canada's poorer regions. The exemption in any event was almost certainly unconstitutional, but before it could be tested in the courts it was withdrawn by the government. Pressure from the importers of fully assembled vehicles, rather than from the hapless Nova Scotians, apparently brought about its demise.

A more publicized, and more successful, case of discriminatory provincial taxation occurred three years later, when the Quebec government removed the sales tax on a list of products carefully selected so as to favour the sectors of Canadian manufacturing that are largely located in Quebec rather than concentrated in Ontario. Unlike the Ontario government in 1975, the Quebec government on this occasion was clearly acting within the letter, although possibly not within the spirit, of the BNA Act. Its action none the less provoked a federal-provincial dispute, since the federal government had earlier offered, in its own budget, compensation to those provinces that would reduce their sales tax on all types of products, rather than eliminating it on a selected list. The other provinces had accepted the federal offer, which had originated in a suggestion by Ontario at a federal-provincial conference on the economy. Quebec predictably, although unjustifiably, denounced the federal offer as an unconstitutional intrusion into provincial affairs and demanded that the federal government subsidize its own manipulation of the sales tax as generously as it subsidized the tax reductions by the other provinces. The federal government offered only a partial subsidy, which it later agreed to supplement by income-tax rebates to Quebec taxpayers.

The marketing of agricultural products is another area in which discriminatory policies have been pursued. Because independent commodity production has continued to predominate in agriculture, individual producers have little power in the market. Because the protection of farmers is considered socially and politically desirable, governments in many parts of the world have intervened to rectify this situation, a tendency that in federal countries can cause legal and political complications. In Canada the effort by the federal government to regulate the marketing of agricultural commodities through a Dominion Marketing Board was declared unconstitutional by the Judicial Committee of the Privy Council in 1937. The provinces then created their own boards, and in 1949 Parliament adopted an act permitting the delegation to the provincial boards of powers to regulate the marketing of produce destined for markets outside the province where it was produced. Two decades elapsed before the question arose as to whether the provinces could legally discriminate in favour of their own producers.

In 1970 the government of Quebec responded to pressure from Quebec egg producers by giving their association, known as FEDCO, the power to control the sale of all eggs within the province. This was bad news for Ontario and Manitoba egg farmers who had enjoyed a substantial share of the Quebec market. FEDCO prohibited imports and raised the price of eggs to a level far above that prevailing in other provinces, permitting less efficient Quebec producers to expand their own production and replace the imports. The Manitoba government responded with a curious but effective use of its power to refer legislation to the provincial Superior Court for a ruling on its validity. It drafted a bill identical to the Quebec legislation of 1970, which it then referred. The bill was declared invalid by the Superior Court and, on appeal, by the Supreme Court of Canada, with the obvious implication that the Quebec legislation also violated the constitution.

Meanwhile a somewhat similar situation had arisen with

regard to broiler chickens, except that Quebec in this case was the victim rather than the instigator of protectionist policies. Ontario gave its broiler board, controlled by the poultry farmers, similar powers to those which the Quebec legislation gave to FEDCO in relation to eggs. The broiler board used its power to prevent imports from Quebec, which produced a surplus of broiler chickens. In both provinces boards were authorized to confiscate products imported without their approval, since a considerable illicit trade in both types of poultry products was taking place across the Quebec–Ontario border. The confusion finally had to be terminated by the intervention of the federal government. In 1972 Parliament adopted the National Farm Products Marketing Act, which permitted the establishment of federal boards and marketing schemes for such products as chickens and eggs and the allocation of production quotas among the provinces. It is not clear that this innovation improved matters from the viewpoint of the consumer, but at least it ended bickering among the provinces and provided protection to producers in all of them. Probably in a federation no more than that could be expected.[10]

Transportation policy, despite the federal government's extensive regulatory powers, offers some scope for the pursuit of economic provincialism. The provinces cannot regulate railway freight rates, unlike the Australian states, but they can build railways and thereby influence the movement of commodities. The Atlantic provinces all owned railways when they joined Canada, but turned them over to the federal government. Quebec sold its provincially owned railways to the expanding CPR not long after Confederation. Manitoba's efforts in the 1880s to build or sponsor railways competitive with the CPR were repeatedly disallowed by the federal government. More recent provincial railways have been intimately associated with resource development. Ontario built the Timiskaming and Northern Ontario (later re-named Ontario Northland) in 1908. It failed in its original objective of encouraging agricultural settlement but assisted greatly in the development of mineral resources. When important mineral deposits were discovered at Noranda in northwestern Quebec, Ontario built a branch line to that locality in 1928, thereby bringing it into the economic orbit of Toronto rather than Montreal.

British Columbia's provincial railway had had a long and somewhat ridiculous history, but it became important for the first time when W. A. C. Bennett was Premier of the province. Besides completing the southern extension to North Vancouver, he extended it north to Fort St. John in the Peace River country, strengthening that area's links with Vancouver and weakening its ties with the much closer metropolis of Edmonton. Not to be outdone, the Alberta government built the Alberta Resources Railway in the same general direction; this remained a white elephant for several years until it was rescued by the discovery of an important coal deposit near its northern terminus. British Columbia meanwhile extended its railway all the way to Fort Nelson, with such disastrous financial results that a provincial Royal Commission was eventually set up to investigate. Bennett's offer to take over the Canadian National railway line west of Prince George was not warmly received by the federal government. His railway also failed to reach the Yukon territory, which is now the principal area of competition for spheres of influence between the two western provinces.

Alberta's purchase of Pacific Western Airlines, which had previously, as its name suggests, had its headquarters in Vancouver, must also be seen in the context of this rivalry for spheres of influence between the two provinces. PWA does not serve the Yukon, but it is the major airline in the Mackenzie Valley and in the interior of British Columbia, two areas of contention that will be more oriented towards Edmonton and Calgary, and less towards Vancouver, as a result of the purchase. It might be noted as a commentary on the often-overlooked artificiality of Canadian provincial boundaries that the B.C. interior is in many ways already more oriented to Alberta than to the Pacific coast. Resentment against coastal domination has a long history and contributed to the rise of Social Credit in British Columbia. The Chamber of Commerce in one interior town even advocated seceding from British Columbia and joining Alberta during the period when the NDP held office in Victoria.

The provincial impact on transportation is greatest, however, in the case of highway transportation. It was mentioned in Chapter 2 that Macdonald had the foresight to want an explicit statement of federal jurisdiction over highways, but was unsuccessful in securing it. Highway-building became a major provincial activity in the early part of the twentieth century. For a long time it appeared as though the increasingly important subject of truck and bus transportation fell under the regulatory jurisdiction of the provinces. In the important Winner case, however, the Supreme Court in 1951 and the Judicial Committee of the Privy Council in 1954 both used the federal power over interprovincial "works" to invalidate the regulation by New Brunswick of buses running through the province on the way from Boston to Halifax. Poetic justice was thus inflicted on the province that had prevented a reference to highways from appearing in the BNA Act. Rather than taking advantage of its newly defined power, the federal government proceeded inexplicably to delegate it back to the provincial regulatory agencies, a rather dubious expedient that had recently been endorsed by the Supreme Court in another case related to the marketing of potatoes. The situation was thus essentially unchanged by the Winner decision.

By not asserting its authority, the federal government allowed a situation to persist in which required weights, dimensions, axle loadings, and so forth of intercity trucks varied from province to province. It also remained possible for provincial authorities to require conditions in the granting of licences that would impose a burden on interprovincial traffic. Beginning in 1959, five years after the Winner decision, the trucking industry urged the provinces to standardize their regulations, but without success. In 1965 the industry appealed to the federal government to bring pressure to bear on the provinces. Not long afterwards Parliament adopted the National Transportation Act, Part III of which provided for the federal government to assume, belatedly, the jurisdiction over trucking that had been given to it by the courts more than a decade earlier. Although the rest of the Act quickly came into force, implementation of Part III was repeatedly postponed because of provincial opposition, mainly from Ontario and Quebec. Finally in 1973 the federal government capitulated and abandoned its efforts to assume control over the trucking industry. The industry itself had meanwhile twice reversed its position on the desirability of federal jurisdiction, which it had more or less favoured between 1966 and 1973, but seems to have had no effect on the outcome, which was largely determined by the federal government's helplessness in confronting the provinces. Provincial control over this vital sector of transportation thus seems likely to last indefinitely.[11]

RESTRICTIONS ON FREEDOM OF MOVEMENT

The freedom to move throughout an extensive territory is one of the major benefits, and perhaps even the most important, that the individual citizen derives from belonging to a large nation-state. The possibility of moving one's place of residence from one province to another in the course of a lifetime should be considered one of the main advantages to individual Canadians of the existence and survival of the Canadian state, and an important reason for rejecting provincial separatism in all of its various forms. Unfortunately the power of the provincial governments in our federal system has been used to create a number of formal and informal obstacles to freedom of movement.

Some Canadians were reminded of this fact in the spring of 1978, when a news item appeared in the Ottawa *Citizen* under the heading "Quebec curbs workers July 1 — Canada Day". Both for its intrinsic importance and as a fairly typical example of the style with which the Canadian media treat the kinds of issue discussed in this book, the item deserves to be quoted at some length.

> Ontario construction workers will soon be asked to pay a price for national unity.
>
> On July 1, Canada Day, the Quebec government will put regulations into effect that will restrict Ontario workers' access to construction sites in *la belle province*.
>
> In certain circumstances Ontario workers will still be able to work in Quebec, but the days of an "open border" will be over.
>
> Predictably, some Ontario tradesmen — notably in the Seaway City of Cornwall — are crying foul. . . .

The provincial government, their employers, even their unions, are all shying away from a confrontation over the dispute.

The reason? National unity. No one, it seems, wants to run the risk of offending Quebec's sensibilities, thereby adding more fuel to the fires of separatism.[12]

It is not at all clear whether the Southam reporter or his employers fully appreciated the irony of the first and last paragraphs quoted. The priority of elite accommodation over the inconvenient complaints of ordinary tradesmen concerned with their livelihood would presumably neither dismay nor astonish the academic proponents of "consociationalism". Some of the *Citizen's* readers, however, may have retained sufficient mental clarity to wonder what kind of "national unity" is maintained by a passive acquiescence in policies that flagrantly contradict the ordinary meaning of the expression.

Whatever indignation this episode deserves, it is perhaps made slightly more intelligible when one is reminded that the BNA Act contains no guarantees for individual freedom of movement. The free movement of goods and commodities is more or less assured by Section 121, which prevents the provinces from imposing tariff barriers, although we have already seen that the Canadian common market, as Premier Robert Bourassa used to call it, is by no means absolute in practice. Free movement of persons, however, is not mentioned at all.

This anomaly is not entirely inexplicable. The economic interests behind Confederation, whether mercantile or industrial, required a common market, while an interprovincially mobile labour force was at best a much lower priority. Few people moved from one province to another in what was still a largely agricultural economy. The expectation that this state of affairs would continue is implied, first, by the fact that federal jurisdiction over immigration was shared with the provincial governments, and, even more strikingly, by the lack of any provision for the French language outside of Quebec, a subject referred to in Chapter 2 of the present volume.

In any event, there have been few legal or political obstacles to the creation of various informal and even formal barriers. The more obvious and explicit barriers are those by which a province discourages "outsiders" from coming into the province. Less obvious and offensive, but perhaps equally real as barriers to free movement, are those public policies, both federal and provincial, which seek to discourage people from leaving a province, and some of which have already been discussed. In spite of both kinds of barrier, many thousands of Canadians have of course managed to change their province of residence. On the other hand, it is impossible to know how many have been deterred from doing so, or to estimate the impact these barriers to free movement have had on our lack of progress in developing a sense of national community that would transcend the artificial boundaries between the provinces.

Perhaps the most important barriers of the first type have been those connected with language. While anglophone Canadians have enjoyed the full use of their language in all provinces and territories, the French language has had practically no legal recognition outside of Quebec. The relatively numerous and compact francophone communities of eastern Ontario and northern New Brunswick have resisted assimilation with considerable, although not total, success, but even they have received little help from their provincial governments. Elsewhere the French language has faced almost insuperable obstacles to survival — even in Manitoba, which terminated its original status as a bilingual province very soon after anglophone settlers from Ontario became a majority of its population. The lack of a francophone presence in the major urban centres outside of Quebec, apart from Ottawa, is particularly striking. Insofar as such a presence exists at all, it is because of the federal government and its agencies, not the provincial governments. Ontario still refuses to make itself officially bilingual, although New Brunswick has belatedly done so. The restrictions on the French language outside of Quebec naturally led francophones to identify their fortunes with that province almost exclusively, creating provincially oriented nationalism, and finally separatism, as a consequence. In turn the Quebec nationalists now seek to deter anglophones from entering their province, and to drive out those who remain there, a process euphemistically but not inaccurately described as making Quebec as French as Ontario is English.

Education is closely related to language, but interprovincial barriers related to education can be established even where no difference of language exists. The scarcity of French-language education outside of Quebec, and even its deliberate suppression by Ontario in the early part of the twentieth century, have naturally been major obstacles to freedom of movement. Such is also the intention of Quebec's provision in its recent language act that persons moving into Quebec from other provinces cannot send their children to English-language schools, unless they apply for and receive a temporary exemption. There are, however, other types of barrier which result from the remarkable, and unnecessary, diversity of Canada's educational systems. The length of time required to reach a given level of education varies from province to province. Ontario adheres to its Grade 13, invented by Howard Ferguson, which has no counterpart anywhere else in the world. Quebec has inserted an intermediate level of education between high school and university, and has recently imposed this alien system on its anglophone minority. Situations of this kind make it difficult for students to move from one province to another while in school, or even to attend university outside their own province. Another difficulty arises from the fact that provincially funded grants and scholarships are restricted to provincial residents. The now almost complete control by provincial governments over the universities suggests even more disquieting possibilities. Some universities already restrict students from outside the province to a fixed quota of total enrolment. The recent imposition of discriminatory fees on foreign students in Alberta, Ontario, and Quebec could very possibly be the prelude to their imposition on Canadian students from other provinces as well.

Students are not the only Canadians who face interprovincial barriers to their mobility. Quebec's policy of excluding Ontario tradesmen from work in the construction industry has already been referred to. The very nature of the construction industry, in which demand for labour in particular localities rises and falls abruptly, would seem to demand maximum freedom of movement in the interests of all concerned. Despite the Southam reporter's observations on national unity, Quebec cannot assume that its own workers will not be subjected to retaliatory restrictions of the same kind, although admittedly the separatist government might be cynical enough to desire this.

Professional standards and licensing requirements are another area in which the provinces have jurisdiction. Apart from the distinction between Quebec civil law and the common law of the other provinces, which has relevance only to the legal profession, there would seem to be no good reason why professional standards in Canada should not be uniform and completely transferable. Such, however, is not the case. It may even be easier to transfer professional qualifications between two member countries of the European Community than between two Canadian provinces.

Interprovincial barriers have successfully been avoided with regard to pensions, family allowances, and medical insurance, although in the latter two cases there are important interprovincial variations in the benefits received. With regard to welfare assistance the situation is less clear. The federal legislation which provides for the sharing of welfare costs with the provinces prohibits them from making eligibility conditional on a prior period of residence in the province. However residence at the time of receiving benefits is a condition in many provinces, and since the meaning of "residence" is not always defined, considerable scope exists for administrative abuses. The federal legislation also does not prevent restrictions from being imposed by the municipalities, which actually administer most of the program.[13] It should also be noted that prominent political figures in Alberta have, recently, like their counterparts in British Columbia at an earlier period, made widely reported public statements intended to deter indigent or unemployed persons from entering the province. The natural tendency of population to move towards prosperous and dynamic localities, a phenomenon at least as old as western civilization, does face institutional barriers under Canadian federalism.

In this connection a final word must be added about the converse phenomenon, namely the policies designed to prevent provinces and regions from losing population. Some of these at the provincial level have already been referred to in the discussion of industrialization and regional development. One cannot omit mentioning in the same connection the constant and pervasive process of socialization, partly under the auspices of the provincial state and partly through more or less independent agencies such as the media of communication, which is designed to attach people more firmly to the province in which they happen to live. An example would be Ontario's absurd attempt to turn the Civic Holiday (actually a transplanted version of the August Bank Holiday observed in Scotland and Ireland) into a commemoration of Governor John Simcoe. The use of provincial flags and other symbols must also be viewed in this connection. Nova Scotia adopted a flag soon after the Second World War and was followed almost immediately by Quebec. The other provinces did the same in the 1960s, many of them for no better reason than that their governments disliked the maple leaf design of the national flag adopted by the government of Lester Pearson. Local chauvinism and prejudice against other parts of the country are still overtly appealed to by provincial politicians, and one cannot discount even the more subtle effect of such appeals as the election slogan, "Is there any other place you'd rather be?", which the Ontario Progressive Conservatives employed with apparent success in 1971.

Finally, it must be noted that the federal government also promotes policies that seem designed to discourage Canadians from moving freely around the country. Equalization payments and so-called policies of regional economic expansion (regional demographic expansion would be a more appropriate expression) slow down the natural outflow of population from poorer provinces by creating artificial incentives to stay there, incentives which are largely paid for by taxpayers in the more rapidly growing parts of the country. Industrial subsidies and artificial "decentralization" of economic activity impose a heavy cost on the whole Canadian economy. Equalization payments have expanded the bureaucracy and the service sector of the economy in Atlantic Canada (and to a lesser extent Quebec) out of all proportion to the real economic base. Yet unemployment continues to rise despite the constant proliferation of jobs in the public sector, because the new jobs are largely filled by people from outside the region, while the indigenous population is encouraged to stay by an artificially high level of social services. If ending poverty were the real object, it would be far better to make payments to individuals and encourage them to migrate to regions where they could be usefully employed, a fact that Premier W. A. C. Bennett was widely criticized for pointing out several years ago. By all available evidence the Atlantic provinces and the eastern part of Quebec are seriously overpopulated. Federal assistance has enabled them to maintain rates of population growth (and rates of unemployment) that far exceed those in the comparable states of Maine, Vermont, and New Hampshire. While the United States encourages its people to move west and south in search of opportunity, Canada encourages its people to remain where they are, even if unemployment and underemployment are the result. Instead of making the best use of its own population, Canada imports immigrants from overseas to areas where the need for labour is increasing. Some discussion of such issues in Canada is long overdue, but it seems to be inhibited by the curious ideological mystique that surrounds many aspects of our federal system.

NOTES

1. See for example the statement of "objectives of Confederation" in Pierre Elliott Trudeau, *The Constitution and the People of Canada* (Ottawa: Queen's Printer, 1969).
2. A. E. Safarian, *Canadian Federalism and Economic Integration* (Ottawa: Information Canada, 1974).
3. M. J. Trebilcock *et al.,* "Interprovincial Restrictions on the Mobility of Resources", in Ontario Economic Council. *Issues and Alternatives — 1977: Intergovernmental Relations* (Toronto, 1977).
4. Joseph Pope, *Correspondence of Sir John Macdonald* (Toronto: Oxford University Press, 1921), p. 176.
5. H. V. Nelles, *The Politics of Development: Forests, Mines and Hydro-Electric Power in Ontario, 1849–1941* (Toronto: Macmillan, 1974).
6. Albert Breton, *Discriminatory Government Policies in Federal Countries* (Montreal: Private Planning Association of Canada, 1967), pp. 53–73.

7. R. T. Naylor, *The History of Canadian Business,* 2 vols., (Toronto: Lorimer, 1975), Vol. II, pp. 104–60.

8. J. R. Smallwood, *I Chose Canada* (Toronto: Macmillan, 1973), pp. 438–39.

9. Canadian Tax Foundation, *The National Finances, 1977–78* (Toronto, 1978), p. 22.

10. For a more complete account see Safarian, *Canadian Federalism and Economic Integration,* pp. 48–54.

11. Richard Schultz, "Intergovernmental Cooperation, Regulatory Agencies, and Transportation Regulation in Canada: The Case of Part III of the National Transportation Act", *Canadian Public Administration,* XIX (1976):183–207.

12. *The Citizen* (Ottawa), May 31, 1978. Several weeks later the Ontario government announced its intention to impose retaliatory restrictions on Quebec workers. While entirely justified in the circumstances, this will not resolve the problem.

13. Trebilcock, "Interprovincial Restrictions", pp. 112–13.

6   Problems of Fiscal Federalism

The financial aspects of federalism have held an enduring fascination for students of the subject, in Canada and elsewhere. Economists who specialize in public finance have had more reason than most other people to be interested in federalism, and have made important contributions, both of a descriptive and of a more theoretical character, to the writing on the subject. Moreover, those who approach federalism from other perspectives cannot ignore the financial aspect, and have rarely done so. Intergovernmental disputes and controversies over financial matters have been a persistent feature of Canadian federalism throughout its history. Changes in financial arrangements have been constantly resorted to as a means of adapting the federal system to new circumstances, although rarely with enough success to avoid the necessity of further modifications a few years later. The management of intergovernmental fiscal relations, especially in recent years, has employed armies of officials and has spawned, as Donald Smiley whimsically observes, a strange proliferation of esoteric and often unintelligible terminology.[1] Thus it would be possible, although somewhat misleading, to write the history of Canadian federalism merely as the history of intergovernmental finance.

The fiscal side of federalism has also attracted interest because it seems to offer a convenient way of measuring the degree of "centralization" in a federal system and the changing distribution of power and importance between the two levels of government. Even for those political scientists who are not quantitatively inclined, the numbers and percentages associated with fiscal federalism provide a reassuring illusion of concreteness and clarity in a field of study whose other aspects seem so often to be obscured by ambiguity, mystification, and the absence of universally shared assumptions.

The precision of fiscal federalism, however, is in some respects more apparent than real. Government revenues need not correspond with government expenditures, and neither revenues nor expenditures form a homogeneous category. Revenue from taxation is only a part of total revenue, and even definitions of taxation may vary, with natural-resource revenues and liquor profits, to take only two examples, being sometimes classified as taxation and sometimes not. Revenues of provincial governments include substantial transfers from the federal government, both conditional and unconditional. When these funds are spent they become part of provincial expenditure, even though they have already been counted as part of federal expenditure. How they are classified, of course, determines how "centralized" the system appears to be. National-accounts statistics treat all intergovernmental grants as expenditures of the recipient government, while public-finance statistics distinguish conditional from unconditional grants, including the former with the expenditures of the government that makes them. These two alternative procedures, although the most widely used, by no means exhaust the list of possibilities.[2]

Expenditure, like revenue, has its ambiguities, quite apart from the question of intergovernmental grants. The amount which a government spends may be related to its economic impact, its political power, or its need for increasing revenues, but all types of expenditure do not necessarily bear the same relationship to all three of these other variables. Expenditures may be at the discretion of the government concerned; they may be fixed; they may even be dictated by another government (as in the case of matching funds required by some conditional grants). Expenditures on goods and services have a totally different economic significance from transfer payments. The entirely different distinction between expenditure on the economic and on the social functions of government (in Marxist terms, accumulation and legitimization) should also be borne in mind. Unfortunately, none of these distinctions is often made in the regrettably abundant polemical statements about government spending. Sometimes these display a total absence of consistency, as when provincial politicians deplore the massive expenditures of the federal government as evidence of its general profligacy, but cite their own increasing expenditures to support the proposition that their "responsibilities" require a larger share of the income tax.

Comparisons of the expenditures or revenues of the two levels of government at various times are often used to support statements about centralization or decentralization. Subject to the reservations noted above, they may have a certain utility for this purpose, but not for the reason that often seems to be assumed. Governments do not necessarily derive "power" from the fact that they have increased their expenditures, and they may exercise power without either raising or spending much money, as they do by permitting, regulating, or prohibiting various kinds of individual or corporate activities. The significance of financial data for the study of how power is distributed between governments is better seen by treating power as the independent variable. The more power a government gains, the better able it is to increase its revenues, and therefore its expenditures, at the expense of the taxpayer and (in a federal state) at the expense of the other level of government. Thus the easily quantifiable shifts in the fiscal balance of Canadian federalism followed the real shifts in the distribution of power between federal and provincial governments, which took place for the reasons discussed in Chapter 4. The often-recounted history of federal-provincial fiscal negotiations and of the imposition of new taxes at one or the other level is significant as an indication of how governments used the power which circumstances had given them, not of how they acquired it. Politically strong governments can get the revenue they want. Politically weak governments (the provincial governments during the Second World War, the federal government more recently) cannot, just as politically weak groups of taxpayers cannot prevent increases in their taxes.

Public-finance economists sometimes refer to the goal of maintaining a "vertical balance" in fiscal federalism, by which is meant an appropriate division of sources of revenue between the two levels of government.[3] Politicians often refer to the desirability of giving each level of government enough revenue to match its responsibilities. What "balance" is considered appropriate depends mainly on how "responsibilities" are assigned. While in theory this may be determined by the constitution, in practice it is determined politically, by a process that reflects the kinds of circumstance described in preceding chapters. Existing state functions may be shifted, in whole or in part, from one level to the other. New ones, when the demand for them arises, will tend to be assumed by the politically stronger level at the time, which can usually, if need be, find a constitutional interpretation to support its position. Even if there is no change in the allocation of functions, the expenses connected with different functions will increase at varying rates, but functions are not often reallocated for this reason. Thus the search for "vertical balance" in a federal state is never-ending, and constant adjustments must be made to bring the fiscal regime in line with the realities of political power.

The problem is complicated, moreover, if an effort is simultaneously made to maintain what the public-finance economist calls "horizontal balance". By this is meant a situation in which all of the provincial governments are equally well-provided with the financial means to perform their functions, assuming that all have roughly comparable rates of taxation. If the same types of taxation are available to all provincial governments, and if all are responsible for the same functions (which is usually the case), the governments of rich provinces may have enough revenue but the governments of poor provinces will not. Either they have to levy higher taxes, or perform their functions less adequately, or both. If this is considered undesirable, horizontal balance could in theory be secured by one of two methods. Either the governments of poorer provinces could hand over some of their functions to the federal government, or else they could receive subsidies to bring their revenues closer to the level enjoyed by the governments of richer provinces. In practice horizontal balance, like vertical balance, is more often sought by adjusting the revenue side of the equation than by adjusting the allocation of functions. Thus in Canada over the last two decades equalization payments have been the main instrument used to bring about horizontal balance.

The history of federal-provincial finance in Canada is one of continual efforts to bring the vertical balance of revenues into line with the constantly changing allocation of functions between the two levels, efforts that have been complicated by a somewhat more sporadic preoccupation with the horizontal balance. At times the system seemed to be largely self-regulating, while at other times more conscious manipulation was required, but at no time could federal-provincial finance be independent of the underlying realities of the Canadian political economy.

THE FIRST SEVENTY-FIVE YEARS

At the time when the BNA Act was drafted the main source of revenue for all the provincial governments was the customs tariff, which by necessity had to become an exclusively federal tax, given the goal of creating a common market. The main business of government was the construction of railways, canals, and other public works, a task which was mainly assigned to the federal level of government both prospectively and, in a sense, retroactively, since it assumed responsibility for most of the debts which the provinces had accumulated in the course of their efforts to perform this function before 1867. Each province was assigned an "allowance" for what was considered a normal level of debt. The Maritime provinces, with actual debts below this level, were rewarded by receiving interest on the difference, while Quebec and Ontario were supposed to pay (although they never actually did) for the higher-than-average debts which the federal government assumed on their behalf.

Since all provincial governments were deprived of the important sources of taxation, their main source of revenue after Confederation was to be subsidies from the federal government. These were of two kinds: one was fixed at eighty cents *per capita* (based on 1861 census returns for Quebec and Ontario, but increasing for the other two provinces until they each reached a population of 400,000); while the other was a fixed sum for each province, ostensibly for the support of the provincial government and legislature. New Brunswick got an additional subsidy for ten years and was explicitly guaranteed the right to continue imposing its lumber dues, which would otherwise have been *ultra vires* as an indirect tax.

These arrangements left the provincial governments with very limited financial resources, even by the standards of the time, and were declared with more optimism than good judgment to be "in full Settlement of all future Demands on Canada". That was not quite how it worked out in practice. Less than two years after Confederation Nova Scotia received "better terms" (a larger debt allowance and a temporary subsidy similar to New Brunswick's) by threatening to secede. The other provincial governments protested that this was unconstitutional, but soon adopted the more fruitful approach of seeking their own "better terms" whenever the opportunity arose. In the words of one subsequent writer, the concession to Nova Scotia "made a breach in the constitution not yet repaired". Surveying the record of more than sixty years, he concluded: "It is not mere coincidence that, of the twenty-six concessions made since 1867 to individual provinces, only five have gone to governments definitely of the opposite political faith. Moreover, all the important concessions have been made immediately before or immediately after a federal election."[4]

Newly admitted or established provinces received terms broadly similar to those of the original ones, sometimes made more generous by highly optimistic estimates of their numbers of inhabitants. In 1907, with nine provinces now in existence, the BNA Act was amended to increase the subsidies for the support of legislatures and to raise the population ceiling for *per-capita* grants to two and a half million, slightly more than Ontario's population at the time. Even above that level a grant of sixty (instead of eighty) cents would be made for each additional person. Special concessions were made to Prince Edward Island and British Columbia, although the latter was still so dissatisfied with the outcome that it petitioned the British Parliament not to make the amendments.

These concessions to the provinces reflected their increasing power and importance, a much greater consequence of which, however, was their increasing ability to extract taxes from their populations and revenues from their natural resources. This ability was unevenly distributed, with the result that some provinces became largely self-supporting while others continued to rely more heavily on federal subsidies. None, however, was as totally reliant on the subsidies as had originally been expected. The reputed unwillingness of British North Americans to tolerate direct taxation — the only kind which the provincial governments could impose — seemed to evaporate as provincial governments demonstrated their usefulness to local economic interests. British Columbia and Prince Edward Island imposed taxes on land not long after Confederation. Quebec pioneered the use of a corporation tax in 1882, an innovation which the Judicial Committee of the Privy Council declared to be acceptable a few years later. Ontario established succession duties in 1892, and was soon followed by all of the other provinces. Even an income tax appeared in British Columbia as early as 1876. One effect of these innovations was to establish in some people's minds the entirely unconstitutional doctrine, which Quebec's Tremblay Commission recited as late as 1956, that the field of direct taxation belonged exclusively to the provincial governments. Even after the First World War began Ottawa hesitated for years before imposing an income tax (Britain had done so during the war against Napoleon a century earlier), and only took the plunge after a coalition government was formed in 1917.

Direct taxes were supplemented by natural-resource revenues, especially in British Columbia and Ontario.[5] (The Prairie provinces of course had none until they received their lands and resources in 1930.) During the golden years between the Klondike gold rush and the First World War, provincial expenditures increased somewhat faster than federal, despite an almost incredible rate of railway-building which occurred largely at the federal taxpayer's expense. Even after the federal subsidies to the provinces were increased in 1907, Ontario relied on them for less than one quarter of its revenue. As some provinces took in more from taxation than others, neither the statutory subsidies nor the various additional grants to dissatisfied provinces could prevent a horizontal imbalance from emerging. Since wealthy capitalists and corporations were concentrated in Toronto and Montreal, succession duties and corporation taxes were mainly collected by the two central provinces, permitting them in effect to tax the wealth that was accumulated by exploiting the eastern and western hinterlands. The hinterland provinces, particularly in the West, had nonetheless to meet many of the expenses associated with rapid economic development, and were forced to supplement their revenues with extensive borrowing.

Increasing provincial power continued to bear fruit in the 1920s, despite the temporary interruption caused by the war. Mackenzie King's government abolished some of the special taxes imposed in wartime and reduced the federal income and corporation taxes to very low levels. There was apparently little demand for an active or expensive government at the federal level. The provincial governments on the other hand were busy assisting the development of mines and forests, building highways, extending public utilities, and opening their northern frontiers. They were also beginning, although with much less enthusiasm, to spend more on health, education, and welfare.[6] The sources of taxation developed before the war were supplemented by automobile licence fees, gasoline taxes, and profits from a newly invented institution that was to become a ubiquitous feature of Canadian life: the provincial liquor control board. By 1929 federal grants accounted for only one tenth of provincial revenue. About two fifths of all revenues went to the federal government, one fifth to the provincial governments, and two fifths to the local governments.[7]

The Canadian system of public finance had not been designed to deal with the depression that followed the collapse of share prices on the New York Stock Exchange in 1929. Relief and welfare costs, ostensibly a municipal responsibility, increased so rapidly that in practice the federal government had to assume about two fifths of them. The Prairie provinces, which were hit by dry weather as well as by disappearing markets, had difficulty even paying the interest on their debts. Municipal property taxes were raised to pay for welfare (producing a decline in property values), and were supplemented by municipal sales taxes in Montreal and Quebec City. Provincial governments tried to make ends meet by increasing their own taxes or inventing new ones (such as sales taxes in Alberta and Saskatchewan and a payroll tax in Manitoba). Federal taxes were also increased, adding to the misery of taxpayers whose incomes were declining. Special federal grants were made to Manitoba, Saskatchewan, and British Columbia, and the special grants to the Maritime provinces, which had begun in 1925, were increased. In 1936 all ten governments agreed to a constitutional amendment that would have opened the field of indirect taxation to the provinces, but it was rejected by the Senate.

In response to this situation the federal government appointed, in 1937, the Royal Commission on Dominion-Provincial Relations, usually known as the Rowell–Sirois Commission.[8] The commission conducted an impressive examination of Canadian federalism and presented its report in 1940. It recommended that the federal government again assume responsibility for all provincial debts, and for a portion of municipal debts in Quebec. The federal government should also take full financial responsibility for emergency relief to agriculture and to the employable unemployed. It should be given power to establish a social-security plan, as the United States had recently done, and to implement the conventions of the International Labour Organization. The provincial governments should surrender their right to impose income, corporation, and succession taxes, receiving some compensation for the contribution of their natural resources to corporation profits. An independent commission (modelled after Australia's) should be established to remove political partisanship from the process of allocating federal grants to the provinces. "Adjustment grants" should be made to provinces insofar as this was necessary for them to provide an "average Canadian standard of government services". It was anticipated that all provinces except Ontario, British Columbia, and (surprisingly) Alberta would require them.

Predictably, the three provincial governments that had been declared ineligible for Adjustment Grants rejected the report, with Alberta's Aberhart denouncing it as a plot by international finance, and Ontario's Hepburn professing to find some arcane significance in the fact that Ontario was unrepresented on the commission. (N.W. Rowell was from Ontario, but he had played little part in the commission's work because of illness.) Thus the commission, by correctly anticipating that these provinces would be the centres of growth in the post-depression economy, provoked them into recognizing their common interest in fiscal decentralization.

In the meantime, the problems of another war had replaced

those of the depression.[9] The report was filed away and replaced by a federal pledge in the 1941 budget speech to raise income and corporation taxes to the maximum level that would be reasonable, on the assumption that the provinces levied no such taxes at all. Provinces that agreed not to tax incomes or corporations would be compensated either by an annual payment equal to their actual revenues from such taxes in 1940 or by a formula based on subtracting their succession-duty revenues from the interest on their debts. Provinces that refused to agree would expose their residents to prohibitive taxation for no apparent purpose. All agreed, with Saskatchewan and the Maritimes choosing the formula based on debts while the more prosperous provinces opted for straight compensation. The system was effective for financing the war but grossly inequitable: British Columbia received about fifteen dollars *per capita* each year, Ontario and the Prairie provinces about eight dollars, Quebec and the Maritimes about six dollars. However, the impact of this fact was softened in that the somewhat chaotic accumulation of "special" and "emergency" grants to individual provinces was retained largely unchanged. In 1945, as the first ministers assembled for a major conference on post-war reconstruction, the most pressing question at hand was whether the wartime fiscal system, the pre-war system, the system recommended by the Rowell–Sirois Commission, or some fourth alternative would be adopted in the post-war period.

FROM TAX RENTAL TO TAX SHARING

At the conclusion of the Second World War the federal government appeared to stand at the height of its power and prestige in relation to the provincial governments. Canada had operated in wartime practically as a unitary state, and the provincial governments had been reduced to insignificance. Popular sentiment appeared to expect a predominant federal role in planning the economy and in extending social legislation after the war, and the greatly expanded federal bureaucracy seemed well-equipped for the task. The temporary and illusory nature of this federal predominance, however, was soon to be revealed. As the underlying logic of the post-war political economy asserted itself, the federal government proved unable to impose its will on the provincial governments, particularly those of the two central provinces. Pressure from these two forced the gradual but inexorable retreat from the post-war design of fiscal centralization and the surrender of a larger and larger share of the direct tax fields to the provincial governments. At the same time direct taxes, especially the personal income tax, were gaining in importance relative to other forms of taxation. Thus the way in which the proceeds of this tax were divided was increasingly important for both levels of government. The fact that the provincial governments were so largely victorious in a conflict where so much was at stake indicated how illusory had been their apparent weakness at the end of the war.

Another interesting feature of the post-war period was the procedure by which federal-provincial negotiations over fiscal matters were carried on. It came to be accepted as a fact of life that the federal government could not in practice impose direct taxation without taking into account the views of the provincial governments, or at least of those in Toronto and Quebec City. This was certainly a very different situation from that which prevailed in the United States or Australia. In addition, power was shifting so rapidly towards the provincial level of government that it became necessary to revise the federal-provincial fiscal regime at least every five years, and in practice somewhat more frequently. The result of these facts has been a new and highly distinctive pattern of policy-making. New arrangements for federal and provincial division of direct taxes and related matters are established every five years, subject to occasional adjustments in the interim. Each five-year period is preceded by a series of intergovernmental conferences, involving officials, finance ministers, and first ministers. Normally the presentation of initial bargaining positions by the federal and provincial governments takes place about two years before the new arrangements are scheduled to come into effect, although bargaining over the 1977–82 fiscal arrangements actually began as early as 1973. Over the months (or years) that follow, a compromise is reached among the views of

the federal, Quebec, and Ontario governments, which becomes
the basis of the tax regime under which Canadians will live for
the next five years.

This process of "executive federalism", which, especially
after 1963, was extended from fiscal matters to other areas of
public policy, places a premium on leadership and negotiating
skill.[10] Except in one case which is discussed below, federal
Prime Ministers have largely left the initiative in fiscal
negotiations to their Ministers of Finance. Provincial Premiers
have not been so self-effacing, although very few have ever
followed the Australian practice of holding the Provincial
Treasurer's portfolio themselves. Both of the two central
provinces have had strong leadership at the provincial level for
most of the post-war period, particularly in the early and crucial
stages. George Drew, who returned the Ontario Conservatives
to their usual position on the government benches in 1943, was
as combative and as obsessed with provincial autonomy as
Mitch Hepburn, but far superior to him in intellect and
character. Leslie Frost in the 1950s and John Robarts in the
1960s continued effectively in the same tradition. In Quebec
the highly progressive (by Quebec standards) Liberal government of Adelard Godbout, who had, with federal assistance,
defeated Maurice Duplessis in 1939, was defeated in its turn by
Duplessis in 1944. Duplessis proved a more formidable
opponent for the federal government after 1944 than he had
been before 1939, either because social and economic forces
were now working in his favour or because, as his biographer
alleges, he had managed to conquer his drinking problem while
in opposition.[11] His policy of using every opportunity to extend
the Quebec government's autonomy was continued without
much change by his successors of all parties, despite the largely
mythical "Quiet Revolution" of the early 1960s.

In 1945 the federal government proposed that a fiscal regime
somewhat similar to the wartime model should be continued in
peacetime. Provinces would "rent" to the federal government
for periods of five years at a time their constitutional right to
impose income, corporation, and succession taxes. In return
they would receive uniform *per-capita* payments, escalating
automatically with the growth in the GNP. Assuming a GNP at
the 1941 level the initial payment would be twelve dollars *per*

capita, but the actual GNP was already at about one and a half times this level, so that the proposed arrangement was more generous than the wartime one even for British Columbia.

The Prairie and Maritime provinces were quite content with this proposal, but British Columbia resented losing its privileged position under the earlier arrangement, and the two central provinces also raised strenuous objections. George Drew unveiled a detailed proposal of his own which included the sharing of income tax between the two levels of government (with the federal government acting as the collector), complete provincial control of succession duties, a formula to allocate the provincial share of corporation tax in proportion to sales (rather than by the location of the head office), and a "National Adjustment Fund" to redistribute some direct-tax revenue from the rich to the poor provinces. None of this was achieved immediately, but Drew lived long enough to learn that he had been a much better prophet than his federal counterparts.

The failure to secure unanimous approval for the federal plan was followed by a more generous federal counter-offer, which satisfied British Columbia but not Ontario or Quebec. In 1946 the federal government announced that it would make tax-rental agreements with those provinces that desired them without waiting for unanimous consent. Provinces that did not agree would receive no tax-rental payments, but they could levy their own taxes which would be partially credited against the federal taxes. The maximum credits would be 50 per cent of the federal tax for succession duty, 5 per cent of the federal tax for personal income tax, and 5 per cent of taxable income for corporation tax. After some additional modification of the tax-rental formula, in January 1947 all provinces except Ontario and Quebec signed tax-rental agreements. Ontario and Quebec imposed their own corporation taxes and succession duties, receiving the federal credits, but neither imposed a personal income tax although they retained the right to do so. Newfoundland signed a tax-rental agreement when it became a Canadian province in 1949.

This tax-rental arrangement was due to expire in 1952. Federal efforts to entice the central provinces into a new one, and to prevent any defections, began in 1950 with the offer of a modified formula for computing the tax-rental payments. The new offer continued the movement, which had begun with the federal government's final offer in 1947, away from strictly *per-capita* payments and towards a more direct relationship between the size of the payment and the value of the taxes rented. It was also more attractive to Ontario, and, after the usual process of bargaining, that province signed a tax-rental agreement in 1952. Unlike the agreements with the other provinces, this one allowed Ontario to levy its own succession duty, which continued to be credited against the federal tax. The federal government also revived the notion of a constitutional amendment to open the field of indirect taxation to the provincial governments, but decided not to proceed with it when Quebec withheld its approval. Presumably Duplessis calculated that the amendment would reduce the likelihood of other provinces supporting Quebec's rigid position on direct taxation.

The Quebec government appeared more isolated than at any time in the past, but it was soon to win a victory of the greatest importance. No province, including Quebec, had imposed a personal income tax since 1941, but in 1954 Quebec adopted legislation which imposed a personal income tax equal to 15 per cent of the federal tax (although with slightly more generous exemptions), despite the fact that the federal tax credit available to it as a non-renting province was still only 5 per cent. The preamble to the Act declared somewhat provocatively (and inaccurately) that the provincial governments had priority in the field of direct taxation under the BNA Act. The Liberal opposition in the provincial legislature denounced the Union Nationale government for imposing "double taxation".

It appeared as though Duplessis had finally miscalculated, but he was saved by Prime Minister St. Laurent, whose behaviour can perhaps most charitably be attributed to advancing senility.[12] The Prime Minister and the Premier, who had barely been on speaking terms, met privately at Montreal's Windsor Hotel in October 1954. Several letters and a telephone conversation followed, and in January St. Laurent agreed to raise the federal income tax credit immediately to 10 per cent. He thus stabbed his provincial Liberal allies in the back, to say nothing of being unfair to other provincial governments which had signed rental agreements in good faith and now saw the only province that had failed to do so rewarded for its intransigence.[13]

Whether intentionally or not, St. Laurent's action signalled the impending demise of the tax-rental system. A few months later the federal government proposed, for the forthcoming (1957–62) set of fiscal arrangements, terms which virtually abandoned any distinction between agreeing and non-agreeing provinces. Provinces that signed an agreement would be given not a fixed rental payment but a percentage of the actual yield from federal taxation of their residents. Provinces that did not sign an agreement would receive exactly the same in the form of tax credits, the only difference being that they would have to handle their own collection and could impose higher taxes if they wished. The provincial share of income tax would be 10 per cent (the same as the credit which Quebec already received), their share of succession duties would be 50 per cent, and their share of corporation tax would amount to 9 per cent of taxable income (or about one fifth of the total tax yield). In effect this was the tax sharing which George Drew had proposed a decade earlier, although the term "tax rental" continued to be used. Since tax sharing naturally meant a very uneven distribution of benefits among the provinces (depending on the incomes of their residents) it would be supplemented by "equalization" payments to all provinces except Ontario and British Columbia, whether or not they signed an agreement.

Shortly after these arrangements came into force, the new Diefenbaker government was elected and promptly increased the provincial share of the personal income tax from 10 to 13 per cent. In 1959, shortly after Duplessis died, it also increased Quebec's corporation-tax credit in return for a promise that the increased proceeds would be used for grants to universities. (Duplessis had prohibited Quebec universities from accepting federal grants, although all universities outside of Quebec received them.)

The demolition of the tax-rental system was completed in 1960. The governments of the two central provinces, like sharks that grow bolder at the smell of blood, escalated their demands at the July conference. Quebec's new Liberal

Premier, Jean Lesage, demanded 25 per cent of personal income tax, 25 per cent of corporation tax, and complete control of succession duties. Ontario's Leslie Frost asked for 50 per cent of both personal income tax and corporation income tax, unless the BNA Act could be amended to give provincial governments access to indirect taxation. Further meetings followed in October 1960 and February 1961, at which the federal government announced its intention to end the tax-rental system. In effect all provinces would be given a deal similar to but more generous than that which Quebec, as a non-renting province, enjoyed under the existing arrangements. As an added concession, the federal government would continue, if provincial governments so desired, to collect direct taxes on their behalf, even though the rates of taxation would no longer be subject to its control. Since equalization would continue, and since it would not even be necessary to establish tax-collection machinery, the Atlantic provinces and Manitoba had no objection to this proposition. The only protest came from Premier Tommy Douglas of Saskatchewan, who had witnessed the ultimate consequences of fiscal decentralization while ministering to a Prairie Baptist church in the 1930s.[14]

With the transition from tax rental to tax sharing completed in form as well as in fact, federal-provincial fiscal relations became largely a process of bargaining over the federal and provincial shares of the three major direct taxes. The process became an almost continuous one, with provincial demands constantly increasing at the expense of the federal government. The 1962–67 fiscal arrangements provided for the provincial share of the personal income tax to begin at 16 per cent in the first year, increasing by one percentage point in each year of the agreement. The new government headed by Lester Pearson agreed in 1964 to accelerate the timetable of federal tax reductions or "abatements" so that the provincial share actually reached 24 per cent (instead of 20 per cent) in the last year of the agreement, and this quite apart from the effect of the higher-than-standard rates that already existed in certain provinces. The same government had earlier agreed to reduce the federal share of death taxes (estate or succession) from one half to one quarter. Another innovation at this time was the so-called "opting out" procedure, by which provinces indicating their desire to assume full responsibility for certain shared-cost programs would be compensated by larger-than-normal abatements. This measure came in response to Quebec's complaints about conditional grants in areas which it alleged were under provincial jurisdiction, and was probably suggested by the precedent of the agreement concerning university grants in 1959. Although all provincial governments were offered the chance to "opt out", Quebec was the only one that accepted.

The Quebec and Ontario governments continued to insist that their "responsibilities" required larger shares of direct taxation, despite the fact that the total yield from such taxation was increasing rapidly as the prosperity of the 1960s pushed more taxpayers into higher income brackets. At the suggesion of Ontario, the federal government agreed to establish a Tax Structure Committee, consisting of three federal ministers and the ten provincial treasurers, to examine the tax-sharing system and report before it became necessary to define the terms of the 1967–72 fiscal arrangements. In view of its composition it was predictable that the committee would support the provincial position, but the new Minister of Finance, Mitchell Sharp, ignored the committee and instead made a somewhat more vigorous defence of the federal primacy in taxation than that to which the provincial governments had become accustomed.

At the 1966 fiscal conference Sharp threw the provinces temporarily off balance.[15] The conference had already been delayed for almost a year by a federal election, leaving the provinces less time than usual to extract concessions from Ottawa before the new arrangements came into force. Ontario again demanded 50 per cent of the personal income tax and was joined by normally docile Manitoba, whose Premier Duff Roblin was already an unannounced candidate for the federal Conservative leadership. Quebec's Daniel Johnson, presumably with tongue in cheek, demanded a complete federal withdrawal from direct taxation in his province. Sharp's position was that since provincial politicians were always talking about their "responsibilities", further abatements would be given to them only if they actually assumed additional responsibilities. He offered them a second opportunity to "opt out" of certain shared-cost programs, as Quebec had already done, but again the other provinces expressed no interest. This offer was followed within weeks by an entirely unexpected announcement that federal grants to universities would be terminated and replaced either by an additional abatement (4 per cent of personal income tax and 1 per cent of corporation income) or by a *per-capita* grant of fourteen dollars (later raised to fifteen) that would increase in proportion to GNP. The abatement, unlike previous ones, would be "equalized" so as to be equally beneficial to all provinces. This proved to be the only abatement that was forthcoming, and it was, in effect, closer to being a conditional grant than a genuine abatement.

These developments infuriated several provincial governments, Ontario's in particular, as did the imposition of an unshared temporary surtax on the personal income tax by the new Trudeau government in 1968. As a symbolic gesture the Tax Structure Committee was revived the following year but accomplished nothing. The 1972–77 fiscal arrangements were little changed from the previous ones, although some complicated adjustments connected with federal tax reforms had the effect of increasing the provincial share of the personal income tax to 30.5 per cent. Provincial tax rates by this time varied so much that these percentages of a theoretical standard had become meaningless. In recognition of this fact the federal government announced that the federal tax alone (except in Quebec) would now be considered as "one hundred per cent" and that provincial taxes would be expressed as percentages of this figure. In Quebec the federal tax continued to be much lower than elsewhere because of "opting out".

The main issue in negotiating the 1977–82 arrangements was again the sharing of personal and corporation income taxes (the federal estate tax had been eliminated in 1971), but it was complicated by the federal government's determination, discussed in the next chapter, to escape entirely from financial responsibility for health insurance and post-secondary education. The end result of three years of negotiation, in the course of which the ten provincial governments for the first time formed a "common front" against Ottawa, was a far more generous abatement of the federal taxes than had originally been offered, plus cash grants for post-secondary education. Provincial revenues from both types of tax will henceforth be more than half as large as federal revenues: a far cry indeed from the situation in the 1940s and 1950s.

It remains to comment briefly on the problem of horizontal balance, and particularly on the system of equalization payments that has existed in one form or another since 1957. Efforts to resolve the problem of interprovincial differences in taxing capacity in fact go back at least to 1927, when special federal subsidies to the Maritime provincial governments were commenced following the recommendation of a Royal Commission. These subsidies were substantially increased during the 1930s, and special subsidies were also given in those years to the western provinces (apart from Alberta which was punished for repudiating its debts under the Social Credit administration). Newfoundland also received special subsidies after it became a Canadian province, although the other special subsidies had by this time been eliminated.

Unless corrective action is taken the problem of horizontal imbalance naturally becomes worse as provincial autonomy increases. If most functions are performed and most taxes collected at the federal level, interprovincial variations in taxing capacity, or in ability to perform the functions, are irrelevant. For this reason equalization payments are unnecessary in the United States, which, despite their absence, has been far more successful than Canada in overcoming the problem of regional disparities. For this reason also, equalization payments were unnecessary in Canada under the tax-rental system, at least in its original form. Uniform *per-capita* grants to the provincial governments, regardless of what proportion of federal revenue actually originated in each province, had the automatic effect of redistributing income from rich provinces to poor ones (apart, that is from Quebec, which had made the deliberate choice to deny its residents the benefits of this redistribution).

The corollary of this fact is that the more fiscal decentralization takes place (i.e., the more federal taxes are reduced to make way for provincial taxes) the greater the conflict of interest that arises between rich provinces and poor ones. Fiscal decentralization improves the position of the rich provinces and worsens the position of the poor ones. The most bizarre aspect of the federal government's behaviour in fiscal negotiations since 1955 has been its persistent refusal to exploit the tactical advantage this fact could have given it in dealing with the provincial governments that pressed for fiscal decentralization. Without equalization, fiscal decentralization would have quickly become intolerable to the poor provinces, a fact which explains why Premier Drew included a form of equalization in his proposals in 1945. Yet instead of rallying the poor provinces as a bloc to resist fiscal decentralization, the federal government at every stage from 1955 onwards took steps to make it acceptable to them. First it offered to pay equalization payments out of its own revenues. (Drew had proposed that the governments of the rich provinces should pay for them, a system subsequently adopted in the Federal Republic of Germany.) Then at each successive stage of fiscal decentralization it made the equalization payments more generous by adding additional types of tax to the calculation on which they were based. Finally, it built additional equalization into the abatement process itself by offering "equalized tax points" rather than straight abatements. This practice began in 1959 with the agreement between Ottawa and Quebec on university financing and was continued with the "opting-out" formula of 1964, the post-secondary education arrangements beginning in 1967, and the new abatements in lieu of contributions to health insurance that began in 1977.

The result of these actions has been to eliminate any serious opposition to fiscal decentralization while leaving the federal government (with a declining share of total revenues) to bear the entire responsibility for its consequences. There is a fundamental lack of logic in an equalization formula based on provincial revenues, with the grants paid out of federal revenues that come from an entirely different mixture of tax sources. This contradiction became apparent in the early 1970s, when the increased price of oil produced a sudden and dramatic increase in the provincial revenues of Alberta and Saskatchewan.[16] Federal revenues did not increase, but the federal government was none the less expected to subsidize the revenues of other provinces so as to bring them up to an average in which Alberta and Saskatchewan were included. This would have meant paying equalization to Ontario! In order to avert a complete fiscal catastrophe the federal government was forced to slow down the increases in the price of oil and then to modify the equalization formula so that oil revenues would be only partially taken into account.

The absurdity of the whole situation is compounded by the fact that the main argument used to justify the ending of the tax-rental system, first by Premier Duplessis and later by Minister of Finance Donald Fleming, was that the government that spent money should also have the responsibility for raising it, rather than depending on another government for financial support.[17] This allegedly sacrosanct principle of British parliamentary democracy would of course rule out any kind of equalization, but the principle was conveniently forgotten once it had served its ideological purpose. In all four Atlantic provinces about half of gross general revenue now consists of transfers from the federal government, a category which does not include the proceeds of provincial direct taxes for which the federal government merely acts as a collector. Equalization payments alone provide almost as much revenue as the total for all kinds of provincial taxes in Prince Edward Island. Even in Quebec and Manitoba, equalization contributes almost as much to provincial revenues as the general sales tax.[18] If responsible government has managed to survive in these circumstances, why could it not have survived in the other provinces under a tax-rental system?

FISCAL FEDERALISM: AN OVERVIEW

One conclusion that can be drawn from the history of federal-provincial finance is that its evolution is almost entirely independent of the written constitution. Apart from the increase in statutory grants and subsidies in 1907 (which in retrospect is clearly a far less dramatic and significant change than many that have happened since), the entire process has been conducted without any formal changes in the rules by which it ostensibly is governed. Yet there have been not one but several changes of an almost revolutionary character.

The assumption that changes have been made in an effort to adjust the revenues of governments to their responsibilities is somewhat more plausible than the assumption that they have been dictated by the constitution, but it begs the question of how "responsibilities" are assigned, for in practice this too is largely independent of the constitution. There is nothing in the BNA Act about air transport or television or manpower training or public housing or industrial relations or hydro-electricity, nothing to suggest that the governments of the larger provinces would conduct quasi-diplomatic activities in foreign countries or that the federal government and two provincial governments would jointly invest in the development of the Athabasca tar sands. There is no evidence that the provincial jurisdiction over education was intended to have anything to do with universities; and the provincial jurisdiction over health and welfare as it is presently understood could only be deduced from the BNA Act with the aid of a singularly fertile imagination. Even the courts have had little to do with the way in which most of these "responsibilities" are in practice assigned.

It appears that governments have in practice selected the "responsibilities" they wanted whenever those private groups and interests with a direct stake in the outcome of the activity concerned found it convenient for them to do so, and have then scrambled for the revenues needed to carry out the task. Governments whose expansion serves the interests of influential classes and class fractions have tended to expand, and to find both the forceful leadership and the revenues required to do so. Constitutional justifications are invented only after the fact.

Although one would never know it from reading the BNA Act, Canada is clearly a rather decentralized federation, both in terms of the division of functions between the two levels of government and in terms of the division of revenues. The reasons for this fact have been explored in Chapter 4. Its consequences are a more complex, less frequently explored, and more controversial subject. A few consequences of decentralization in terms of functions were discussed in Chapter 5, but the observations in that chapter barely scratch the surface of the subject.

The consequences of decentralization in terms of revenues constitute another subject well worth exploring. With some of its more arcane aspects the author is quite unqualified to deal, although he is comforted slightly by the fact that in recent years economists appear to have lost some of the self-assurance that so aroused the envy of political scientists in the past. Even the Keynesian theory of using fiscal policy to manage aggregate demand, often used in earlier years as an argument for fiscal centralization, seems to have lost much of the magic it had a generation ago.

One set of consequences, however, is quite easy to explore. Under the present Canadian form of fiscal federalism the provincial governments have freedom to set the rates of several important types of taxation, which consequently vary from province to province. What kinds of variations have resulted?

The four major provincial sources of tax revenue are the personal income tax, the general sales tax, the corporation tax and the motor-fuel tax. Together these account for about four fifths of the revenue from provincial taxation.[19] In the case of the personal income tax, variations in the rates have been possible since 1962 (apart from the special case of Quebec, which imposed its own tax in 1954), and have gradually become more pronounced since that time. The variations have also, of course, become more significant to the taxpayer as the provincial share of his total income-tax payment has increased. There is a clear tendency for rates to be higher in poorer provinces. In Alberta the provincial tax in 1977 was 38.5 per cent of the federal tax, in Ontario 44.0 per cent, and in British Columbia 46.0 per cent, but in all the Atlantic provinces it was 50.0 per cent or more and in Newfoundland 57.5 per cent, or almost one and a half times the level in Alberta. Quebecers pay less federal tax than other Canadians, and their provincial income tax is unrelated to the federal one, making comparison more difficult, but it appears that the effective rates in Quebec (combined federal and provincial) were higher even than Newfoundland's for all tax brackets. If the personal income tax were entirely under federal control, and thus uniform across Canada, one suspects it would be closer to Alberta's present rate than to Newfoundland's.

The situation is similar for the general sales tax, where Newfoundland has the highest rate, Alberta none at all, and the provinces east of the Ottawa River all have higher rates than the provinces west of the Ottawa River. This of course increases the cost of living in provinces where incomes are lower than average. In the case of motor-fuel tax the interprovincial differences are less pronounced, but all the Atlantic provinces have above-average rates and Alberta's rate was by far the lowest even before it abolished the tax entirely in 1978.

In the case of corporation tax the situation is entirely different. There is relatively little variation from province to province, but the lowest rate in 1977 was in the poorest province, Prince Edward Island, and the highest rates were in Manitoba and British Columbia. Poor provincial governments can try to fill their treasuries by imposing heavy taxes on their residents and consumers, but the mobility of capital and the competition for investment and "jobs" makes it hazardous to impose heavy taxes on corporations, and there is even a slight tendency for the provinces that have the greatest difficulty in attracting private investment to do the reverse. Since all provinces compete for investment it is probably not unreasonable to assume that if the corporation tax were entirely under federal jurisdiction, and were imposed uniformly across the country, it would be higher than it now is in any province, although admittedly Canada would still be competing for investment against the United States.

The higher rates of personal income, sales, and motor-fuel taxes in the poorer provinces may seem strange in view of the fact that they receive equalization payments. It is apparent, however, that equalization payments have been used to increase provincial government expenditures, not to reduce taxes.[20] Provincial government expenditures *per capita* are fairly uniform from one province to another, and the differences that exist do not suggest that rich provinces spend more. In the 1976–77 fiscal year expenditures were well above average in the two provinces that receive the most equalization *per capita* (Prince Edward Island and Newfoundland) and in the province that receives the most equalization in absolute terms (Quebec). They were significantly below average in Ontario. The major beneficiaries from equalization are provincial public servants, and, to a lesser extent, politicians in the provinces that receive them. The major sufferers from fiscal decentralization, with which equalization has been intimately associated, are the taxpayers in the same provinces. Unlike the politicians and public servants, these people do not appear at the federal-provincial conference table to state their case.

NOTES

1. Donald V. Smiley, *Canada in Question, Federalism in the Seventies,* 2nd ed. (Toronto: McGraw-Hill, 1976), p. 114.
2. Richard M. Bird, *The Growth of Government Spending in Canada* (Toronto: Canadian Tax Foundation, 1970), pp. 33–38.
3. The concepts of vertical and horizontal balance are discussed in R. L. Mathews, ed., *Intergovernmental Relations in Australia* (Sydney: Angus and Robertson, 1974), Chapters 9 and 10.
4. J. A. Maxwell, "Better Terms", *Queen's Quarterly,* XL (1933):125–39 at p. 136.
5. See the table of estimated resource revenues, by province and year, in Anthony Scott, ed., *Natural Resource Revenues: A Test of Federalism* (Vancouver: University of British Columbia Press, 1976), pp. 42–43.
6. Christopher Armstrong, "The Politics of Federalism: Ontario's Relations with the Federal Government, 1896–1940" (unpublished Ph.D thesis, University of Toronto, 1972), Chapter 9.
7. Canadian Tax Foundation, *The National Finances 1977-78* (Toronto: 1978), table on p. 19.
8. The report was published by the King's Printer in Ottawa, and reprinted in 1954. A useful abridgment is Donald V. Smiley, ed., *The Rowell–Sirois Report* (Toronto: McClelland and Stewart, 1963). A companion volume in the same series reprints the most interesting of the many studies done for the commission: W. A. MacKintosh, *The Economic Background of Dominion-Provincial Relations* (Toronto: McClelland and Stewart, 1964).
9. From this point onwards the reader in search of more detail should consult A. Milton Moore, J. H. Perry, and Donald I. Beach, *The Financing of Canadian Federation: The First Hundred Years* (Toronto: Canadian Tax Foundation, 1966), as well as the Foundation's annual volumes on federal and provincial finances.
10. Smiley, *Canada in Question,* pp. 54–82, discusses the concept of "executive federalism".
11. Conrad Black, *Duplessis* (Toronto: McClelland and Stewart, 1977), pp. 262–63.
12. St. Laurent's deterioration from 1954 onwards is discussed in Peter C. Newman, *Renegade in Power: The Diefenbaker Years* (Toronto: McClelland and Stewart, 1963), pp. 34–35.
13. Black, *Duplessis,* pp. 432–46 gives a fuller account. See also

Reginald Whitaker, *The Government Party: Organizing and Financing the Liberal Party of Canada, 1930-1958* (Toronto: University of Toronto Press, 1977), p. 297, for the impact on relations between federal and provincial Liberals.

14. Newman, *Renegade in Power,* p. 126.
15. For a good account of the negotiations see Richard Simeon, *Federal-Provincial Diplomacy: The Making of Recent Policy in Canada* (Toronto: University of Toronto Press, 1972), pp. 66-87.
16. Thomas J. Courchene, "Equalization Payments and Energy Royalities", in Scott, *Natural Resource Revenues.*
17. See Duplessis' statement at the 1955 conference, reprinted in Moore, Perry, and Beach, *The Financing of Canadian Federation,* pp. 121-25.
18. Canadian Tax Foundation, *Provincial and Municipal Finances, 1977* (Toronto: 1977), table on p. 23.
19. Information in this and subsequent paragraphs is from Canadian Tax Foundation, *Provincial and Municipal Finances, 1977,* pp. 33, 67, 72, 76, 78, 82, and 91.
20. In fact under the present system of equalization there is an incentive for a "poor" province to increase rates of taxation with respect to sources of taxation for which its tax base is relatively low. By doing so it will increase both its tax revenue and its equalization revenue. See T. J. Courchene and D. A. Beavis, "Federal-Provincial Tax Equalization: An Evaluation", *Canadian Journal of Economics,* VI (1973):483-502.

Conditional Grants and Shared-Cost Programs

An aspect of federal-provincial finance that was only briefly referred to in the preceding chapter is the whole area of conditional grants and shared-cost programs. The omission was an important one, not only because conditional grants and shared-cost programs have been an important feature of Canadian federalism at least since the Second World War, but also because their fate has become increasingly inseparable from the question, discussed in the preceding chapter, of how revenue sources are distributed between the two levels of government.

Like so many other aspects of federalism, conditional grants originated in the United States, where their history can be traced well back into the nineteenth century. The United States constitution contains no explicit provision for "grants-in-aid" (the term customarily used in that country), but their constitutional basis is often said to reside in Article 1, Section 8, which enumerates the powers of Congress, including "to lay and collect taxes, duties, imposts and excises, to pay the debts and provide for the common defense and general welfare of the United States". The first conditional grants actually involved the disposal of public lands rather than the proceeds of taxation, but cash grants were not long in following.

In the twentieth century the American practice of making conditional grants has been extensively imitated in both Canada and Australia, although less so in other federations. In Australia they are usually known as special-purpose grants, and the constitution makes explicit provision for them in Section 96: "During a period of ten years after the establishment of the Commonwealth and thereafter until the Parliament otherwise provides, the Parliament may grant financial assistance to any State on such terms and conditions as Parliament sees fit."

The Canadian and Australian (although not the American) expressions both suggest the basic characteristics of such grants, which distinguishes them from unconditional or general-purpose grants such as the statutory subsidies and equalization payments discussed in the preceding chapter. A conditional grant is earmarked for a particular program or activity, and is offered only insofar as the recipient government agrees to undertake the program or activity in a way that falls within the guidelines set by the donor government. Usually this means that the recipient government must spend some of its own funds, over and above what it receives in the grant. Activities financed in this way are sometimes known as shared-cost programs.

In Canada, however, it is not always easy to draw a clear distinction between conditional and unconditional grants. The conditions have characteristically been less rigid, even on paper, than those that prevail in the United States and, as J. A. Corry pointed out more than forty years ago, it has never in practice been politically feasible to punish a province for failing to carry them out by terminating its grant.[1] Both of these facts tend to dissolve the distinction between conditional and unconditional grants. Additional ambiguities have been added to the picture through the development of post-war fiscal arrangements. The tax-rental payments were in effect conditional grants, although they were not earmarked for any specific purpose. On the other hand the federal payments to the provinces for post-secondary education from 1967 onwards were ostensibly earmarked for a specific purpose but are practically never considered to be conditional grants. Federal payments for "medicare", at least up to 1977, approximated much more closely to the characteristics of a conditional grant, but Donald Smiley none the less described them as "an alternative to conditional grants" on the grounds that they were simple to implement, involved no problems of defining shareable costs, and allowed for broad variations in the character of provincial programs.[2] Both post-secondary education and medicare are shared-cost programs, even if they do not involve conditional grants. On the other hand there may be a conditional grant without cost-sharing, although examples are fairly rare in Canada. In such a case the federal government pays the entire cost of the program to the provincial government and no provincial funds are required. Provincial governments are only involved because it is easier or cheaper for the federal government to purchase a service from them than to perform the task itself. An example would be the enforcement of the Canadian Labour (Safety) Code by provincial inspectors.

In Canada, as in the United States, the constitution makes no explicit provision for conditional grants, but the freedom of Parliament to dispose of its own consolidated revenue as it sees fit would seem to be an inevitable conclusion from its jurisdiction over "The Public Debt and Property" and "The raising of Money by any Mode or System of Taxation". In fact one could reasonably conclude on similar grounds that Section 96 of the Australian constitution is an unnecessary statement of the obvious. The so-called "spending power" of Parliament, however, is not entirely unrestricted by judicial enactment. The Judicial Committee of the Privy Council stated in 1937 that legislation disposing of Dominion property would still be *ultra vires* if it invaded fields of provincial jurisdiction.[3] Since the legislation overturned by this opinion was not a conditional grant to the provincial governments, but rather the establishment of an unemployment insurance fund, the relevance of the opinion to conditional grants is not clear. It is probably significant that no provincial government has ever sought directly to challenge their legality. A provincial government that objects to them on principle can protect its autonomy by refusing to accept them, as Quebec did on more than one occasion.

Most of the voluminous arguments for and against conditional grants in Canada have not been based primarily on legal criteria. Opponents of conditional grants often state that it is improper for the federal government to seek to influence the decision-making priorities of the provincial governments. This view cannot be derived from the BNA Act, even if it may be justified on other grounds. Perhaps its real basis lies in another argument which both J. A. Corry and Donald Smiley have used against conditional grants, which is that they destroy the accountability of governments to their electorates.[4] Since every Canadian citizen entitled to vote in a provincial election can also vote in a federal election, and vice versa, this argument does not seem exceptionally persuasive. A better one, strongly emphasized by Corry in his work for the Rowell–Sirois Commission, is that the "divided jurisdiction" inherent in shared-cost programs prevents bureaucracy from operating in the rational and orderly manner prescribed by Max Weber since there is no single hierarchical chain of command when more than one government is involved. On the other hand, some recent studies of bureaucracy suggest that the Weberian model may, in any event, have little resemblance to reality since different departments and agencies of the same government enjoy considerable autonomy in practice, even though they may be formally subject to one centre of authority.

Smiley, in his monograph for the Canadian Tax Foundation, has enumerated a number of other arguments against conditional grants: no objective criteria of "national interest" can be discovered, the provinces are in practice just as competent to determine their spending priorities as the federal government, the effort to impose conditions and standards is usually futile, provinces that have already established a program qualifying for grants are given an unfair advantage over other provinces, poorer provinces must reduce their spending in other fields of activity so as to match the federal grants, provincial programs will gradually tend to become more uniform even without federal pressure, and "national standards" of public-sector activity can more effectively be achieved by unconditional equalization.

Supporters of conditional grants argue that some degree of uniformity in provincial government programs and activities is desirable on grounds both of equity and convenience, and that under a rigid constitution it can only in practice be achieved through conditional grants. The first argument, like its opposing counterpart argument about the impropriety of intruding on provincial priorities, must have, *a priori,* a moral justification if it has any at all. The argument about constitutional rigidity must be qualified seriously, for in practice rigidities in the sense of obstacles to federal action seem to be much more political and economic than legal. Whatever their source, conditional grants are not necessarily immune to them, as events from the time of Maurice Duplessis to the present have suggested.

A more sophisticated argument used in favour of conditional grants is based on the economic concept of spillovers or externalities.[5] Certain things that provincial governments do, or fail to do, have consequences outside the territorial boundaries of the province. For example, if Ontario fails to build and maintain an adequate highway across its northern hinterland, communication between Quebec and Manitoba may suffer. The scarcity of votes in northern Ontario and the southern orientation of the provincial government provide little incentive for action, while the adversely affected residents of Quebec and Manitoba have no way of influencing the provincial government at all. Thus it may be appropriate for the federal government, over which Quebec and Manitoba residents do have some influence, to use financial incentives in an effort to do so. This example of course is not hypothetical; it was precisely the justification for one of the most important and successful of shared-cost programs, the Trans-Canada Highway. The fact that the largest and wealthiest province was not crossed by a paved road until well into the second half of the twentieth century, and then only as a result of a federal initiative, provides grounds for great scepticism as to the widely reputed virtues of untrammelled provincial autonomy.

A somewhat more complex example of the external impact of provincial policy is provided by the field of education. The incentive for provincial governments to spend in this area may be reduced by the mobility of the population, to the extent that over-all spending on education in Canada will be prevented from reaching an optimum level. A province with a net outflow of population, such as New Brunswick, may be reluctant to invest in the education of residents who are likely to move elsewhere as soon as they join the labour force. On the other hand, a province with a net inflow of population, such as Alberta, may consider that it will attract so many educated people from elsewhere that it need not worry about educating its own residents.

This state of affairs would seem to provide a justification for federal action to ensure that spending on education is maintained at a high enough level to meet national needs. In fact the federal governments of both the United States and Australia have become increasingly involved in all levels of education for this very reason, mainly by means of conditional grants and, in Australia, by assuming total responsibility for financial support of the universities. In Canada, unfortunately, Quebec nationalism has succeeded in virtually preventing any federal activity in the educational field. Even Pierre Elliott Trudeau expressed vigorous opposition when the federal government offered grants to universities in the 1950s, and the practice was eventually abandoned in favour of channelling the funds through provincial governments as a virtually unconditional abatement.[6] The federal role in elementary and secondary education is confined to a partial involvement in the education of native peoples, immigrants, linguistic minorities, and the dependents of military personnel stationed in Europe.

This example suggests the validity of the point made earlier, that even conditional grants are not an infallible cure for the "rigidities" of federalism. Yet the economists, with their externalities and spillovers, do provide not only a valid argument in favour of conditional grants, but also some clues to explain why conditional grants and shared-cost programs have been developed so extensively, particularly in the three federations that have the most geographically mobile populations.

THE ORIGINS OF CONDITIONAL GRANTS

Conditional grants are basically a device to stimulate public expenditure that would not otherwise take place. It is thus no accident that they have become unpopular in recent years at a time of well-orchestrated hostility to public expenditure and "big government". It is also no accident that the political party most critical of public expenditure, the Progressive Conservative party, is one whose five incumbent provincial premiers in 1977 collectively demanded a constitutional restriction on the spending power of Parliament, by which is meant its power to make conditional grants. This is so despite the fact that a

government of the same party, when it was uncharacteristically led by the Prairie populist John Diefenbaker,
contributed significantly to the proliferation of conditional
grants and shared-cost programs.

An analysis along these lines, however, is misleading unless
it takes into account the direction, as well as the volume, of
public expenditure. Both the history of Canadian conditional
grants and contemporary controversies over them must be
seen in the context of the tendency of governments, especially
provincial ones, to prefer some kinds of expenditure over
others. As discussed in an earlier chapter, Canadian governments have traditionally preferred the types of expenditure
that contribute directly to capital accumulation, a tendency
first noticed by Lord Durham when he visited the country in
1839. Although Confederation ostensibly conferred most of
the responsibility for stimulating capital accumulation on the
federal level of government, the provincial governments, as we
have seen, quickly found ways to become involved and,
predictably, found such activities far more congenial than the
social and "cultural" matters which had been entrusted to
them by the BNA Act.

There were and are strong reasons for emphasizing expenditures on accumulation over other types of expenditure. Such
an emphasis accorded with traditional British North American
expectations and assumptions that long pre-dated Confederation. Accumulation expenditures directly benefited the influential classes in the provinces — businessmen and in some
cases farmers — persuading them that they received good
value in return for their taxes and thus increasing the
legitimacy and authority of the provincial level of government.
Another advantage, directly relevant to the present discussion,
was that the benefits of accumulation expenditures (public
works, resource development, subsidies to business, and so
forth) largely remained within the province; in other words,
there were few spillovers.

On the other hand, the provinces showed little disposition to
spend heavily on legitimization, by which is meant such areas
as health, welfare, social insurance, pensions, protection of the
environment, or support of the arts, letters, and the sciences.
These activities did not directly and in the short run benefit

the dominant classes; taxes levied to support them would be viewed as a burden disproportionate to the benefits received. Those residents of the province who would benefit directly were politically weak and poorly organized, usually without even a political party that reliably represented their interests. Ideology and tradition provided no impetus towards such expenditure. In addition, the mobility of the population ensured that the direct benefits of expenditure on legitimization might be largely reaped outside the province. The result of all these factors was a tendency of provincial governments to neglect their responsibilities for social policy even after twentieth-century urbanization and industrialization began to produce a pressing need for greater social expenditure. Faced with a choice between a dam and hospital, between a railway and a university, between industrial subsidies and pensions, provincial governments chose the first alternative. By the 1920s it was painfully evident that Canada lagged far behind the United Kingdom, Australia, New Zealand, and other advanced countries in developing what would later be known as the welfare state.

Conditional grants were developed in Canada primarily as a means of overcoming this situation, by stimulating the provinces to spend more on legitimization than they would otherwise have been inclined to do. It is true that some of the earliest grant-aided programs were related to agriculture; the use of the conditional-grant mechanism in this field was presumably suggested by the fact that agriculture is a shared jurisdiction under Section 95 of the BNA Act. It is also true that a number of provincial projects and works related to economic development have been partly financed by federal grants, especially under the Diefenbaker and Trudeau governments. Significantly, this latter type of "conditional" grant appears totally immune to the criticisms which provincial governments direct against conditional grants in general, and it should probably be regarded as the modern equivalent of the politically inspired ad-hoc subsidies or "better terms" described in the early part of the preceding chapter. The Trans-Canada Highway was another major exception to the general rule that conditional grants are related to legitimization rather than accumulation, but the specific motivation for it has already been described. In only a very few special cases, of which this was one, do provincial governments need any federal encouragement to spend money on economic development.

Generally speaking, however, conditional grants have been mainly devoted to legitimization, precisely because the provinces cannot be relied upon to spend enough on this field of policy without substantial incentives, and in some cases actual coercion. The history of grant-aided programs in Canada shows this clearly, as does the functional distribution of conditional grant funds at any given time. In 1969–70, a time at which the present structure of ongoing grant-aided programs was virtually complete, and before the Trudeau government had begun its efforts to escape from responsibility for the programs, health and welfare accounted for about 88 per cent of the funds disbursed in conditional grants to the provinces.[7] This fact also, of course, explains the close connection between hostility to conditional grants and the familiar North American rhetoric about the evils of government spending. When businessmen and right-wing politicians complain about government spending they are really, of course, referring to spending on health and welfare. Spending on transportation, resource development, industrial subsidies, and so forth is never singled out for criticism, and the same persons who complain most loudly about "spending" in general frequently advocate more spending, rather than less, on the military forces, the police, and penitentiaries. Expressing opposition to spending in general, rather than admitting frankly what kind of spending is resented, is a deliberate strategy of mystification to attract the support of the very people who would suffer most from the demolition of the welfare state.

This interpretation of the impact of conditional grants does not explain why the federal government would be more likely to take an interest in legitimization than the provincial governments. Actually the similarity between the two levels in this regard has been more apparent than the contrast; federal governments, like provincial governments, have traditionally given more emphasis to economic than to social policy, and still do, as will be apparent even from a cursory reading of *Hansard*. None the less there are reasons why the motivation to spend on legitimization, weak as it is, is slightly stronger at the federal level. Usually the federal government has had more funds at its disposal than the provincial governments, and its control over the currency means that it can spend more than it receives in taxes and other revenue without having to worry about the state of the bond market. Thus it can afford to devote some attention even to secondary priorities like health and welfare. The federal government also has less need to worry about spillovers, because the persons who benefit directly from spending on health and welfare are not likely to leave the country permanently, however likely they may be to move from one province to another. Although Canada does compete against foreign countries, particularly the United States, for capital investment, the international competition is less intense than the interprovincial one, so there is less need to spend every available dollar of public funds on activities that contribute directly to capital accumulation.

It would be wrong, however, to overestimate the federal enthusiasm for spending on legitimization. Major health and welfare programs have usually been conceded grudgingly, often at times when "minor" parties of social reform enjoyed unusual influence in Parliament or unusual support among the electorate. Moreover, the very fact that such programs are so often financed by conditional grants to the provinces, rather than being fully supported by federal revenues, suggests a certain lack of enthusiasm for them. By accepting only partial financial responsibility and leaving the provinces to assume the rest, the federal government purchases the political benefits (or avoids the political cost) of inaction, at minimum expense to its treasury. If some provincial governments refuse to accept the conditional grants, a risk that is always present, it will simply be too bad for the potential beneficiaries of the program. They can always be encouraged to blame the provincial level of government for their troubles.

These generalizations can be illustrated by reference to the first major shared-cost program (there had been minor ones as far back as 1912), which was the Old Age Pensions Act of 1927. Contrary to a persistent myth, there was no legal reason why the federal government could not have assumed full responsibility for this program from the outset, as it was urged to do at the time by J. S. Woodsworth and his colleagues. Even Viscount Haldane could not possibly have invented a constitutional obstacle to the granting of pensions directly by the federal government. No provincial government would have objected either — apart, that is, from Quebec, which adhered to the ideological principle that the family rather than the state was responsible for supporting elderly persons. Since Quebec considered the financing of pensions by conditional grants to be just as objectionable as a strictly federal program, if not more so, provincial sentiments were certainly not the reason why a shared-cost program rather than an exclusively federal one was adopted. In fact the governments of British Columbia, Alberta, and Saskatchewan all urged the federal government to proceed with an exclusively federal program.[8]

The argument that a conditional grant had to be used because pensions fell under "provincial jurisdiction", a belief now deeply embedded in Canadian mythology, was a justification invented after the event. The original text of the BNA Act contained no reference to pensions. For that matter, the supposed constitutional obstacle did not prevent Mackenzie King, who was Prime Minister in 1927, from adopting a federal program of family allowances several years later, when the surging popularity of the CCF made it politically too hazardous to waste time waiting for the agreement of the provinces. The real reason why an exclusively federal pension plan was not adopted in 1927 is suggested by the response of the Deputy Minister of Justice in 1925 to a parliamentary committee's request for a statement of the constitutional position. While stating that "the subject matter of pensions has been entrusted to the provincial legislatures", he continued, more significantly, as follows:

I do not mean to suggest that Parliament has not the power to legislate upon the subject so as to assist the provinces or to establish an independent voluntary scheme, provided that in either case the legislation does not trench upon the subject of property and civil rights in the provinces, as for example by obligating any person or province to contribute to the scheme. The enactment of such legislation would, however, involve the assumption by the Dominion of obligations involving heavy expenditures with regard to a matter which does not fall specifically within the Dominion field of legislation.[9]

"Heavy expenditures" were the last thing Mackenzie King wanted, so the persistent pressure from Woodsworth and other progressive members of Parliament were met with the half-measure of a shared-cost program dependent on provincial consent for its implementation. The western provinces and Ontario were fairly prompt in joining the program, but the provinces east of Ottawa, where the need for pensions was presumably even greater, were not. Nova Scotia and Prince Edward Island waited until 1933, New Brunswick until 1935, and Quebec until 1936, almost a decade after Parliament had adopted the legislation.

The Depression painfully underlined the inadequacies of the Canadian welfare state but did not produce a major expansion of shared-cost programs or other innovations in social policy. The so-called "Bennett New Deal", which was invalidated by the Judicial Committee of the Privy Council in a series of reference cases after Mackenzie King returned to office, did not rely on the cost-sharing mechanism. Presumably, the rapidly approaching end of Parliament's term made it politically essential for Bennett to act quickly and unilaterally, rather than waiting for provincial collaboration, particularly since all of the provincial governments except New Brunswick and Prince Edward Island were politically hostile by the beginning of 1935. Both the Bennett and King governments assisted the provinces in carrying the burden of emergency relief expenses, but the only major ongoing shared-cost program established in the 1930s was allowances for the blind, which began in 1937. Although even the United States finally embraced the welfare state with Roosevelt's Social Security legislation, Canada lagged far behind.

The Rowell–Sirois Commission was naturally aware of the problem, but it disapproved of conditional grants for reasons already discussed. The argument of J. A. Corry's monograph, *Difficulties of Divided Jurisdiction,* was reflected in the conclusions of the commission's report, which recommended a transfer of both legislative and taxing powers from the provincial to the federal level of government, federal assumption of provincial debts, and unconditional subsidies to the poorer provinces. These recommendations were ignored, however, and the years that followed the Second World War saw a massive proliferation of conditional grants and shared-cost programs. Predictably, they were heavily concentrated in the fields of health and welfare. In most other areas the provinces needed no urging to expand the scope of their activities.

The first major step, in 1948, was a National Health Program consisting of nine separate conditional grants: health survey, hospital construction, professional training, crippled children, mental health, tuberculosis control, health research, cancer control, and general public health. This was followed by a major revision of pension legislation in 1951, including a probably superfluous constitutional amendment which stated pensions to be a concurrent field of jurisdiction with provincial paramountcy. In place of the means-tested, shared-cost pensions of the 1927 legislation there were now two separate programs known respectively as Old Age Security and Old Age Assistance. The former established universal pensions for persons over seventy, exclusively financed by the federal government. The latter provided additional support for persons over sixty-five who were in need, and was administered by the province with the aid of conditional grants.

In 1954 a new shared-cost program provided allowances for the disabled, similar to the allowances for the blind that had commenced in 1937. In the following year another shared-cost program provided unemployment assistance to those who were not eligible for benefits under the contributory scheme of unemployment insurance. This institutionalized the recognition of the fact, which had become obvious two decades earlier, that responsibility for "relief" could no longer safely be left to the provinces and muncipalities. In 1966, following three years of federal-provincial negotiation, all three of these welfare programs, as well as Old Age Assistance, were combined into a new shared-cost program known as the Canada Assistance Plan (CAP). The CAP also included provision for federal cost-sharing of child welfare, mothers' allowances, medical expenses of welfare recipients, rehabilitation and preventive welfare services, and certain special programs for native peoples. These increased federal responsibilities were largely undertaken in response to the demands of Ontario and British Columbia, which at that time were the only provinces with a sizeable net inflow of population. Both had complained loudly and persistently about the burden of welfare costs, despite their prosperity and rapid rates of economic growth.[10]

In the meantime, health had eclipsed welfare as the major area of expenditure on conditional grants. The Liberal party had proclaimed a vague commitment to the principle of health insurance as early as 1919, which was not a particularly startling move inasmuch as a Liberal government in the United Kingdom had actually implemented a form of health insurance several years earlier. The subject was raised again as part of the "Green Book" of federal proposals to the provinces in 1945. Legislation to provide for cost-sharing of hospital insurance was finally adopted in the last months of the long post-war Liberal regime, although it did not come into effect until after John Diefenbaker had formed his first government. Saskatchewan under the CCF had established its own plan long before the federal grants became available, and the remaining provinces joined promptly — with the exception of Quebec, which waited until the end of 1960 and, as will be seen, chose to "opt out" at the first opportunity.

Hospital insurance was soon followed by medical insurance. Prime Minister Diefenbaker's appointment of the Royal Commission on Health Services, headed by Justice Emmett Hall (the Hall Commission) was interpreted by some observers as a delaying tactic. If so it was not a particularly successful one, for the commission recommended, in 1964, a shared-cost program of medical insurance even more comprehensive than the one that had recently been adopted in Saskatchewan at the cost of a doctors' strike that helped to overturn the long-established CCF government. The following year Prime Minister Pearson placed "health services" near the top of the agenda at the federal-provincial conference of first ministers and offered in his opening statement "to co-operate with the provinces in making medicare financially possible for all Canadians". Somewhat confusingly, he assured his audience that he was "not proposing a new shared-cost program", given the fact that the mechanics of such programs were currently under review by the Tax Structure Committee.[11] His proposal did differ from existing shared-cost programs in the extreme flexibility and permissiveness of the terms and conditions on which federal aid would be offered. There were only four requirements for a plan to be eligible, and two of these were subsequently watered down or eliminated. No federal auditing or supervision of provincial plans would be required or expected.

Although the premiers were not enthusiastic in their response to this proposal, it was embodied in legislation in 1966 and adopted by Parliament with only the western remnants of Social Credit dissenting. However, its proclamation was delayed by the right wing of the Liberal party, including Minister of Finance Mitchell Sharp, who argued that it would contribute to inflation. It did not actually come into effect until July 1, 1968, by which time Pierre Elliott Trudeau was Prime Minister. Only Saskatchewan and British Columbia were immediately eligible for grants. Ontario, which had opposed the whole idea, soon produced a plan which violated at least one of Pearson's four conditions, since it was initially administered on the government's behalf by private insurance companies, but which was none the less declared eligible. The remaining provinces had all launched their plans by the beginning of 1971, so that "medicare" became the second-largest shared-cost program, hospital insurance being the first.

It seemed likely, however, that medicare would be the last major shared-cost program to be established, for reasons that must now be discussed.

THE DECLINE OF CONDITIONAL GRANTS

During the two decades that followed the end of the Second World War, a period characterized by the rapid proliferation of conditional grants and shared-cost programs, the provincial governments presented little opposition to the trend. It appears that a rapid increase in spending on health and welfare was considered acceptable and inevitable so that in the circumstances the federal government's willingness to bear a large share of the expense was welcomed. The very expansion of grant-aided health and welfare programs produced a large number of provincial officials who benefited directly from the federal largesse and who had a vested interest in maintaining and expanding it.

The exception to this general rule was the province of Quebec, where the Liberal government of L. A. Taschereau, as noted above, had delayed for almost a decade the provision of shared-cost pensions to the province's residents. A similar policy was pursued in the post-war years by the Union Nationale government of Maurice Duplessis, whose political and social philosophy was basically similar to that of Taschereau. Provincial expenditures were relatively low and heavily oriented towards activities that directly assisted the accumulation of capital, a major reason for the cordial relations that Duplessis enjoyed with both Canadian and American corporations. The legitimization function of the provincial state remained unusually underdeveloped, even by Canadian standards. Admittedly, however, there was a partial justification for this in the fact that many of the responsibilities of providing for education, health, and welfare were assumed by the Roman Catholic Church, whose multitudes of largely unpaid personnel could perform the task of legitimization cheaply and fairly effectively.

Conditional grants were thus deeply resented, because they would tend to distract attention from the goal of economic development, undermine the traditional division of labour between church and state, and introduce the alien doctrine that the public authorities were directly responsible for social welfare. Moreover, they would tend, as in the other provinces, to create a group of officials with a vested interest in federal-provincial collaboration. Despite these reservations, most of the federal grants were reluctantly accepted by the Duplessis government, although two of the largest ones — those pertaining to hospital insurance and to the Trans-Canada Highway — were not. The Quebec universities, both anglophone and francophone, were also forbidden to accept federal subsidies.

To justify this policy, an ideological view of federalism was invented and expounded at great length in the report (1956) of the Tremblay Commission. This asserted that the entire field of legitimization fell exclusively under provincial jurisdiction, and that this was appropriate because the provinces were distinct societies with their own "cultures" and values. Each provincial government must therefore be given complete freedom to perform the function of legitimization in its own way, or not to perform it at all. Moreover, it was asserted that the federal Parliament had no right to spend in areas outside of its legislative jurisdiction, which was defined as narrowly as possible. If in fact it had the funds with which to do so, this was treated as proof that it was taxing too heavily and should withdraw from direct taxation in favour of the provinces.

The Liberal government headed by Jean Lesage, who took office in June 1960, deviated only partially from this philosophy. At his first federal-provincial conference the following month Lesage described shared-cost programs as undesirable, although he failed to present any convincing justification for such a view. He proposed that the federal government should withdraw completely from the funding of existing programs and should compensate the provinces for the additional expenditures they would have to assume by giving them tax abatements and unconditional subsidies. Meanwhile, he announced, Quebec would participate in the programs to which Duplessis had refused assent, such as hospital insurance and the Trans-Canada Highway. It would be unjust to do otherwise since Quebec residents were already "participating" through the payment of federal taxes which supported these programs in the other provinces.[12]

Despite Lesage's assertion that his decision to participate was only a temporary expedient, the Diefenbaker government did not respond to his suggestion that the federal government should replace the conditional grants already in force with abatements and unconditional subsidies. In 1964, however, the Pearson government introduced legislation that would allow any province, within a stated time, to "opt out" of a number of shared-cost programs, including hospital insurance, vocational training, old age assistance, allowances for the blind and the disabled, unemployment assistance, health grants, and several minor agricultural and resource programs. If a province opted out of any program the federal government would terminate the relevant conditional grant to that province, but would pay compensation in the form of a tax abatement (for the larger programs) or a cash payment (for the smaller). The abatements would be "equalized" to the level of the average *per-capita* yield in the two richest provinces. When the legislation came into effect in 1965 Quebec opted out of all the major programs, receiving 20 equalized percentage points of the personal income tax, and out of some of the minor ones as well, for which cash compensation was offered. No other province expressed any interest.

Even before this Quebec had benefited from a special deal with respect to two new programs, youth allowances and student loans, both of which represented the fulfilment of campaign promises made by the federal Liberals in 1963. Neither was a shared-cost program, but Quebec already had comparable programs of its own and Lesage argued that it should therefore receive fiscal compensation. The Pearson government agreed to this demand in both cases.

In 1966 the provincial governments were offered a second chance to opt out of hospital insurance and certain health grants, as well as the Canada Assistance Plan which had just replaced several of the welfare programs from which Quebec had opted out earlier. Once again the other nine provinces expressed no interest.

The introduction of medicare, however, brought about a drastic change in provincial attitudes towards shared-cost programs. Only British Columbia and Saskatchewan were pleased by Pearson's announcement of the proposal in 1965, and the distress of the other eight provincial governments was increased by the federal government's uncharacteristically firm position on tax-sharing in the fiscal negotiations a year later. Minister of Finance Mitchell Sharp, the architect of the new position on tax-sharing, was himself not noted as an enthusiast for medicare; whether by accident or design his rigidity served to enlist the provinces as allies in his efforts to delay the implementation of the program. Faced with the prospect of at least a temporary halt to the escalation of federal tax abatements, provincial governments decided that the rate of growth of public expenditure on health and welfare must be reduced. Medicare, a new and major program of unpredictable expense, was certain to make this impossible. Ontario and

Manitoba argued that the objectives of the Hall Commission could be achieved by providing public health insurance only for those unable to afford private insurance, but the federal government insisted that only plans which were universal, or nearly so, could qualify for federal assistance. Most of the provinces established medicare very reluctantly, and only after the Trudeau government had practically forced them to do so by imposing a special medicare tax, known as the Social Development Tax, on their residents. The Ontario government in particular was bitterly resentful, as suggested by Premier Robarts' celebrated outburst at the televised constitutional confernce in 1969, when he called medicare a "Machiavellian fraud".[13]

Resentment against medicare, and against what was viewed by the provinces as federal determination to coerce them into excessive spending on social policy, was soon transformed into a generalized hostility towards conditional grants, a position that had hitherto had little support outside of Quebec. Ontario's Ministry of Treasury, Economics, and Intergovernmental Affairs (TEIGA) took the lead in expressing such sentiments, producing in 1972 a lengthy staff paper which listed and described the shared-cost programs in which the province participated as well as their alleged disadvantages.[14] Over and above the usual rhetoric about provincial autonomy, the gist of the argument was that shared-cost programs lessened the ability of TEIGA to control the total volume of provincial expenditure, and, incidentally, to assert its authority over the program departments such as Health, Education, or Community and Social Services. Clearly there was some concern on the part of TEIGA at the tendency of conditional grants to increase the autonomy and expand the importance of the program departments, especially those concerned with social policy. On the other hand, J. A. Corry had argued long before that this tendency could never go so far in Canada as in the United States because of the hierarchical and centralizing nature of parliamentary cabinet government.[15] The growing power of TEIGA and of co-ordinating agencies in other provinces, although it had other causes, seemed to lend substance to this view.

At the same time as the provincial governments were

developing a generalized opposition to conditional grants, the federal government was also losing much of its enthusiasm for them. At the federal level, as at the provincial, the new perspective was largely motivated by the view that public expenditure on health, education, and welfare was growing too rapidly, and that public policy should be re-oriented towards a greater emphasis on the more traditional and congenial role of promoting the accumulation of capital. This theme was expressed in the Liberal election campaign of 1968, which proved highly successful, especially in high-income urban and suburban areas and in the three "rich" provinces, where Liberal members elected increased by almost half. It was given added emphasis by the evidence of an inflationary trend, which led to the formation of a Prices and Incomes Commission in 1969. The government could not escape from its commitment to medicare, but its subsequent promise of "no more medicares" was as much an expression of its own sentiments as a concession to the provinces.

So strong had this view become that the federal government was now prepared to propose a constitutional restriction on its own power to make conditional grants. This it did in a working paper entitled *Federal-Provincial Grants and the Spending Power of Parliament,* which was submitted to the Constitutional Conference in June 1969. The main recommendation of the paper read as follows:

> The power of Parliament to make general conditional grants in respect of federal-provincial programmes which are acknowledged to be within exclusive provincial jurisdiction should be based upon two requirements: first, a broad national consensus in favour of any proposed programme should be demonstrated to exist before Parliament exercises its power; and secondly the decision of a provincial legislature to exercise its constitutional right not to partici-pate in any programme, even given a national consensus, should not result in a fiscal penalty being imposed upon the people of the province.[16]

This proposal must be interpreted in the light of two facts. In the first place, a subsequent working paper declared that health insurance and social services (although not family allowances or pensions) were, and should remain, under exclusive provincial jurisdiction.[17] In the second place, the "broad national consensus" as defined had nothing to do with the ordinary meaning of the term, but was a euphemism for a requirement that any proposed program must be supported by the governments of both Quebec and Ontario, and by at least four of the other provincial governments as well, including a minimum of two western provinces and two Atlantic provinces, not counting Prince Edward Island.

As the new decade began, the federal government commenced its efforts to escape from financial responsibility for hospital and medical insurance, to say nothing of post-secondary education. An ostensible reason for this move was to place Quebec on the same footing as the other provinces; the fact that only Quebec had opted out of hospital insurance seemed dangerously close to the heresy of "special status", but if the federal government itself opted out the other provinces would be placed in the same position. A more important reason was to reduce the drain of health, education, and welfare expenses — all of which seemed to be increasing faster than tax revenues — on the federal treasury. In addition, if the provinces were forced to bear the full financial responsibility they would have a greater incentive to economize and reduce the over-all rate of growth of expenditure on legitimization.

The first target of the federal effort to reduce the growth of expenditure was post-secondary education. In 1966 the federal government, while terminating any direct relationship with the universities, had agreed to pay the provinces an annual subsidy equivalent to half of university operating costs, presumably to be used for that purpose. Less than five years later Ottawa informed the provincial governments that these subsidies would be allowed to increase by no more than 15 per cent each year, regardless of the actual operating costs of the universities.

At the same time the federal government unveiled a new proposal for the financing of health insurance. Instead of being related to the actual costs of the programs, federal contributions would be allowed to increase no faster than the *per-capita* GNP. To sweeten the pill, an additional sum of $640 million over five years would be made available for the improvement of health services. Since the costs of health insurance were more difficult for the provinces to control than the costs of the universities, this suggestion met with firm and unanimous opposition. The provinces differed, however, as to what alternative should be proposed. Quebec and Ontario, with some support from Alberta and British Columbia, suggested that federal contributions to health insurance should be replaced by an abatement of the personal income tax. The smaller provinces, on the other hand, preferred the status quo. No agreement was reached, although the federal government indicated that it would be willing to consider the alternative of an abatement, provided that it retained enough control over the income tax to pursue Keynesian policies.

As a federal election year, 1972 saw virtually no progress in federal-provincial negotiation. In the following year the federal government produced a new set of proposals. Federal contributions to post-secondary education would be through a *per-capita* grant based on the population of each province in the eighteen to twenty-four age group, increasing by 7 per cent each year, a proposal apparently based on the curious assumption that all students attended a university in their own province. Federal grants for health insurance would be replaced by an income-tax abatement of 6 equalized percentage points, removal of the federal excise taxes on liquor and tobacco so that the provinces could occupy this field, and a cash adjustment grant. This proposal proved no more acceptable than its predecessor, and the same division of opinion among the provinces as had existed earlier reappeared. Ontario and Quebec both demanded huge abatements, while most of the smaller provinces indicated a preference for the existing system. No province was interested in the liquor and tobacco taxes. The hostility of the federal NDP, on whose support the minority government depended, made it unwise for the federal government to insist on implementing its own proposal.

In 1974, however, the Liberals regained their majority in the House of Commons. In the budget speech of 1975 Minister of Finance John Turner announced the government's intention to terminate the cost-sharing agreement for hospital insurance in five years, the minimum period of notice required by the legislation. He also announced that a ceiling would be placed on the *per-capita* rate of growth of federal contributions to medicare, regardless of its actual costs. The maximum increase allowed would be 13 per cent in the first year, 10.5 per cent in the second, and 8.5 per cent in subsequent years. Legislation to provide for this was given first reading almost immediately. Ontario offered to take full responsibility for both kinds of health insurance in return for 17 percentage points of the personal income tax, a reasonable offer considering that Quebec had received 14 points when it opted out of hospital insurance only, but the offer was rejected.

In the spring of 1976, with the expiry of the current fiscal arrangements only a year away, negotiations resumed under a new Minister of Finance, Donald Macdonald. Parliament meanwhile proceeded to adopt the legislation limiting federal contributions to medicare. The polarization between the four largest provinces and the six smaller ones was initially more complete than in any previous round of negotiations, with the former group demanding generous abatements and complete provincial control over health insurance while the latter group continued to prefer a cost-sharing arrangement. By the end of the year, however, all ten provincial governments had managed to agree on a proposal that combined income-tax and corporations-tax abatements, both equalized, and cash grants related to gross national expenditure. This was probably the first time the federal government had faced a provincial common front on a fiscal issue. The result was an agreement at the very end of the year that was basically similar, although not entirely identical, to what the provincial governments had proposed.[18]

The federal retreat from responsibility for social policy was pursued in other ways as well during the 1970s. In 1973, after years of agitation from the government of Quebec, the federal government agreed to channel family-allowance payments through the provinces, permitting Quebec to redistribute payments in an effort to encourage large families (so far without success), and permitting Alberta to implement a singularly bizarre and regressive scheme by which payments escalate as the children grow older. Federal plans to supplement the incomes of "the working poor" were abandoned in 1976, partly because of determined resistance by the government of Ontario. A number of existing federal programs devoted to legitimization were cut back or terminated as part of the anti-inflation program in the autumn of 1975. Finally, Ottawa and the more influential provinces agreed in 1978, despite protests from Saskatchewan, to replace the Canada Assistance Plan with a single general-purpose block grant for the sake of greater "flexibility", an idea borrowed from Richard Nixon's administration in the United States. This was ardently desired by the Progressive Conservative provincial governments; few doubted that its real purpose was to reduce over-all expenditure on welfare.[19]

It seems likely, therefore, that Canada is returning to the pre-war situation in which each level of government seeks to attribute the responsibility for social policy to the other level, while concentrating its own efforts on activities that contribute directly to the accumulation of capital. The result, as in the past, is likely to be an inadequate level of expenditure on legitimization. The federal government in particular seems consciously to have pursued under Mr. Trudeau's direction a strategy of shifting emphasis from social to economic policy so as to win the support of business interests away from the provinces, and thus reverse the centrifugal tendencies that were so evident in the 1960s. As should be apparent from Chapter 4, there are many obstacles to the success of this strategy, but it may bear some fruit if the central-Canadian corporate elite become sufficiently worried about Quebec separatism, Alberta resource diplomacy, and an increasingly organized and militant working class.

NOTES

1. J. A. Corry, *Difficulties of Divided Jurisdiction* (Ottawa: King's Printer, 1939), pp. 28–36.
2. Donald V. Smiley, *Constitutional Adaptation and Canadian Federalism since 1945* (Ottawa: Queen's Printer, 1970), pp. 66–67.
3. Attorney General for Canada *v.* Attorney General for Ontario and Others (1937) AC 355. This reference dealt with the Employment and Social Insurance Act.
4. Corry, *Difficulties of Divided Jurisdiction,* and Donald V. Smiley, *Conditional Grants and Canadian Federalism* (Toronto: Canadian Tax Foundation, 1963).

5. A good example of the argument is George E. Carter, *Canadian Conditional Grants Since World War II* (Toronto: Canadian Tax Foundation, 1971), especially pp. 5-20.

6. See Trudeau's essay, "Federal Grants to Universities", first published in 1957 and reprinted in his *Federalism and the French Canadians* (Toronto: Macmillan, 1968).

7. See the table in Carter, *Canadian Conditional Grants Since World War II*, pp. 114-16.

8. Kenneth Bryden, *Old Age Pensions and Policy-Making in Canada* (Montreal: McGill-Queen's University Press, 1974), pp. 61-101 has a good account of the 1927 legislation.

9. Quoted in Ibid., p. 68.

10. Rand Dyck, "The Canada Assistance Plan: The Ultimate in Co-operative Federalism", *Canadian Public Administration,* XIX (1976):587-602.

11. *Federal-Provincial Conference, Ottawa, July 19-25, 1965* (Ottawa: Queen's Printer, 1968), pp. 15-16.

12. *Dominion-Provincial Conference 1960* (Ottawa: Queen's Printer, 1960), pp. 31-32.

13. *Constitutional Conference, Proceedings, Second Meeting* (Ottawa: Queen's Printer, 1969), p. 161.

14. *Federal-Provincial Shared-Cost Programmes in Ontario* (Toronto: Ministry of Treasury, Economics, and Intergovernmental Affairs, 1972).

15. J. A. Corry, "Constitutional Trends and Federalism", in A. R. M. Lower and F. R. Scott, *Evolving Canadian Federalism* (Durham, N.C.: Duke University Press, 1958).

16. Pierre Elliott Trudeau, *Federal-Provincial Grants and the Spending Power of Parliament* (Ottawa: Queen's Printer, 1969), p. 36.

17. Pierre Elliott Trudeau, *Income Security and Social Services* (Ottawa: Queen's Printer, 1969), pp. 102, 104, 106.

18. For a detailed analysis of the new arrangements, see George E. Carter, "Financing Health and Post-Secondary Education: A New and Complex Fiscal Arrangement", *Canadian Tax Journal,* XXV (1977):534-550.

19. See Leonard Shifrin, "Horse sense loses out to politics of federalism", in *The Citizen* (Ottawa), March 20, 1978.

8 Intergovernmental Conflict and Its Resolution

Conflict between federal and provincial governments has been an enduring feature of Canadian political life for more than a century. Indeed it has been so ubiquitous that it tends to be taken for granted or treated as almost synonymous with federalism, rather than as a distinct phenomenon to be analysed in its own right. Consequently there have been no systematic studies of federal-provincial conflict and not much attention has been paid by students of the political system to the mechanisms by which federal-provincial conflicts are managed and resolved.

Some degree of conflict between the two levels of government is probably best viewed as an endemic and almost universal condition, but its incidence has none the less been unevenly distributed, both in space and in time. Certain episodes and sources of controversy stand out conspicuously in the history of federal-provincial relations, from Macdonald's conflicts with Mowat over navigable rivers and provincial boundaries to the recent struggles over energy prices, resource taxes, and cable television. Certain periods in Canadian history appear to have been relatively lacking in federal-provincial controversy, while in other periods, such as the 1960s and the 1970s, it seems to have been unusually intense. Certain provinces, like Ontario and British Columbia in the past, or Quebec and Alberta more recently, have seemed particularly prone to become involved in conflict with the federal authorities over a variety of issues, while others have appeared more docile and passive in their disposition.

If the study of federal-provincial conflict had been pursued as extensively and as systematically as the subject of international conflict, there would doubtless be as many competing and conflicting explanations for the phenomenon as the students of international relations have devised to explain the causes of war. In both cases it seems likely that no single explanation will suffice, and in other ways, too, it would not be unduly fanciful to draw a parallel between them. Provincial policies towards the federal government, like the foreign policies of sovereign states, seem to have elements of continuity that survive regardless of parties, issues, and personalities. One historian has referred to "the Mowat heritage in federal-provincial relations" as characteristic of Ontario's behaviour ever since.[1] Alberta appears as truculent under Peter Lougheed as it was under William Aberhart. Manitoba was as cautious and conciliatory under Ed Schreyer as it was under John Bracken. The government of René Lévesque was surely recognizing a real affinity, which its anglophone sympathizers appear to ignore, when it erected a statue of Maurice Duplessis in a place of honour near the "National" Assembly.

Conflict with Ottawa seems also to affect the provinces in the same ways that war and cold war affect the development of sovereign states. Local chauvinism and hostility towards the external foe are stimulated by enhancing the ceremonial and symbolic aspects of political life. Administrative resources are expanded and strengthened, the power of the legislature to control the executive is curtailed, and the state intervenes more directly in economic life to shape it for its own purposes. Powerful, combative, and effective leaders emerge and become symbols of the province's determination to defend its interests. Just as war and external danger produced a Lloyd George, a Churchill, a Stalin, or a de Gaulle, so federal-provincial conflict seems to produce a Mowat or a Mercier, a Duplessis or a Drew, a Lesage or a Lougheed.

None of this is intended to suggest that federal-provincial conflict is artificial or contrived, although there have undoubtedly been cases where a display of truculence towards the federal authorities was used to win elections or to distract attention from internal cleavages. In general, however, federal-provincial conflict is not deliberate or contrived but arises from more fundamental causes. It is necessary to write "causes" in the plural, because no single explanation will cover every case.

Some federal-provincial conflicts have been expressions of class conflict, in cases where the influence of different classes predominated at different levels of government. Ontario in its very early years as a province, the Prairie provinces for much longer, and Saskatchewan perhaps even today, represented the interests of farmers in opposition to the financial and other capitalists that influenced the federal government in Ottawa. Their struggles with Ottawa were mainly over the traditional sources of agrarian discontent: tariffs, transportation, agricultural marketing, mortgages, and credit, supplemented by controversies over whether the local farmers or the distant capitalists would capture the benefits of natural-resource development.

Another type of class conflict leading to federal-provincial conflict is illustrated by the recent experience of Quebec, although some observers may prefer to view this as "national" rather than class conflict. Within Quebec there has been a long history of conflict between a largely anglophone *bourgeoisie* and an almost entirely francophone *petite bourgeoisie,* a conflict reinforced by linguistic and cultural barriers and by the rather tenuous economic and geographic ties between the anglophone citadel of Montreal and the rest of the province. In recent years the weakening· of the Montreal *bourgeoisie* in relation to its counterpart and rival in Toronto has upset the local equilibrium and allowed the francophone *petite bourgeoisie* to assume a dominant position in relation to the provincial state apparatus. That apparatus has in turn been strengthened and transformed into a instrument of conflict against the declining *bourgeoisie* and its external allies, while in the process the *petite bourgeoisie* has evolved from the traditional sort of professional class into a much more numerous class of technocrats and officials. For this class the expansion of state power at the provincial level becomes an end in itself, a fact that places it on a collision course with the federal authorities.

More frequently, federal-provincial conflict has represented the conflict between different class fractions within the dominant world of corporate capitalism. Christopher Armstrong and H. V. Nelles have documented a number of such struggles in early twentieth-century Ontario: between electric utilities and manufacturers, between the promoters of electric and steam railways, between different sectors of the insurance industry, and between a variety of natural-resource interests.[2] Each fraction identifies its interests with a level of government at which it finds a sympathetic hearing, and the economic conflict becomes institutionalized as a federal-provincial one, complete with the usual ideological justifications on both sides. More recent examples have been the efforts of Premier John Robarts to protect the insurance industry (particularly influential in his own city of London) against the competition of government pensions and medicare, the lobbying of western provincial governments against federal tax reforms that threatened the privileges of the mining industry, and the recent disposition of several provincial governments to participate in the making of tariff policy.

Conflicts of this kind exist in virtually all countries, with or without federal institutions, and intergovernmental conflict is not the only form they could take, even in Canada. There are a number of reasons, however, why in Canada they are particularly likely to take this form. The regionalized nature of the Canadian economy increases the probability that a particular sector of the economy will be largely concentrated in one province and will exercise significant economic and political power within that province. The fact that the provinces are few in number and that most of them are relatively large increases the likelihood that a determined provincial government can influence federal policy or place obstacles in the way of federal initiatives.

An even more important circumstance is the fact that the mechanisms for expression and representation of specific fractional interests (especially regionally concentrated ones) at the federal level of government are rather weak and ineffective. In both the United States and Australia the Senate is effective in this regard, especially as the representative of agricultural and resource interests whose geographical bastions are over-represented there to compensate for their weakness in the House of Representatives. The Canadian Senate cannot play this role because it is federally appointed, lacks the legitimacy that would come from election by the people, and has an unsuitable distribution of seats among the provinces. Responsible government and the premium placed on "party discipline", as well as the national prejudice against coalition governments, ensures that regional interests find little expression in the House of Commons either. The abolition of political patronage in the federal bureaucracy, and its tendency to become a hereditary caste largely recruited from the Ottawa Valley, closes off another possible avenue of representation which the American system provides. Thus by default the task of representing regionally concentrated economic interests is left to the provincial governments, which are more than happy to assume this role since it enhances their own power and importance.

It would be wrong, however, to view the provincial governments only as the direct representatives of specific interests or to view federal-provincial conflict entirely as an expression of economic rivalries. The modern capitalist state invariably has a certain degree of autonomy, which seems to be increasing, in relation to the specific interests whose collective purposes it serves, and it can only be effective insofar as this is the case.[3] The provincial level of Canadian government is no exception to this rule. To a large degree the increasingly complex and sophisticated apparatus of provincial government, like any organization, has its own interests which it defends, although it may or may not serve other interests as an incidental consequence of doing so.

Thus a large part of federal-provincial conflict is really no more than conflict between competing organizations, each with its own imperatives of expansion, survival, and self-defence. No class analysis is needed to explain why provincial governments seek to expand their revenues, through equalization or abatement as the case may be, or to exclude the other level of government from functional areas of jurisdiction over which they have already staked a claim. Nor is class analysis needed to explain why politicians quarrel over patronage or campaign funds, although the expansion and bureaucratization of government at both levels has made this kind of conflict far less important than it was in the days of Mitch Hepburn.

Federal-provincial conflict thus has a number of different

causes, each of which has a long history in Canada and none of which is capable of being removed except through very fundamental changes in the society. Moreover, the institutional type of conflict is really an inevitable consequence of the existence of federalism, whose rationale is that it is the only basis on which even a semblance of national unity can be achieved in the face of the other types of conflict. Despite this rather paradoxical dilemma, federal-provincial conflict has historically been managed, and at times resolved, with a fair degree of success. Various institutional mechanisms or procedures have been employed for this purpose, although not all of them seem equally suitable for every circumstance or every type of conflict. In the next section these mechanisms or procedures will be examined in what is roughly the chronological order in which they emerged to a position of importance. The progression begins with the quasi-federal devices of disallowance and reservation, continues through political, judicial, and administrative approaches to conflict management and resolution, and concludes with the phenomenon variously described as executive federalism or federal-provincial diplomacy.

DISALLOWANCE AND RESERVATION

Enough has been written concerning the powers of disallowance and reservation that it is not necessary in this context to describe them in detail. In theory they offered a means of "resolving" federal-provincial conflicts through an assertion of the federal authority against which the province had no redress. In so doing they accorded both with the monarchical and hierarchical philosophy of the Fathers of Confederation and with the apparently overwhelming strength of the economic interests that favoured a centralized and quasi-federal union in 1867.

Yet in practice the use of these powers was not particularly convenient or successful, with the result that they were used only rarely and with decreasing frequency even against the new and supposedly immature provinces of the West. Almost half the acts that have been disallowed or reserved since the death of John A. Macdonald were from the single province of

British Columbia, and after Laurier's defeat in 1911 both powers became virtually extinct, apart from the brief revival of disallowance in relation to the Alberta Social Credit legislation between 1937 and 1943.[4]

One reason for this was surely the fact that with the gradual growth of democratic sentiment the use of these powers, particularly that of reservation, came to appear increasingly illegitimate and anachronistic. The Judicial Committee's opinion in the Maritime Bank case also conferred the ideological support of the imperial connection on the notion that the provincial legislatures should enjoy equal dignity and status with the federal Parliament. Moreover, it was politically hazardous to use disallowance and reservation, especially against the larger provinces whose support was crucial in federal elections. If the provincial government affected was of the same party as the federal one it might refuse its assistance, while if it was of the other party it might redouble its efforts in support of the federal opposition. In either case the provincial electorate would be unlikely to look with favour on the disallowance or reservation of acts approved by their elected representatives in the legislature. In fact it is possible that the peculiar Canadian tendency for the party that holds office in Ottawa to enjoy little success in provincial elections is in part a legacy of resentment against the frequently partisan interventions of federally appointed lieutenant-governors.

An additional defect of disallowance and reservation was that there was nothing to prevent the provincial legislature from adopting the same act, or a practically identical one, a second time, thus forcing the federal government or the lieutenant-governor either to admit defeat or to repeat the process, again with no assurance of ultimate success. There were some notable cases of provincial defiance, such as Mowat's Rivers and Streams Acts which the Macdonald government disallowed on three occasions, or the repeated attempts by the Manitoba government to charter railways in competition with the CPR. Such protracted episodes could only increase popular sympathy for the provincial government and give the federal government an appearance of heavy-handed ineptitude and callous disregard for the principles of representative government. Thus it is not surprising that the powers eventually fell into disuse.

Disallowance and reservation seem to have been used successfully in some cases, although the over-all record was not particularly encouraging to their proponents. In some cases the provincial government did not persevere with its intention, and the federal initiative was successful. It is not clear exactly what variables contributed to success or failure in the use of the federal powers. It does appear that they were used in response to several types of federal-provincial conflict. In a very large number of cases the federal government seems to have acted on behalf of either transcontinental railways or financial institutions when it disallowed provincial acts. Examples of disallowed acts that offended these interests would include the Manitoba railway charters, three efforts by Saskatchewan to incorporate trust and loan companies, anti-Oriental legislation in British Columbia (which threatened to interfere with construction of the CPR and later the Canadian Northern), and the Social Credit legislation in Alberta. Some of these episodes can certainly be regarded as cases of class conflict (capitalists *versus* farmers) while others were in the nature of conflicts between fractions of the dominant class. Still other cases of disallowance resulted from expressions of institutional self-interest on the part of the two levels of government. This category would include such episodes as the Rivers and Streams Acts in Ontario, the Alberta Mineral Tax Act of 1923 which was disallowed because it seemed to threaten the federal ownership of lands and resources in the province, or the disallowance at about the same time of a Nova Scotia private bill that attempted to reverse a decision of the Supreme Court of Canada.

POLITICAL PARTIES AND CONFLICT RESOLUTION

A less contentious response to federal-provincial conflict, and one that could conceivably have been used, would be to seek accommodation through the machinery of a political party. By definition, of course, this method of resolving conflict would only be available when the same party held office both

federally and provincially. There are, however, more fundamental reasons why it has become relatively insignificant.

Donald Smiley's lament that Canadian political scientists
have ignored the subject of federal-provincial party relations is
still largely justified, although a major gap in our knowledge
has since been filled by Reginald Whitaker's outstanding work
on the Liberal party under King and St. Laurent.[5] Most
students of Canadian federalism have dismissed parties as of
little importance, in contrast to non-Canadian writers on
federalism such as K. C. Wheare and W. H. Riker, both of
whom attribute to parties a decisive role in facilitating the
operation of a federal system. Smiley himself concludes that
Canadian parties and the party system are too loosely
integrated or, as he puts it, "confederal" to have any impact on
federal-provincial relations. By this he means that Canadian
voters do not typically support the same party at both levels
and that federal and provincial parties, even if they bear the
same name, have separate organizations, elites, platforms, and
sources of financial support.[6]

While few would argue today with Smiley's description of
the Canadian party system, it did not always have the
characteristics he describes. At least until 1917, when the
federal Liberal party split over conscription and a coalition
government was formed, the party system was in fact quite
integrated according to all of Smiley's criteria. Although
detailed knowledge is lacking, it also appears that party had a
significant impact on federal-provincial relations, in the sense
that relations were much more cordial when the same party
held office at both levels. Relations between Ottawa and the two
central provinces were very close in the first few years, when
the provincial governments were controlled by allies of
Macdonald and Cartier. The Interprovincial Conference of
1887 was basically a meeting of Liberals to denounce a
Conservative federal government, apart from the presence of
the nominally Conservative Premier Norquay of Manitoba.
British Columbia and Prince Edward Island, both governed by
more orthodox Conservatives, were not represented at the
conference. The bitter struggles between Ontario and the
federal government occurred between 1878 and 1896, when
the former was Liberal and the latter Conservative. Between
1905 and 1911, when the positions were reversed, relations

again deteriorated. Federal politicians depended on the organizational support of friendly provincial governments to win elections, and the provincial allies were rewarded with "better terms", and sometimes with appointments to the federal cabinet. It seems reasonable to conclude that many conflicts were avoided or quietly resolved through political channels.

At the same time this method of resolving and managing conflicts had its limitations. In some cases, Norquay's experience as Premier of Manitoba being a good example, the objective conflicts of interest between a provincial government and the federal authorities were too serious to be accommodated within the party machinery. The provincial government was forced to disagree publicly with the federal one and thus fell between two stools, being regarded by the federal government as untrustworthy and by the electorate as too closely tied to the federal government. It is not accidental that Ontario, with its long history of federal-provincial conflict, has usually been governed by the federal opposition party, but it is arguable that the latter fact is more the result of conflict than the cause of it. Ontarians may have believed that the federal government and, by implication, the party that controlled that government were too closely tied to the economic interests of Montreal. The use of anti-French bigotry in Ontario by both nineteenth-century Liberals and twentieth-century Conservatives could be viewed as an ideological smokescreen to conceal what was basically an economic rivalry between Toronto and Montreal. Significantly, the bigotry ceased to be respectable, because it had ceased to be necessary, once Toronto replaced Montreal as the major economic centre.

There were, however, other reasons why the partisan method of dealing with federal-provincial conflict became obsolete. The events of 1917 disintegrated the party system and produced as one consequence the formation of provincial governments in Alberta, Manitoba, and Ontario by parties that had no realistic chances of success at the federal level. The Saskatchewan Liberals survived, but at the cost of loosening their ties with the federal party. With the rapid disappearance of the federal Progressive party, the governments of all three Prairie provinces in effect adopted a position of quasineutrality with respect to federal politics, and were able to deal impartially with federal governments of either party.[7] The ambiguity was increased when Manitoba's Progressive government became a coalition including the Liberals and eventually even the Conservatives. A coalition of the two major parties also governed British Columbia between 1942 and 1952, largely as a means of keeping the CCF out of office.

Another milestone in the transformation of the party system was reached in 1935, when Maurice Duplessis formed his Union Nationale, the first major Canadian political party to operate at the provincial level exclusively. Quebec continued to support the Liberal party in federal elections while giving the Union Nationale the largest share of its votes in provincial ones. Shortly afterwards Mitch Hepburn severed the ties between his Ontario Liberal party and the federal party, with ultimately fatal consequences for his own career, but with the long-term result that Ontario, as well as Quebec, tended to support one party in federal elections and another in provincial ones. Subsequently the Union Nationale's practice of operating exclusively at the provincial level has been imitated by the Social Credit parties in Alberta and British Columbia, as well as by the Parti Québécois.

This peculiar separation of the party system into federal and provincial layers is perhaps in part a consequence of the intensity of federal-provincial conflict, which makes it difficult for a party affiliated with the federal government to appear as a credible defender of provincial interests. Significantly, the traditional two-party system has survived at the provincial level only in the Atlantic provinces, which are so dependent on federal largesse that affiliation with the federal government is still an electoral asset. At the same time, the separation of the federal and provincial party systems was facilitated by, and might not have been possible without, the bureaucratization and depoliticization of government at both levels, especially the federal, which limited the functions of parties to recruiting candidates and conducting election campaigns. The conduct of federal-provincial relations was one of the functions that was largely transferred from the parties to the non-partisan bureaucracy.

Whitaker's account shows how far this process went in the

federal Liberal party, which remained in office for so long that it became virtually a part of the machinery of state and, in a sense, the political and electoral arm of the federal bureaucracy. The bureaucracy supplied the party with ideas, programs, and even personnel such as Pearson and Pickersgill. In return the federal party's behaviour in federal-provincial relations was determined by bureaucratic rather than partisan considerations. It ruthlessly undermined its faltering provincial affiliates so as to improve relations with the non-Liberal governments of Quebec, Ontario, Alberta, and British Columbia, as in the episode of the Quebec income tax discussed in Chapter 6. Interestingly enough, this did not happen in Saskatchewan; apparently it was considered more important to maintain a viable "free enterprise" party there than to form a friendly relationship with Tommy Douglas. In the four largest provinces, however, the indifference of the federal Liberal party to the fate of its provincial affiliates was both a cause and a consequence of the perceived irrelevance of party ties to federal-provincial relations.

None the less, the importance of party ties in resolving or avoiding federal-provincial conflict can not yet be completely dismissed, particularly in the Atlantic provinces where the federal and provincial parties remain fairly integrated. The history of Newfoundland's relations with the federal government since 1949 is particularly suggestive in this respect; they were clearly very cordial when the Liberals reigned at both levels but rather hostile at other times. Even elsewhere, parties may not always be irrelevant. Maurice Sauvé, who had contacts in both the federal and provincial wings of the Liberal party, seems to have played an important part in resolving the dispute between the Pearson and Lesage governments over pension legislation in 1964–65, and relations between Ottawa and Quebec were generally better under Pearson and Lesage, who had been colleagues in the St. Laurent government, than they were either before or subsequently.[8]

JUDICIAL CONFLICT RESOLUTION

The judicial method of resolving federal-provincial conflicts had a rather slow start in Canada, and has remained controversial. As Canada was a part of the British Empire, the acts of its various legislatures were automatically subject to review by the Judicial Committee of the Privy Council. Allegedly this safeguard was required for the security of British investors, although its absence does not seem to have prevented them from investing in Latin America or the United States. On the other hand, judicial review of the federal Parliament's Acts was a somewhat American notion, and logically incompatible with the expressed desire to have a form of government similar to that of the United Kingdom.[9] The BNA Act did not establish a general court of appeal for Canada but provided that one could be established at a later date. Although a bill for this purpose was introduced by the government as early as 1869, the Supreme Court was not actually established until 1875, not fully separated from the Exchequer Court until 1887, and did not become the final court of appeal until 1949.

Judicial review is primarily a means of defining the powers of legislatures in relation to private interests, not a means of resolving intergovernmental disputes. None the less it can play the latter role not only in the relatively rare cases where governments are litigants on both sides, but in other cases as well. Since Canada lacks an entrenched bill of rights (that is, an area in which neither level can legislate), and since the enumerated powers of both Parliament and the legislatures are mainly exclusive rather than over-lapping (at least in theory), narrowing the jurisdiction of one level of government tends to enlarge that of the other. For this reason, a federal or provincial government may have enough interest in the outcome to become an intervener or even a co-plaintiff when the constitutionality of legislation by the other level is at issue.

Another way in which the courts can be used to settle intergovernmental disputes is through reference cases, by which legislative powers can be defined without waiting for private parties to launch litigation. The federal government can refer either its own legislation or that of a province to the Supreme Court of Canada while a provincial government can refer either its own or federal legislation to the superior court of the province, from which the case may go to the Supreme Court of Canada on appeal. Until 1949 both kinds of references could go on appeal to the Judicial Committee of the Privy Council. In contrast to the United States and Australia, where the courts have refused to hear reference cases, they have comprised about half of all constitutional cases in Canada. It has been very common for governments other than the one that made the original reference to intervene on one or the other side. For example Ontario's reference of the Canada Temperance Act in 1939 was opposed by the federal government and supported by four other provinces.

Certain types of conflict are more easily resolved through the judicial method than others. The courts can conclusively determine which level of government has the power to regulate an industry, but they are of little help in resolving such questions as the proportion in which the income tax should be shared between the two levels of government. They also cannot resolve disputes that arise because a province perceives itself as receiving less than its fair share of benefits from federal expenditures and other policies. The limited capabilities of the judicial method largely explain the statement, frequently made in the 1960s, that the courts were declining in importance as a means of resolving intergovernmental disputes. In the 1970s disputes over fiscal matters have abated somewhat while disputes over regulatory jurisdictions have increased and intensified, mainly because both levels of government have been trying to shift their emphasis from policies of legitimization to the less expensive and more politically profitable task of promoting accumulation. As a result the courts have assumed much greater prominence and importance. Bora Laskin is probably the first Chief Justice whose name is familiar to large numbers of Canadians, although his complaint that the media have underestimated the importance of the Supreme Court still has some justification and could also be directed at Canadian political scientists.

Because the agenda of intergovernmental issues changes in its composition, the judicial method of resolving disputes, like other methods, has varied in importance from time to time. In earlier times the major decisions of the Judicial Committee of the Privy Council established the locus of jurisdiction over liquor control, the regulation of insurance companies, agricultural marketing, and various other matters. A large proportion of these cases originated in references, often references of provincial legislation to the Supreme Court by the federal government, a circumstance which almost by definition indicates the existence of an intergovernmental dispute.

In the last decade the judicial method of resolving disputes has again come into prominence, for the reason already described, with the important difference that the Supreme Court, rather than the Judicial Committee of the Privy Council, is now the final court of appeal. The offshore minerals reference, by which Lester Pearson's government sought a solution to a dispute with British Columbia, was perhaps the beginning of a trend back to the judicial method.[10] More recent cases, some of them originating in private litigation rather than references, have dealt with such matters as the constitutionality of federal wage and price controls, provincial resource taxation in Saskatchewan, and the right of the federal rather than the Quebec government to license cable-television operators.

Even in relation to such matters. however, the judicial method of resolving disputes has its defects. By its very nature a judicial solution tends to be clear cut and uncompromising; the winning side wins totally and the losing side receives nothing. This makes the decision to seek a solution in the courts something of a gamble and, more importantly, may make the atmosphere of intergovernmental relations somewhat rancorous in the aftermath of the decision. A decision may also not accord with the realities of political power, a commodity which appears to be quite evenly distributed between the two levels of government. A significant and recurring pattern is for the federal government to surrender through political negotiation a large part of what it has won through judicial decision. The case of the Winner decision on highway transport was mentioned in Chapter 5. Federal victory in the offshore minerals reference was followed by years of negotiation and a generous compromise with the Maritime provinces. Federal victory in the cable-television case produced an immediate statement by the Minster of Communications, Jeanne Sauvé, that she would welcome a negotiated solution with any interested province.

This federal generosity is in part a response to the

widespread belief among provincial governments that the Supreme Court is biased against them. The evidence for this view is not particularly overwhelming; Peter Russell has calculated that between 1949 and 1969 the Supreme Court's decisions were pro-federal in 54.7 per cent of constitutional cases, or only slightly more than half.[11] None the less the suspicion of bias will inevitably exist for as long as the members of the court are appointed unilaterally by the federal government. Provincial statutes are tested before the courts far more frequently than federal ones, and they are far more likely to be overturned. The fact that more than half of them are upheld may not comfort the provincial governments when they reflect that only one section of one federal statute has been declared unconstitutional since 1949 on the grounds that it intruded on provincial jurisdiction. The federal government's high batting average possibly indicates no more than that it receives good legal advice from the Department of Justice, but some provincial nostalgia for the days of Watson and Haldane may be understandable.

CO-OPERATIVE FEDERALISM

The administrative approach to managing and resolving intergovernmental conflicts did not really begin to develop before the turn of the century, and reached its fullest development in the period roughly from 1945 until 1970. During the two decades following the Second World War it was the predominant method of dealing with federal-provincial conflict, largely supplanting both the party-political and the judicial approaches. This was the heyday of "co-operative federalism", a phrase borrowed from the United States, which both celebrated and purported to describe the way in which the federal system operated at that time. By the late 1960s, however, administrative or "co-operative" federalism was already being transformed into executive federalism, which will be considered subsequently.

Administrative or "co-operative" federalism, its proponents liked to argue, was based on the virtues of compromise, flexibility, and pragmatism.[12] It was also based on the assumption that all disputes and problems could be resolved through the application of these virtues and that some mutually acceptable position midway between the demands of both parties could always be discovered. Certainly the administrative approach to the resolution of conflict contrasted with the judicial approach in that it did tend to promote such compromises and was thus more effective in resolving certain kinds of dispute, such as those over fiscal matters. The administrative approach also appealed to governments which for one reason or another preferred not to seek a clear definition of jurisdictional boundaries, or which did not believe it was possible to find one.

While it had certain advantages over the judicial approach, the administrative approach tended to replace the party-political approach to conflict resolution for somewhat different reasons. As bureaucracies became larger, more powerful, more functionally specialized, and more removed from partisan influence and pressure, they assumed increasingly autonomous roles in seeking accommodation with their counterparts at the other level of government. As specialists of various kinds came to predominate in certain sectors of the public service they tended to discover that they held interests, goals, and assumptions in common with similar specialists at the other level of government, and that these took precedence over considerations of intergovernmental competition, party rivalry, or even constitutional propriety. Thus administrative methods of problem-solving were preferred to other methods. Politicians acquiesced in this, partly by necessity (since they could no longer control all the detailed activities of their departments), partly because it lacked the risks of the judicial approach, and partly because they were themselves acquiring bureaucratic perspectives. It is significant that the administrative character of federalism became most pronounced under the St. Laurent government, at a time when the governing federal party had become almost a part of the bureaucratic machinery.

The growth of administrative or co-operative federalism was very closely associated with the growth of conditional grants and shared-cost programs, a phenomenon discussed in the preceding chapter. Inseparable from both was the proliferation of federal-provincial committees, councils, meetings, and other forms of contact at various levels of officialdom, which served as the mechanisms by which problems were resolved in an administrative manner. These bodies have been catalogued and described by a number of writers. Gérard Veilleux discovered in the 1960s that about four fifths of them were concerned with the areas of general government (including finance), statistics, health and welfare, natural resources, and agriculture.[13] This list suggests the areas in which administrative approaches to the resolution of intergovernmental conflict were generally successful and popular. Finance is the area least amenable to solutions achieved through the judicial process. Health and welfare, for reasons already described, was the area where conditional grants and shared-cost programs were most important. Agriculture is a shared jurisdiction under the BNA Act. The inclusion of resources appears anomalous from our present perspective, but at the time Veilleux wrote they would have been mainly renewable resources, which are closely associated with agriculture.

Donald Smiley has suggested some of the circumstances under which co-operative federalism is most likely to be successful. The officials who do the negotiating should have real authority to speak on behalf of their governments. They should have a common frame of reference, such as might result from shared professional training and expertise. They should be more committed to the success of the program than to other types of goals. They should be willing to compromise, and also to share confidential information with one another. Finally, there should not be too much public interest or involvement in the matters at issue.[14]

Viewed in a somewhat different way, co-operative or administrative federalism seems to be a fairly effective remedy for the types of conflict that arise from the organizational imperatives of different levels of government. It can prevent or resolve such conflicts, at least to some degree, through the countervailing impact of professional or programmatic goals that cut across, instead of reinforcing, the jurisdictional rivalries between the two levels. Co-operative federalism cannot, however, deal very successfully with the conflicts that originate outside the governmental and bureaucratic milieu and that result from more fundamental antagonisms between the interests of different classes or class fractions. Whether producers or consumers benefit from resource developments, whether industries are established in the East or in the West, whether jobs go to anglophones or francophones — these are not the types of question to which co-operative federalism provides answers. This is one reason for its obsolescence.

EXECUTIVE FEDERALISM

In recent years the term "executive federalism", first coined by Donald Smiley, has come to be used more frequently than "co-operative federalism".[15] Although the fact may not always be explicitly stated or even recognized, the change in terminology corresponds to a real change in the nature of intergovernmental relations, and one that began to take place a few years before the terminology was changed to correspond with it. Although one cannot state any precise date at which it occured, the change is in fact fundamental. Co-operative federalism was characterized by the fragmentation of authority within each level of government, the absence of linkages between different issues and functional domains, the forging of specific intergovernmental links by different groups of specialized officials, and the lack of publicity or public awareness of what was happening. Executive federalism, on the other hand, is characterized by the concentration and centralization of authority at the top of each participating government, the control and supervision of intergovernmental relations by politicians and officials with a wide range of functional interests, and the highly formalized and well-publicized proceedings of federal-provincial conference diplomacy. While co-operative federalism tended to subordinate the power, status, and prestige of individual governments to programmatic objectives, executive federalism does exactly the opposite.

Despite its recent rise to prominence, the origins of executive federalism and of its most characteristic institutional manifestation, the first-ministers' conference, can be traced back fairly far in Canadian history. Contacts between the Prime Minister and individual Premiers were fairly frequent in the early period when partisan political considerations exercised a decisive influence on federal-provincial relations. Laurier summoned all of the Premiers to a conference in 1906 to discuss the proposed changes in statutory subsidies to the provinces. There was a one-day conference in 1910 to discuss company law reform and a longer one in 1918, mainly to discuss problems of post-war reconstruction. In 1927 Mackenzie King organized a major conference to commemorate the sixtieth anniversary of Confederation, at which a long agenda of topics was discussed. There were four more conferences during the depression, mainly to discuss problems of relief and federal-provincial-municipal finance, an abortive conference to discuss the Rowell-Sirois Report in 1940, and a conference on post-war reconstruction and fiscal arrangements in 1945. As it turned out, the post-war pattern of federal-provincial finance required a first-ministers' conference to discuss the arrangements at least every five years, and two additional conferences were also held in 1950 to consider the amendment of the constitution, a topic that had also been discussed in 1927 and 1935.

Federal-provincial first-ministers' conferences were thus by no means unknown, but they took place at fairly infrequent intervals and could hardly be considered the predominant mechanism of interaction between the two levels of government, at least as regards the more mundane topics that dominated the federal-provincial agenda. Only for major changes in fiscal arrangements or for the consideration of amendments to the BNA Act were they considered essential. For the most part federal-provincial relations in the post-war period remained fragmented, specialized, uncoordinated, and dominated by officials. Gérard Veilleux estimated in his book that only one-tenth of federal-provincial meetings and conferences involved elected politicians as participants.[16] By contrast, a study done for the government of Alberta in 1975 found that by that time politicians participated in almost one out of every four meetings.[17] It is also significant that at least one first-ministers' conference took place almost every year from 1963 onwards. The federal government in fact proposed in its "Victoria Charter" that the obligatory requirement of an annual conference be written into the constitution, corresponding to the requirement that there be an annual session of Parliament.

The most important reason for the shift from co-operative to executive federalism was the fact that federal-provincial conflicts were becoming too serious, too profound, and too sensitive to be safely entrusted to the diplomatic and managerial skills of subordinate officials. In particular the evident dissatisfaction of the Quebec government under Jean Lesage and his successors, and of the francophone *petite bourgeoisie* which that government represented, could not be accommodated by the traditional means. Federal-provincial relations had to be politicized and conducted at the highest level, as in the case of the Pearson–Lesage negotiations over the Canada and Quebec pension plans. At the same time or subsequently a number of other serious conflicts emerged which involved provinces other than Quebec: conflicts over tax-sharing and the financing of health, education, and welfare, over economic relations with the United States, over regional development and the competitive scramble for investment, and over the division of benefits from mineral resources. All of these matters were clearly "political" rather than "administrative", in the sense that large numbers of people outside the bureaucracy were aware of their significance and deeply interested in their outcomes. In fact the complex of problems (and particularly the situation in Quebec) provided grounds for apprehension that the survival of the federal state itself might be called into question.

This exacerbation of conflict led to a renewed emphasis on intergovernmental competition and to a tendency to give the institutional interests of governments priority over functional or programmatic objectives. A distrust of co-operative federalism followed, accompanied by a belief that the fragmentation of authority and the lack of co-ordination that it entailed were luxuries that no self-respecting government could afford. Quebec nationalists had always argued, correctly from their point of view, that the proliferation of specialized and fragmented intergovernmental relationships, such as those that arose from shared-cost programs, was a potential menace to the integrity of their provincial state and its ability or willingness to defend its own interests. This belief had caused Maurice

Duplessis to refuse some conditional grants and had caused a later generation of Quebec nationalists to denounce the co-operative federalism of the 1960s as a fraud and a delusion.[18] Increasingly, similar reasoning began to be apparent on the part of other provincial governments, and even of the federal government itself. This led to the development of new mechanisms for the conduct of intergovernmental relations.

These sentiments arising out of intergovernmental competition reinforced certain incentives towards centralization and concentration of power within each of the eleven governments that had arisen simultaneously from other causes. There was a widespread conviction in the 1960s, partly inspired by the reorganization of the United States Department of Defense under the Kennedy administration, that administrative structures and procedures could and should be reformed to make them more "rational". The centralized setting of priorities and control of expenditure, through a process that related decisions on expenditures to more fundamental decisions on objectives, were viewed as fundamental to successful administration and policy-making. The desire to control expenditure was particularly strong on the part of Canadian provincial governments, which saw themselves after 1966 as faced with mounting expenditures on legitimization coupled with the diminishing likelihood that the "tax room" made available to them by the federal government would increase proportionately.

All of these pressures to centralize and concentrate authority were manifested in organizational changes at both the federal and the provincial levels. Intergovernmental competition certainly played a part in promoting these changes, although they occurred so rapidly that it is not easy to say which level of government initiated the trend and which responded. At the federal level the establishment of the Treasury Board as a separate department and the proliferation of cabinet committees and support staff took place under Prime Minister Pearson. It was followed under Prime Minister Trudeau by a dramatic expansion of the Prime Minister's Office and the Privy Council Office, and later by the creation from the latter of a separate Federal-Provincial Relations Office reporting directly to the Prime Minister. Subsequently a Minister of State for Federal-Provincial Relations in the person of Marc Lalonde was appointed.

At the provincial level there was a general tendency to expand and develop the Premier's Office, which in most of the provinces was given a general responsibility for co-ordinating and supervising relations with other governments. Usually an official reporting directly to the Premier is concerned exclusively with intergovernmental relations. Quebec went a step further under Jean Lesage by establishing a Department of Intergovernmental Affairs with its own minister, and Alberta later did the same. Newfoundland also has such a department, but with the Premier as the responsible minister. Ontario initially followed a different pattern by giving the major responsibility for intergovernmental relations to the Treasury, which was expanded and given the new name of Treasury, Economics, and Intergovernmental Affairs. In 1978 this Ministry was divided so that Ontario now has a full-time Minister of Intergovernmental Affairs.

All of these changes were in part a response to intergovernmental competition, but at the same time they tended to exacerbate that competition by strengthening the influence of politicians and officials who were predisposed by the nature of their responsibilities and institutional perspectives to emphasize the power and prestige of their government in relation to other governments rather than to give priority to programmatic objectives or the avoidance of intergovernmental conflict. At the same time and as a consequence, the influence of program specialists was reduced and their authority curtailed. The growing distaste of both levels of government for shared-cost programs was in part a reflection of this redistribution of power and influence within their respective bureaucracies. The lessened importance of such programs tends in turn to lessen intergovernmental contacts among the specialists. Thus all of the conditions that Smiley specified as conducive to the success of co-operative federalism have tended to disappear. Only in the Atlantic provinces, where federally assisted programs of regional economic development comprise a large share of total government activity, does anything resembling the co-operative federalism of the post-war period seem likely to continue.[19]

Despite the triumph of executive federalism, there is little evidence to suggest that it is a very effective method of resolving intergovernmental conflicts. In fact the apparently increasing tendency to seek solutions through the judicial process might be in part a testimony to its ineffectiveness. The system is open to other objections as well. Although any kind of public interest in the politics of federalism is perhaps better than none at all, there are some disquieting implications for national unity in the extent to which media coverage of intergovernmental relations tends to emphasize conflict, competition, and personal rivalry, whether real or imagined, among the first ministers. Another problem which cannot be dismissed as insignificant is the way in which executive federalism erodes the power and influence of the legislatures at both levels. Admittedly, executive federalism may be as much a consequence as a cause of the weakness of legislatures in a system of responsible government where a single, disciplined party normally holds a majority of the seats. There is no doubt, however, that legislatures are further weakened when they must legislate within the parameters of executive agreements arrived at in secret and without their participation. Opposition parties, especially at the federal level, are also placed in the position of being forced either to acquiesce in the agreements arrived at or to criticize the members of their own party who have participated in making them.

It would seem however that the vicious circle of executive federalism will not be easily broken. Part of the problem is certainly the very intensity of intergovernmental conflicts and of the more fundamental conflicts that lie behind them. Another part of it, and one that has recently attracted much attention, is the inability of the current parliamentary system to provide much meaningful representation at the federal level for regionally concentrated interests.[20] Those who put their faith in the separation of powers, proportional representation, a German type of second chamber, and various other nostrums must none the less recognize the force of the institutional self-interest that leads provincial governments and politicians to oppose any institutional change that threatens their own roles as the principal defenders of regional interests.

NOTES

1. Christopher Armstrong, "The Mowat Heritage in Federal-Provincial Relations", in Donald Swainson, ed., *Oliver Mowat's Ontario* (Toronto: Macmillan, 1972).

2. Christopher Armstrong, "The Politics of Federalism: Ontario's Relations with the Federal Government, 1896-1940" (unpublished PhD thesis, University of Toronto, 1972), and H. V. Nelles, *The Politics of Development: Forests, Mines and Hydro-Electric Power in Ontario, 1849-1941* (Toronto: Macmillan, 1974).

3. This argument is persuasively presented in Leo Panitch, "The role and nature of the Canadian state", in Leo Panitch, ed., *The Canadian State: Political Economy and Political Power* (Toronto: University of Toronto Press, 1977).

4. A brilliant analysis and interpretation of the latter episode is J.R. Mallory, *Social Credit and the Federal Power in Canada* (Toronto: University of Toronto Press, 1954). See also Eugene Forsey, "Canada and Alberta: the Revival of Dominion Control Over the Provinces", his *Freedom and Order: Collected Essays* (Toronto: McClelland and Stewart, 1974).

5. Reginald Whitaker, *The Government Party: Organizing and Financing the Liberal Party of Canada, 1930-1958* (Toronto: University of Toronto Press, 1977).

6. Donald V. Smiley, *Canada in Question, Federalism in the Seventies,* 2nd ed. (Toronto: McGraw-Hill Ryerson, 1976), pp. 83-113.

7. An argument that this fact was an essential "safety valve" for regional conflict is presented in Steven Muller, "Federalism and The Party System in Canada", in Aaron Wildavsky, ed., *American Federalism in Perspective* (Boston: Little Brown, 1967).

8. Peter C. Newman, *The Distemper of Our Times: Canadian Politics in Transition, 1963-1968* (Toronto: McClelland and Stewart, 1968), pp. 295-332 contains reflections on the Pearson–Lesage relationship, and a detailed account of the pension negotiations.

9. This was A. V. Dicey's view, and is also argued by Paul Weiler, *In the Last Resort: A Critical Study of the Supreme Court of Canada* (Toronto: Carswell/Methuen, 1974). Weiler argues that the judicial process is unsuitable for the resolution of federal-provincial disputes.

10. A useful account is Neil Caplan, "Offshore Mineral Rights: Anatomy of a Federal-Provincial Conflict", *Journal of Canadian Studies,* V (1970):50–61.

11. Peter Russell, "The Politicial Role of the Supreme Court of Canada in its First Century", *Canadian Bar Review,* LIII (1975): 576–96.

12. See for example Jean-Luc Pépin, "Co-operative Federalism", in J. Peter Meekison, ed., *Canadian Federalism: Myth or Reality,* 1st ed. (Toronto: Methuen, 1968), pp. 320–29.

13. Gérard Veilleux, *Les Relations intergouvernementales au Canada 1867–1967* (Montréal: Les Presses de l'université du Québec, 1971), p. 90.
14. Donald V. Smiley, *Constitutional Adaptation and Canadian Federalism since 1945* (Ottawa: Queen's Printer, 1970), pp. 111–18.
15. Smiley, *Canada in Question,* pp. 54–82.
16. Veilleux, *Les Relations intergouvernementales au Canada*, p. 73.
17. R. D. Olling, "Canadian Conference Activity 1975: Alberta Participation", in J. Peter Meekison, ed., *Canadian Federalism: Myth or Reality,* 3rd ed. (Toronto: Methuen, 1977), pp. 229–38.
18. See for example Jean-Marc Léger, "Le Fédéralisme co-operatif ou le nouveau visage de la centralisation", in Meekison, *Canadian Federalism,* 1st ed., pp. 317–20, and Claude Morin, *Quebec versus Ottawa: The Struggle for Self-Government 1960–72* (Toronto: University of Toronto Press, 1976).
19. This fact is explored, and criticized, in Anthony Careless, *Initiative and Response: The Adaptation of Canadian Federalism to Regional Economic Development* (Montreal: McGill-Queen's University Press, 1976).
20. For an extended discussion and proposals for reform see David Elton, F. C. Engelmann, and Peter McCormick, *Alternatives: Towards the Development of an Effective Federal System for Canada* (Calgary: Canada West Foundation, 1978).

9   Constitutional Amendment and Reform

In all of the federations that have lasted for any extended period of time — and Canada is no exception — the way in which federalism operates has been altered more extensively and more frequently by informal changes in practice than by formal amendments to the constitution. Occasionally federal constitutions may have to be amended because the judicial interpretation of the existing constitution imposes an obstacle to necessary adaptation, but such occasions are in fact quite rare. In Canada the only real case of this kind was the unemployment insurance amendment of 1940. The BNA Act has in practice been remarkably adaptable (some would say too adaptable) to shifts in the distribution of political and economic power.

Constitutional amendment, however, plays an important role in the politics of federal countries, and ironically this is more true in Canada, whose constitution was drafted without specifying a procedure for its amendment, than almost anywhere else. One suspects that the reason why constitutional amendment is so important, especially to politicians, is that it brings with it symbolic benefits that no mere informal change in practice can provide. Constitutional amendment is not so much a cause of changes in the distribution of political power as it is a means of legitimizing and giving explicit recognition to changes that have already taken place. Yet the substance of changes may often be more easily achieved than the symbol. The provincial government of Quebec, and the *petit-bourgeois* class which it represents, have greatly enlarged their freedom of action in practice since 1963, but they have been unsuccessful in securing symbolic recognition of the fact through constitutional changes.

Constitutional controversy is none the less important for an understanding of Canadian federalism since it draws attention to the issues that politicians consider important and to the economic and social forces that they represent. Although frequently expressed in arcane language, the controversies can be recognizably related to the familiar complex of conflicts and cleavages — between different sectors of the economy, between English and French, metropolis and hinterland, large and small provinces, rich and poor provinces — that has shaped the evolution of Canadian federalism. If formal changes have been rare, it is because these forces have usually been too evenly balanced to allow the imposition of any proposed amendment. The relations between the forces and the symbols can be illustrated by examining two related aspects of constitutional discussion. The long search for a "formula" to amend the BNA Act, and the closely associated problem of "repatriation", will be examined first. Attention will then be focused on the more wide-ranging constitutional review that has continued inter-mittently from the latter part of the 1960s to the present.

THE SEARCH FOR AN AMENDMENT FORMULA

It is generally known that the British North America Act of 1867 contains no procedure for its own amendment. This fact appears more anomalous and unsatisfactory today than it presumably did at the time. The Act, after all, was a statute of the Parliament at Westminster, one out of many, before and since, that have made provision for the government of various colonies. Presumably if it ceased to be suitable for its intended purpose it could be modified or repealed by the body that enacted it, a fate that had already overtaken such previous enactments as the Constitutional Act of 1791, which created Upper and Lower Canada, or the Act of Union of 1840, which united them into a single province.

Admittedly the convention had become established after the middle of the nineteenth century that the colonies populated mainly by British settlers would have virtually complete control over their internal affairs, and the corollary of this was that their internal constitutions would only be changed by Westminster at the request of the colonial politicians concerned, and would be changed whenever such a request was made. Presumably this meant that if the government of Canada subsequently requested an amendment to the BNA Act, Westminster would make the amendment with as little difficulty or hesitation as it had shown in adopting the original Act in 1867. Since the Fathers of Confederation were generally not very concerned with symbolic matters, they saw no reason to specify the procedure more precisely.

It is hindsight to say that this ignored the complexities of federalism, since the men of 1867 thought they had avoided those complexities by discarding the unwanted features of the American model. It will be recalled from Chapter 3 that John A. Macdonald, only a year after Confederation, expressed the view that a province's representatives in the federal Parliament at Ottawa were the only "constitutional exponents of the wishes of the people" with regard to federal-provincial relations, and that the provincial legislatures should not be concerned with such matters.[1] Logically this could only mean that a request to Westminster for a constitutional amendment would be a unilateral act by the federal government or Parliament. As long as the Macdonald view of federalism prevailed, the question of involving provincial governments or legislatures in the process of amendment could not arise.

F. R. Scott has suggested an additional although related reason why the BNA Act was not provided with an amendment formula of the kind normally found in federal constitutions.[2] The reason was the belief held by the Fathers of Confederation that their distinctive and un-American approach to the problem of dividing legislative powers between the two levels of government had ensured that amendments would be largely unnecessary. In the United States, and subsequently in Australia, the national government was given only a few specified legislative powers, with the residue being left to the states. As time went on and the national government required legislative authority over new subjects, the constitution had to be amended accordingly. In Canada, on the other hand, the national government was supposedly given from the outset almost complete legislative powers, and any authority over unspecified or unanticipated matters was contained in the general power to make laws for the peace, order, and good government of Canada. Thus there was little reason to suppose that many amendments would be necessary.

For both of these reasons the question of adding an American-style amending procedure to the BNA Act only arose in the twentieth century, after Lord Watson and other members of the Judicial Committee of the Privy Council had placed their official stamp of approval on an American-style theory of federalism. In the nineteenth century several amendments were made, but the only procedural question that was raised in regard to them was whether the federal cabinet could make the request without reference to the federal Parliament. As always in Canada, the "rights of Parliament" served as a convenient rallying cry for the opposition party, to be forgotten as soon as that party itself became the government. Thus the Liberals protested because Parliament was not involved in the request for the amendment of 1871, an amendment which ratified the rather hasty creation of Manitoba in the previous year and also authorized Parliament to create additional provinces out of federal territories. However, a Liberal government four years later secured without reference to Parliament an amendment to Section 18 of the BNA Act (dealing, ironically, with parliamentary privilege) and this time it was the Conservatives who protested. In 1886 a formal address by both houses of Parliament was used to secure the amendment allowing for the parliamentary representation of territories not included in any province.

The practice of consulting the provincial governments before making such an address was not invented until as late as 1906, when it was used prior to the amendment the following year which revised the provisions for financial subsidies to the provinces. Alexander Brady is almost certainly right in attributing the practice, which incidentally produced the first federal-provincial conference in Canadian history, to political expediency rather than constitutional principle.[3] Even then, Wilfrid Laurier's government did not consider it necessary to secure the unanimous consent of the provincial governments. The request was made despite the vigorous objections of the government of British Columbia, which made its own representations to Westminster and was only partly placated by the latter's decision to delete from the amendment a statement to the effect that the new terms would not be subject to further revision.

Subsequent practice was not entirely consistent, confirming the validity of Brady's observation about political expediency. The provincial governments were not consulted about the amendment of 1915, which revised the formula for representation of regions in the Senate and also enacted the rule that no province should have fewer members in the lower than in the upper house of Parliament. They were also not consulted the following year about the amendment which allowed Parliament to extend its own term beyond the five years permitted by the BNA Act. The BNA Act of 1930, transferring natural resources to the western provinces, was discussed at a federal-provincial conference in 1927 and all provincial governments agreed in principle, even though this was not really an amendment to the original act at all.[4]

This sort of pragmatic expediency might have continued indefinitely, had not Canada's emergence as a virtually sovereign state after the First World War produced the problem of "repatriating" the BNA Act. It is not clear who invented this unhappy expression, which has left generations of undergraduates with the belief that a dusty document lies waiting to be carried across the North Atlantic, like the Ark of the Covenant that accompanied the children of Israel on their biblical wanderings through the Sinai desert. In any event, it began to appear absurd that a Parliament at Westminster whose authority over Canada had vanished in all other respects had still to be involved in the amendment of Canada's constitution. Yet if Westminster formally divested itself of that power it would have to state where the power now resided, a rather delicate point that was far more conveniently left to the imagination. Unfortunately, it had become politically inexpedient and unrealistic by the 1920s to state what Macdonald would have considered obvious in the circumstances, that the power now resided in the federal Parliament. Provincial premiers, with Ontario's Howard Ferguson in the lead, revived the "compact theory" of the Mowat-Mercier era and used it to argue that the unanimous consent of all nine provincial governments should be both a condition of "repatriation" and a requirement written into the subsequent amending procedure itself.

This problem was inconclusively discussed at the federal-provincial conference in 1927, and again in 1935. It soon became apparent that the procedures used in other federations, which typically require that a majority (but not all) of the provinces or states give their approval either through their legislatures, special conventions or referenda, were not easily adaptable to Canadian circumstances. In the first place the two central provinces, with more than three fifths of the population and an even more overwhelming concentration of economic and political power, would settle for nothing less than a power of veto. This meant that any formula would either have to extend the same power to all the provinces, producing an unprecedented degree of constitutional rigidity, or else explicitly concede that the provinces were unequal in status. In the second place the BNA Act itself contained a remarkable variety of provisions, some not really of constitutional significance, others pertaining to only one or a few provinces, so that no single procedure seemed appropriate for all types of amendment.

In response to these problems the idea emerged of classifying the sections of the Act into categories that would be subject to different procedures of amendment. It was hoped that Ontario and Quebec would thus be persuaded to confine their insistence on unanimity to a few selected sections of the Act, which were so unlikely to need modification that a requirement of total unanimity would be acceptable. Thus the need to make invidious distinctions between the provinces would not arise. Other sections would be amendable by procedures similar to those used in other federations, or even by the federal Parliament alone in the case of sections that did not really pertain to provincial interests.

This approach, first suggested at the 1927 conference by Minister of Justice Ernest Lapointe, governed all further discussion of the subject for more than forty years. Four different efforts were made by the federal and provincial governments, in 1936, 1950, 1961, and 1964, to classify the sections of the BNA Act. The first effort seemed close to agreement but was terminated by the election of Maurice Duplessis and the Union Nationale. In 1950 and 1961 the CCF government of Saskatchewan insisted on a more centralist formula than either Quebec or Ontario was willing to accept. The 1964 formula was finally rejected by Jean Lesage, who succumbed to heavy pressure from Quebec nationalists.

The first formula, devised by a federal-provincial committee of officials in 1936, required unanimous consent for amendments to the sections dealing with education and language, the section vesting executive power in the British monarch, and the sections dealing with provincial representation in both houses of Parliament. Parts of Section 92 were likewise "entrenched", but other parts, including the "property and civil rights" clause, could be amended with the consent of six provinces comprising at least 55 per cent of the population. This meant that an amendment could be carried over the objections of either Quebec or Ontario, but not both. In effect, however, there was a provision for "special status", in that a province which opposed an amendment relating to "property and civil rights" or "matters of a merely local or private nature" could continue to retain exclusive legislative jurisdiction over these subjects, regardless of the amendment.[5]

In 1949 Louis St. Laurent's government, without consulting the provinces, secured from Westminster an amendment to the Act which gave the federal Parliament the power to make all further amendments, except for amendments in relation to certain specified matters. The list of exceptions was confined to education, language, the division of powers, the "rights or privileges" of provincial governments, and the requirements that Parliament meet at least once a year and be dissolved at intervals of no more than five years. Notably absent from this list were the sections dealing with provincial representation in the House of Commons (which had been amended without consulting the provinces in 1946) and in the Senate.

This initiative was presumably intended to stake out a bargaining position and also to precipitate an early decision on a formula to amend the excluded sections. Its chief effect, however, was to antagonize the provincial governments. A series of discussions in 1950 made little progress, with Ontario and Quebec insisting that the whole division of legislative

powers be "entrenched" and Saskatchewan expressing vigorous opposition. The federal government had implicitly
accepted the Ontario and Quebec position by waiting for
unanimous consent before proceeding with the unemployment
insurance amendment in 1940, a procedure it was to follow
again with the amendments relating to pensions in 1951 and
1964.

In the Fulton formula of 1961, named after the federal
Minister of Justice, the central provinces achieved their
objective of entrenching the whole division of legislative
powers, as well as the educational and linguistic guarantees.
The requirement of unanimous consent for amendment was
also extended to the "Senate rule" which guaranteed each
province a fixed minimum representation in the House of
Commons, but not to the provisions for an annual session and
a dissolution every five years. Most of the other important
sections would be amendable with the consent of seven
provinces comprising at least half of the population. The
Fulton-Favreau formula of 1964 was almost identical, but
differed from both the 1949 amendment and the 1961 formula
in that Parliament would no longer be able unilaterally to
abolish the monarchy or to alter the scheme for allocating seats
in either house among the provinces.

The most striking and controversial feature of both the 1961
and the 1964 proposals was the provision whereby Parliament
could delegate any of its legislative powers to a minimum of
four provinces (presumably the four largest) and whereby a
minimum of four provinces could delegate certain of their
legislative powers to Parliament. This was intended to compensate for the rigidity of the amending procedure that would apply
to Sections 91 and 92. While the federal power to delegate was
unrestricted, the provinces could only delegate their powers
over prisons, local works and undertakings, property and civil
rights, or matters of a merely local or private nature, all
subjects that had been excluded from the unanimity rule under
the 1936 formula. (Only Saskatchewan argued in 1961 that the
provinces should be able to delegate all their powers.) The
provision for delegating provincial powers to Ottawa was
perhaps defensible, but the open-ended provision for delegating federal powers to the provinces was disturbing, in view of

the political power that the governments of the larger provinces had acquired by this time and the tendency of newly elected federal governments or those dependent on the support of minor parties to defer to provincial demands. Although Parliament could in theory take back what it had delegated, this might prove difficult once the larger provincial governments had become accustomed to exercising delegated power over economic matters.

The amendment formula in the so-called "Victoria Charter" of 1971 differed from all of its predecessors in that it eliminated the distinction between entrenched sections of the constitution and those amendable by the ordinary procedure. Apart from a few sections (mostly of little importance) that could be amended unilaterally by the government to which they pertained, all of the BNA Act was to be subject to amendment by a standard formula, closely resembling the Trudeau formula for establishing a "consensus" with respect to conditional grants that was described in Chapter 7. For the first time it was openly proclaimed that the provinces were, or should be, unequal in status. Ontario and Quebec would have a veto over all amendments, even to the point where they could veto efforts by one another to extend the terms of their respective legislatures. In addition to the support of the two central provinces, amendments would require only the approval of two western and two eastern provinces. In the final version this was modified slightly to require that the consenting western provinces have at least half of the total western population, a concession to the anxiety of British Columbia's Premier W. A. C. Bennett that Manitoba and Saskatchewan might be insufficiently militant in defending western interests.

In 1971 only Quebec opposed the Victoria Charter, but when discussion of it was renewed five years later, the premiers of Alberta and British Columbia each demanded a veto for his province. This reflected a conviction that the new centres of economic power should be equal in status to Ontario or Quebec, although in Alberta's case it was also partly based on anxiety lest the other provinces unite to deprive Alberta of its control over energy resources. Prime Minister Trudeau threatened to "repatriate" the constitution unilaterally, but it was soon apparent that he had no serious intention of doing so. For the foreseeable future (assuming the federation survives at all) the defacto situation will remain as it has been since 1949. Parliament can unilaterally amend those sections of the BNA Act pertaining to the institutions of central government, apart from the five-year rule and the requirement that there be an annual session of Parliament. Other amendments, including any related to the division of powers, require the participation of Westminster and will not be made without the unanimous approval of the provincial governments.

Certain conclusions emerge from the history of efforts to devise a formula for amending the BNA Act. The most obvious is the unequal power and status of the provinces, and particularly the special position of the two largest. In one way or another this primordial fact of Canadian life has been recognized in all the efforts to devise a formula, most obviously in the Victoria Charter. The fact that British Columbia and Alberta are beginning to assert claims to a similar privileged status, which they did not do in the past, also suggests how intimately constitutional discussions are related to the realities of economic and political power.

A second conclusion to be drawn from these events is the declining power and legitimacy of the federal level of government. In the 1930s those who argued for constitutional change usually thought in terms of transferring legislative powers from the provincial to the federal level, and it was politically possible to contemplate a formula that would make this relatively easy to do. In 1949 the federal government was still strong enough to assert a unilateral right to amend most of the constitution, including some of the most cherished provincial guarantees. Since that time each succeeding formula has restricted the scope of unilateral federal action more narrowly than its predecessor. Yet amendment proposals have not become more rigid as regards the division of powers. Significantly, it is now Quebec and Ontario, rather than Saskatchewan, that call for greater "flexibility" in this part of the amending formula.

This suggests a less obvious conclusion about the real implications of "rigidity" and "flexibility", and indeed about the underlying motivation behind the search for a formula itself. Students of federalism, whatever their personal preferences, tend to assume that a more flexible constitution is more conducive to centralization, and should thus be preferred by those who wish to strengthen the forces of national unification. In Canada since 1963 the reverse is arguably true, both because the formal constitution is actually more centralized than the informal reality (unlike most other federal constitutions) and because political and economic pressures are predominantly in a centrifugal direction. Paradoxical as it may seem, a centralist in Canada should support the rule of unanimity, since it permits the least-adventurous provincial government to prevent the formal transfer of additional powers to other provincial governments.

If this is so, why seek a new amendment formula at all? "Repatriation" is an obvious red herring, since Westminster presents no obstacle in practice to anything that Canadians might wish to do. The real reason why so many politicians want a new formula is to escape from the convention of unanimity, and their reason for wishing to do so is precisely the fact noted above: the convention is an obstacle to the desire of the larger and richer provincial governments to be formally endowed with greater powers. A new formula of the kind contained in the Victoria Charter would serve their purposes much better. By denying a veto to the small provinces it would facilitate amendments that would weaken the central government. On the other hand by giving a veto to the large provinces it would prevent amendments that would strengthen the central government. The stage would be set for an indefinite process of decentralization.

In the light of this analysis it may seem strange that the government of Quebec prevented adoption of both the Favreau formula and the Victoria Charter. But its reasons for doing so must be examined. The Favreau formula was rejected because it gave the smaller provinces a veto over permanent changes in the distribution of legislative powers. The provision for delegation of federal powers, although tempting, was not considered quite reliable enough to be a substitute for an easier procedure of amendment. The Victoria Charter went further in the direction of Quebec's demands, by permitting the federal government to surrender its powers even if Manitoba, Saskatchewan, and two Atlantic provinces were opposed.

Quebec rejected that formula not on its merits but because it was still not satisfied; it wanted a simultaneous transfer of legislative powers over what it called "social policy". Whether this too will ultimately be granted remains to be seen.

Finally, and perhaps most importantly, some fundamental characteristics of Canadian political life are revealed by the extent to which concern for the "rights" of various governments has excluded any preoccupation with democracy or with a widening of participation in the process of constitutional change. The consent of "the provinces" to constitutional amendments has always in practice meant no more than the consent of the provincial cabinets, meaning that fundamental decisions about the nature of the Canadian state are entrusted to no more than a few hundred people. Admittedly the various formulas have all tried to improve on this situation by proposing that the provincial legislatures, rather than the cabinets alone, would have to give their approval. However, the tight control of the legislature by the cabinet under our system of government would make this only a slight improvement, leaving us with a formula still far less conducive to wider participation than is the approval of amendments by state legislatures in the United States.

The limits of Canadian democracy were revealed even more strikingly by the provincial response to a federal suggestion, in August 1978, that referenda might be used as an alternative to approval by provincial legislatures, or in certain circumstances by Parliament, in amending the constitution under a new "formula". If the Prime Minister had been caught spitting in church the hullabaloo from provincial politicians and the news media could scarcely have been louder, notwithstanding the fact that constitutional referenda have been used in Australia since its inception and have rarely, if ever, approved any amendment not desired by the governments of the individual Australian states. Possibly Canadian provincial politicians fear — and with good reason — that the voters are less obsessed with the virtues of provincial autonomy than their own rhetoric would lead one to believe. It is surely remarkable, however, that while one provincial government proposes to break up the federation on the basis of a referendum confined to its own province, both that provincial government and others besides consider it illegitimate and subversive to amend the constitution on the basis of a referendum in which all Canadians would be able to participate. The weakness of democratic ideals in Canada and the weakness of national unity both have deep roots in our history, and both are closely related to our national obsessions with regionalism and provincial autonomy.

CONSTITUTIONAL REVIEW

Canada is probably unique among federations in that the procedures of constitutional amendment have been the subject of more discussion and controversy than the substantive content. Yet concern for the latter has not been absent, and implicit assumptions about the kinds of amendment that are desirable can usually be discovered lurking behind the procedural discussions. At times of crisis or breakdown they have emerged in demands for wide-ranging constitutional review. Thus in the 1930s changes were desired that would extend the legislative powers of Parliament; those who wished to do so were emboldened by the evident inability of the provincial governments to respond to the consequences of the depression, and the loss of legitimacy and power that they suffered as a result. It was these types of change, some of which would soon afterwards be proposed by the Rowell–Sirois Commission, that provided the incentive to seek an amending formula in 1935–36.

In the last two decades, as already suggested, the most powerful and effective demands for substantive changes have come from those who wish to extend the powers of the provincial legislatures at Parliament's expense, and the discussions of procedures for amending the constitution have again been shaped by the prevailing set of demands, even if this fact is not fully apparent to the general public. Yet once again, as in the 1930s, the demand for substantive change has emerged into the open. Since 1965 there have been a number of efforts and initiatives by federal and provincial governments in the direction of constitutional "review", and even demands for a completely new constitution.

Although most of the impetus for formal constitutional change has come directly or indirectly from Quebec, other provinces have contributed significantly to it. One of the first government-sponsored bodies to be spawned by the current round of constitutional review was in fact the Ontario Advisory Committee on Confederation, established by the government of John Robarts in January 1965. Both the establishment of this committee and the related decision to revive the historic alliance between the governments of the two central provinces were the outcome of Ontario's resentment at the federal government's penchant for launching expensive health and welfare programs and for occupying tax room that Ontario wished to occupy itself. By 1965 the time seemed ripe to apply some pressure in the hope that these tendencies could be abated.

Jean Lesage and his colleagues, on the other hand, had their own more effective ways of influencing the federal government. The results were to be seen in the concessions made with regard to "opting out", youth allowances, student loans, and the Quebec Pension Plan. Formal constitutional change was not a high priority, as long as concessions could be won within the existing legal framework. The re-writing of the formal constitution would be more likely to proceed in the desired direction if it were postponed until after the substance of provincial power had already been achieved, and after anglophone opinion had been softened up to accept a drastic weakening of the central government.

None the less, by 1965 a considerable sector of articulate opinion in Quebec was too impatient to await the results of this strategy. Nationalism has been rising in the province for at least a decade, and some inhibitions had doubtless been removed in 1961 when a former federal civil servant, Marcel Chaput, published his book *Pourquoi je suis séparatiste.*[6] Nationalist parties and pressure groups began to proliferate, each with its own preferred plan to enlarge Quebec's freedom of action and symbolic sovereignty while minimizing the economic consequences of doing so. Their impatience permeated some sectors of the provincial bureaucracy, the Liberal party, and even the cabinet.

Quebec's interest in constitutional change, in fact, extended beyond the traditional *petit-bourgeois* nationalist milieu. One of its early expressions was a book, and a proposed constitution, jointly authored by two leading Montreal businessmen: the President of the Canadian Pulp and Paper Association, Robert M. Fowler, and the ultra-reactionary financier Marcel Faribault, who was later to serve as an advisor to Daniel Johnson and as Robert Stanfield's "Quebec lieutenant" in 1968.[7] The dust jacket of their book proudly stated that one author was a Presbyterian and the other a Roman Catholic, a circumstance that might have had some bearing on constitutional controversy during the protectorate of Oliver Cromwell but was of rather questionable significance in 1965. Although it did contain a remarkable number of sections dealing with religious matters, their constitution was chiefly notable for the extensive powers given to the provincial governments. They were to have all powers not explicitly assigned to the federal government, which was declared to exist only at their volition. They could appoint their own lieutenant-governors, control offshore mineral resources, and sign treaties with foreign states. Federal powers over interprovincial trade and transportation were to be drastically reduced. The most bizarre provision was that all federal Crown corporations, except for a few of a "supervisory" character, must be liquidated within two years after the constitution came into force.

In the same year the leader of the Union Nationale, Daniel Johnson, published a book entitled *Egalité ou Indépendance,* the timing of which was largely occasioned by its author's intense opposition to the Fulton-Favreau formula.[8] Johnson also demanded a new constitution, although he was far less explicit in outlining its terms than Faribault and Fowler. He said that Quebec must be recognized as a national state, and Canada must be a bi-national state if it were to include Quebec, but neither then nor later did he indicate how these two principles could be compatible with one another or what would happen to the governments of the other provinces if both were incorporated in a new constitution.

Johnson's accession to the Premier's office in 1966 ended the Lesage strategy of winning piecemeal concessions, partly because of his own preference for a new constitution and partly because the federal government was less prepared to make concessions now that it was dealing with a political opponent. The provincial throne speech at the end of the year called for a new constitutional order in terms that were no surprise to readers of *Egalité ou Indépendance.*

The Ontario government had meanwhile been moving in a somewhat similar direction. In the autumn of 1966, following the disappointing results of the federal-provincial fiscal negotiations, the decision was reached to hold an interprovincial conference on the constitution, partly to put pressure on the federal government and partly as a means of forming a closer relationship with Daniel Johnson.[9] Although Johnson's vision of a bi-national Canada might appear to leave little obvious *raison d'être* for the government of Ontario, the short-term tactical objectives of the two central provinces were, as usual essentially the same. The proposed conference would underline this fact, and the Ontario throne speech in January 1967 announced that it would be held towards the end of the year.

This news was decidely unwelcome to the federal government, which professed to see little need for constitutional change, and no need at all for a conference hosted by John Robarts. None the less, the Department of Justice, now headed by Pierre Elliott Trudeau, established a constitutional task force in May, and in July Prime Minister Pearson privately proposed to the premiers that he too might hold a conference on the constitution, although not before the end of the year. For the moment he had clearly been outmanoeuvred by Robarts, whose conference had been several months in preparation. A long-awaited media event with even more disquieting implications occurred in November when a gathering of traditional French-Canadian elites, picturesquely although somewhat absurdly styling themselves the Estates General of French Canada, adopted a resolution which declared the province of Quebec to be the homeland of the French-Canadian nation and as such to have the right of "self-determination". The resolution was moved by the nationalist patriarch François-Albert Angers, previously known for his interminable campaign to establish a corporate state on the model of Italian fascism and for his battles against conscription, family allowances, Keynesian economics, and a host of other bugbears.

The Ontario spectacle, which had been hopefully dubbed the "Confederation of Tomorrow" conference, assembled in the last week of November, and was featured on the Canadian cover of *Time* magazine. The circumstances and much of the rhetoric irresistibly recalled the Interprovincial Conference of 1887, although Mowat and Mercier might have been rather ill at ease amid the glittering ambience of the then brand-new Toronto-Dominion Centre, from whose towers, on a clear day, one can see almost as far as Buffalo. Premier Bennett, like his predecessor in 1887, sent his regrets, but all the other premiers participated with varying degrees of enthusiasm. Probably none of them remembered the famous opening words of Marx's *The Eighteenth Brumaire of Louis Bonaparte:* "Hegel remarks somewhere that all the great events and characters of world history occur, so to speak, twice. He forgot to add: the first time as tragedy, the second as farce."[10]

But farce or not, the conference could not be dismissed by Lester Pearson with the same casual disdain that John A. Macdonald had bestowed on its predecessor. The two central provinces were in a strong bargaining position. Both had experienced rapid economic growth in the 1960s, largely on the basis of accelerating integration with the United States, and had reinforced their advantage over the outlying regions of Canada. They possessed a powerful bargaining tool in the shape of the federal Progressive Conservative party, which had recently dismissed John Diefenbaker and appeared to be transforming itself into an instrument of provincial purposes, even to the point that its ruling oligarchy was persuaded by Marcel Faribault to endorse the somewhat ambiguous doctrine of "deux nations".

The federal government's response, largely the work of Minister of Justice Pierre Elliott Trudeau, was to agree that the constitution should be changed but to propose that the entrenchment of a bill of rights, stronger language guarantees, and the reform of central institutions like the Senate and the Supreme Court should be given priority over changes in the allocation of legislative powers, even though the latter were not ruled out at some future date. These basic themes were presented in a white paper, *Federalism for the Future,* which appeared early in the new year. Although published under Pearson's name it revealed the handiwork of the Minister of Justice in such lines as "the division of powers between orders of government should be guided by principles of functionalism, and not by ethnic considerations."[11] No mention was made of repatriation or an amendment formula.

This document was inconclusively discussed at the first session of the federal-provincial Constitutional Conference in February 1968. Most of the premiers were predictably opposed to a bill of rights, a fact which reflected both their deeply rooted suspicion of the Supreme Court and their determination to protect the "property and civil rights" clause of the BNA Act. Federal effrontery in introducing such a subversive and American idea into constitutional discussion was denounced most vigorously, if implausibly, by premiers notorious for their encouragement of American direct investment. The hinterland provinces, of which only British Columbia had much cause for satisfaction in its economic circumstances, were more interested in discussing economic grievances than constitutional change, which they rightly suspected would reinforce the predominance of Quebec and Ontario at their expense.

At the second session a year later the federal government, now headed by Trudeau, unveiled its plans in more detail. The white paper entitled *The Constitution and the People of Canada* contained little that was striking, apart from a proposal that the Senate should be partly selected by the provincial governments and should be able to veto certain appointments, particularly appointments to the Supreme Court. Other papers that followed soon afterwards dealt with taxing powers, conditional grants, and social services. Federal enthusiasm for the constitutional review process appeared to have increased considerably during 1968, a reflection of the belief that the federal government's bargaining position had been improved by its fresh electoral mandate and by the death of Daniel Johnson, who was replaced by the less experienced and less militant Jean-Jacques Bertrand.[12] However, the Prime Minister was unable to stimulate any interest in a bill of rights or to prevent a rather heated discussion of fiscal matters that occupied much of the conference. The third meeting in December 1969 revealed little more progress towards agreement, despite the intensive work by both federal and provincial officials during the intervals between the public sessions.

The televising of the three main sessions, following a

precedent established by the Confederation of Tomorrow conference, had possibly provided some political benefits to federal politicians, but its chief effect had been to publicize intergovernmental and interprovincial differences and conflicts, both real and imaginary. Despite fashionable slogans about participatory democracy, the people of Canada were left in their accustomed role as political spectators rather than participants. In 1970, however, they were offered a somewhat more meaningful chance to participate by the formation of a parliamentary committee on the constitution, a move which the government had previously resisted. The committee held public sessions at forty-seven locations, from Inuvik to St. John's, many of which provided real opportunities for the expression of grass-roots opinion. (A notable exception was the session in Ottawa, where the mayor of the city read aloud from a tedious brief for half an hour before he was forced to desist by the boos and hisses of his constituents. He did not run for re-election.)

The committee finally produced a report in 1972, although by that time the collapse of the Constitutional Conference following Quebec's rejection of the Victoria Charter had made it somewhat anticlimactic.[13] The report endorsed the idea of a new constitution, but its proposals were actually not much different in substance from the existing constitution, suggesting possibly that the general public was less convinced of the need for drastic change than many politicians and other prominent persons. Insofar as changes were proposed, the committee mainly called for a return to the original intentions of the BNA Act by assigning most accumulation functions to the federal government and leaving the provinces with mainly "social" and "cultural" responsibilities. However defensible in theory, this was a somewhat unrealistic suggestion. The committee's lack of attention to economic, as opposed to cultural, cleavages partly reflected the fact that it had been bombarded with briefs from ethnic and cultural organizations but had received very few from organized farmers, business, or trade unions. It was also in part a result of the composition of the committee itself, which had only three (out of thirty-two) members from the provinces west of Manitoba and none from Nova Scotia or Newfoundland.

The establishment of the parliamentary committee was not regarded as a substitute for the work of the Constitutional Conference, since Ottawa was committed to the view that constitutional change could only come through intergovernmental agreement. Little was heard from the Constitutional Conference in 1970, but by early 1971 agreement seemed to be near on the package of amendments that came to be known as the Victoria Charter. Apart from the amendment formula which has already been referred to, this contained a number of substantive provisions. It opened with a list of entrenched "political rights" which incorporated, and extended to the provincial level, the familiar provisions for an annual session of Parliament and a dissolution at least every five years. A second part dealing with "language rights" entrenched bilingualism at the federal level and at the provincial level in all but the three most westerly provinces. The Charter also included a commitment to remove regional disparities and a requirement that there be a federal-provincial conference at least annually.

Almost one third of the Charter was devoted to the Supreme Court. There was to be a new and more complex procedure for appointments, whereby the Minister of Justice would be required to seek the agreement of the Attorney General of the province from which an appointment was made. If they could not agree, they were to establish a "nominating council" consisting either of themselves and a mutually selected chairman, or else consisting of themselves and the attorneys general of all the other provinces. This council would make the final selection from a list of at least three nominees submitted by the Minister of Justice. Another provision related to the Supreme Court was a requirement that judges belonging to the Quebec bar be a majority of the bench in any case involving an interpretation of the Quebec civil code, and that this result be achieved, if necessary, by appointing ad-hoc judges.

In contrast to the heavy emphasis on the Supreme Court, the Charter contained no mention of the federal government's earlier plans to reform the Senate. Predictably, it also said little about the division of powers; the only change would be the addition of family, youth, and occupational training allowances to Section 94A of the BNA Act, the section which now provides for shared jurisdiction over pensions with provincial paramountcy. This change was not enough to satisfy Quebec's opposition parties, nationalist pressure groups, and intellectual elites, including Claude Ryan of *Le Devoir*. Repeating their earlier performance in response to the Fulton-Favreau formula, they forced Premier Bourassa to reject the Charter. By doing so, they temporarily ended the federal government's enthusiasm for constitutional review. The Constitutional Conference was wound up and the secretariat that had served it was disbanded.

In the spring of 1975, however, the persistent federal government re-opened negotiations with Quebec. The result was a revised version of the Victoria Charter which declared that "preservation and the full development of the French language and the culture based on it" was a fundamental purpose of Canadian federalism. More concretely, although more obscurely, it also provided that the federal government and any province or provinces could enter into agreements concerning "the manner of exercise" of their powers in relation to such matters as immigration, communications, and social policy. This would be done "especially in order to reduce the possibility of action that could adversely affect the preservation and development in Canada of the French language and the culture based on it."[14] Beneath the tortured prose there lurked the spectre of unilateral delegation of powers, and indeed of "special status for Quebec", a term long banished from polite conversation in official Ottawa.

Yet Quebec failed to rise to the bait, despite an empty threat from the Prime Minister that he might "repatriate" the BNA Act on the basis of less than unanimous intergovernmental agreement if unanimity could not be achieved. Moreover, the new economic power of the western provinces had added another factor to the equation. Both British Columbia and Alberta demanded a veto over at least certain types of amendment. Meeting in Alberta in August 1976, the ten provincial premiers agreed unanimously to a long list of demands for additional powers, some of which reflected Quebec's preoccupations and others those of the West. In the former category were references to culture, communications, and immigration. Western concerns were shown in demands for strengthened jurisdiction over resource taxation, for a provincial veto over the use of the federal power to declare "works . . . for the general advantage of Canada", and for "any amending formula consensus" to apply to the creation of new provinces.[15]

Alberta feared that the declaratory power might be used to assume jurisdiction over the petroleum industry, even though Alberta's ownership of the resources and its power to collect royalties would not be affected by such a move. British Columbia wanted a veto over the attainment of provincial status by the Yukon territory, possibly as a means to facilitate absorbing the territory itself on some future occasion. Although Manitoba and Prince Edward Island subsequently assured the federal government that they would not make their agreement on "repatriation" conditional on the satisfaction of these demands, the four largest provinces at least were determined to do so. Thus another stalemate had been reached even before the separatist victory in the Quebec election of November 1976.

That event terminated the second attempt at constitutional review, but almost immediately launched a third one, which was apparently predicated on the assumption that the separatist government could more easily be defeated in its own referendum if a "third option" of reformed federalism were made available. Another objective was probably to isolate the Quebec government by agreeing to as many as possible of the demands of the other provincial governments. A new working group to draft constitutional proposals was established under the direction of a former deputy minister of Justice. Simultaneously, and perhaps redundantly, a Task Force on National Unity was formed under the joint chairmanship of Jean-Luc Pépin and John Robarts, who retraced the transcontinental path followed by the parliamentary committee almost seven years previously. Robarts had retired as Premier of Ontario in 1971, but his mysterious reputation as an architect of national unity, like the smile of Lewis Carroll's Cheshire cat, had lingered on inexplicably after his departure. Early reports of the task force's travels did not, however, suggest that two personages so closely associated with central-Canadian big business, and with the politics of the Pearson era, would find a formula to solve the riddle of national unity in the 1980s. What the task force would propose was unknown at the time of writing, but the background of the two co-chairmen suggested that something similar to the Faribault and Fowler proposals of 1965 was a not unlikely prognosis.

The in-house constitutional review was destined to bear fruit more quickly, although not necessarily with more beneficial results. In June 1978 the government released a document entitled *A Time For Action: Toward the Renewal of the Canadian Federation,* which was advertised as a white paper but contained a remarkable scarcity of specific proposals. It began with lengthy excerpts from the correspondence of Intendant Jean Talon, who was said to have been concerned, although not unduly so, about national unity back in 1667. The remainder of the document was filled with odes to the beauty of the northern landscape, national purpose, racial tolerance, multiculturalism *et al.*: in general an unconscious parody of the most sterile and shallow variety of Canadian nationalism, dressed up in the sort of language a Toronto advertising agency might have employed to promote the latest brand of low-calorie beer. Among the many questions left unanswered by *A Time For Action* was how a man as genuinely eloquent as Pierre Trudeau could have allowed his name to appear on such a ghost-written monstrosity.

Despite its absence of detail in other respects, the white paper did reveal what was said to be the government's timetable for this latest attempt to revise the constitution. Changes to those portions of the BNA Act and other constitutional documents which Parliament could (since 1949) amend by itself should be completed by July 1, 1979. This was described as Phase One. Phase Two would cover "those matters which require joint action by federal and provincial authorities", presumably meaning the division of legislative powers, and "repatriation". This was to be completed by July 1, 1981, which, it was noted, corresponded more or less with the fiftieth anniversary of the Statute of Westminster.

A week after tabling the white paper, the government introduced legislation to implement Phase One. After an interval of another week the parliamentary committee on the constitution was re-established on the motion of the Prime Minister. It seemed none the less that the deadline for Phase

One would be difficult to achieve, in view of the fact that a general election would have to take place beforehand.

The government's legislation, Bill C-60, revived some of the ideas it had first suggested to the Constitutional Conference between 1968 and 1971, such as provincial appointment of half the members of the upper house and involvement of provincial attorneys general in appointments to the Supreme Court of Canada. An entrenched charter of rights, including language rights, was again proposed, with the unusual proviso that individual provinces could "opt in" to the charter individually at times of their own choosing. As an incentive for them to do so it was provided that the powers of disallowance and reservation would no longer apply to provinces that had opted in.

This was not the only respect in which Bill C-60 broke new ground. The number of justices on the Supreme Court would be increased to eleven, with four from Quebec and guaranteed representation for each of the other main "regions". The Senate, re-named the House of the Federation, would have only the power to delay most kinds of legislation, but with respect to matters of "special linguistic significance" it could be overruled only by a two-thirds majority of the House of Commons. Furthermore, such matters would be voted upon in the upper house according to a "double majority" formula, requiring concurrence by a majority of both anglophone and francophone members.

Although it contained some valuable suggestions, the government's latest proposal for a new constitution reflected in some ways a remarkable insensitivity to the concerns of the provincial governments, and even of the general public. Section 109 of the BNA Act, guaranteeing provincial ownership of mineral resources, was omitted, an almost unbelievable oversight, if not worse. The proposed charter of rights would invalidate not only Quebec's language legislation, but also Saskatchewan and Prince Edward Island legislation restricting non-resident ownership of land. There were at least symbolic changes in the respective roles of the Queen and the Governor General, unattractive new names were conferred on familiar institutions like the Senate and the Privy Council, and a few of the other provisions were simply inexplicable and bizarre.

Predictably, although regrettably, the provincial premiers issued a unanimous communiqué rejecting the contents of the bill, as well as the unilateral method of its introduction, after their annual conference in August 1978. The circumstances did not augur well for the success of Phase Two, which would require provincial concurrence.

At the time of writing, then, the story of constitutional review must be left in its usual state: unfinished. Whether any conclusion will in fact be reached is a question distinct from, and obviously subordinate to, the more fundamental and equally uncertain question of whether the Canadian federal state will survive at all. Some aspects of that question will be examined in the concluding chapter.

NOTES

1. See Chapter 3, note 8.
2. "The special nature of Canadian Federalism", in F. R. Scott, *Essays on the Constitution: Aspects of Canadian Law and Politics* (Toronto: University of Toronto Press, 1977), at p. 189.
3. Alexander Brady, *Democracy in the Dominions,* 3rd ed. (Toronto: University of Toronto Press, 1958), pp. 59–60.
4. The early history of constitutional amendment is outlined in Paul Gérin-Lajoie, *Constitutional Amendment in Canada* (Toronto: University of Toronto Press, 1950), and, more briefly, in Guy Favreau, *The Amendment of the Constitution of Canada* (Ottawa: Queen's Printer, 1965). The latter includes both the Fulton and the Fulton–Favreau formula.
5. Favreau, *Amendment of the Constitution of Canada,* p. 22.
6. Marcel Chaput, *Pourquoi je suis séparatiste* (Montréal: Editions du Jour, 1961).
7. Robert M. Fowler and Marcel Faribault, *Ten to One: The Confederation Wager* (Toronto: McClelland and Stewart, 1965).
8. Daniel Johnson, *Égalité ou Indépendance* (Montréal: Les Editions de l'homme, 1965).
9. Richard Simeon, *Federal-Provincial Diplomacy: The Making of Recent Policy in Canada* (Toronto: University of Toronto Press, 1972), p. 91.
10. Karl Marx, *Political Writings,* Volume II, *Surveys from Exile,* ed. David Fernbach (New York: Random House, 1973), p. 146.
11. Lester B. Pearson, *Federalism for the Future* (Ottawa: Queen's Printer, 1968), p. 36.
12. Simeon, *Federal-Provincial Diplomacy,* pp. 103–04.

13. The Special Joint Committee of the Senate and the House of Commons on the Constitution of Canada, *Final Report* (Ottawa: Queen's Printer, 1972).

14. Quoted in John Saywell, ed., *Canadian Annual Review of Politics and Public Affairs 1976* (Toronto: University of Toronto Press, 1977), p. 43.

15. Quoted in Saywell, *Canadian Annual Review of Politics and Public Affairs 1976,* pp. 46–48.

10   The Prospects of Canadian Federalism

Only twenty years have elapsed since A. R. M. Lower and F. R. Scott published their book, *Evolving Canadian Federalism.* Contributors to that volume portrayed Canadian federalism as a stable and successful system that was evolving gradually and inevitably towards greater unity. Yet today even the title of their book has a quaint sound, contrasting with such recent efforts as *Canada in Question, Must Canada Fail?, Canada and the Burden of Unity,* or *Divided Loyalties.* The existence in Quebec of a provincial government dedicated to separatism is the most striking, but by no means the only, indication of general malaise. The numbness of the federalist response to that phenomenon is in some ways even more discouraging. Even among self-styled federalists there are some who would reduce the federal government's powers so drastically as to leave it more nearly resembling an intergovernmental organization than a modern state.[1] Public opinion polls consistently rank "national unity" far down the list of important issues. A student conference in the autumn of 1977 found support for national unity so weak among its participants that it concluded: "The only challenge to the supremacy of regionalism is provincialism."[2]

What has happened in twenty years to produce this situation? Why does Canada, after well over a century of reasonably successful existence, appear so fragile, so lacking in sustained support from either masses or elites, so lacking in permanence? What, if anything, can be done about it?

Donald Smiley referred several years ago to the "compounded crisis" of Canadian federalism, and the phrase seems even more apt today than when he coined it. Smiley was referring to the interlocking relationships among three problems, each of which, in his words, has "a jurisdictional-territorial dimension".[3] The problems are the relationship between the anglophone and francophone communities, the relationship between central Canada and its western and eastern hinterlands, and the relationship between Canada and the United States. A recent analysis of the political views expressed in the Confederation Debates of 1865 has suggested that these three problems preoccupied Canadians even at that time, and that their importance was recognized both by supporters and by opponents of the BNA Act.[4] The serious difficulties faced by Canadian federalism in recent years are the result of changes that have occurred in the nature of all three sets of relationships. A change in any one of the three, had it occurred in isolation, could probably have been handled with little difficulty. Unfortunately for Canadian federalism, the three sets of changes have coincided, but they are related in such a way that efforts to resolve one problem may exacerbate the others.

Readers who have persevered this far in the present volume will have noted references to all three problems throughout the various chapters, for their influence on Canadian federalism is such that hardly any aspect of the subject can be discussed without reference to them. To deal exhaustively with any one of the problems would require a book in itself. This concluding chapter will merely outline some of the recent changes that have upset the balance of Canadian federalism and will discuss the challenge with which those changes confront Canadians who wish to preserve the unity of their country.

ENGLISH AND FRENCH

Ethnic conflict, of which the English–French conflict in Canada is one example has no logical or necessary connection with federalism. In some federations, such as the Federal Republic of Germany or Australia, it is insignificant. On the other hand, it is of major importance in a number of non-federal countries. One could cite for example the conflicts between the Flemings and the Walloons in Belgium, between Greeks and Turks in Cyprus, between Jews and Arabs in Israel, or between "Catholics" and "Protestants" in Northern Ireland.[5] Federalism has often been recommended as a solution to conflicts of this kind, particularly where each group has a geographically distinct sphere of influence, but it is not universally regarded as an appropriate solution. Its most obvious defect, fully demonstrated by Canadian experience, lies in the fact that it is almost always impossible to draw provincial boundaries that correspond exactly with cultural ones. As a result ethnic conflict will continue to exist in microcosm within the provinces, as it does in both Quebec and Ontario.

Although a great deal of racist mythology argues the contrary, there is nothing in "human nature" or in the characteristics of particular ethnic groups that makes this conflict inevitable. Its source is almost always to be found in a particular economic division of labour among the ethnic groups or an inequitable distribution of economic benefits, frequently, although not always, reinforced by the discriminatory policies of a state that has become an instrument in the hands of a single ethnic community.

In the Canadian case, English–French conflict became partially identified at a fairly early stage with federal-provincial conflict, as discussed in Chapter 3. However, French Canada has never been completely synonymous with Quebec (although Quebec separatists and some of their English-speaking sympathizers would like to make it so), and there has been important English–French conflict within Quebec and within certain of the other provinces.

The adoption of a federal constitution in 1867 did not end the underlying causes of English–French conflict, but it did provide a framework within which the conflict could be managed with considerable success. In recent years, however, important and rather complex changes have occurred in the distribution of power between the two language groups both within Quebec and in Canada as a whole. These changes have contributed to the present crisis of Canadian federalism.

As was suggested in Chapter 4, recent developments have tended to increase the power of the French-speaking *petite bourgeoisie* in relation to the English-speaking minority within Quebec. At the same time the relative weight of the French-speaking community in relation to the English-speaking community of Canada as a whole has declined. One effect of both these trends is that both English and French are increasingly likely to regard Quebec and French Canada as synonymous. Recognizing this danger, the Trudeau government has sought to reverse or at least slow down both trends, particularly the second, but there are obviously limits to the impact of action by the state on socio-economic developments.

Within Quebec the power of the English-speaking community has traditionally been based on its control over the commanding heights of the provincial economy and on the importance of Montreal as a national and not merely provincial metropolis. The first has been challenged by the increasing role of American and European, not to mention French-Canadian, capital, while the second has been greatly lessened by the rise of Toronto, itself largely a result of economic integration with the United States. "The Commercial Empire of the St. Lawrence" has long vanished, and today Montreal is no more than a regional sub-metropolis comparable to Calgary or Vancouver.

More in response to the pull of economic opportunity elsewhere than to the push of political uncertainty at home, the English of Quebec have been trickling out of the province over the last few decades. While this trend was counterbalanced until very recently by the arrival of immigrants who were more likely to learn English than French, there has been a net loss of political and economic power, as suggested by the failure to prevent the adoption of increasingly restrictive language legislation by the last three provincial governments. At the same time the economic power of the French-speaking *petite bourgeoisie* within the province has been increased both by long-overdue reforms in the French-language educational system and by the increasingly effective use of the provincial state as an instrument for economic objectives.

The effect of these developments has been to place the English-speaking community of Quebec in the dangerous position of a conspicuous minority whose apparent privilege far exceeds its real power and importance. Such minorities are in danger of attack by competitors who resent their privilege while recognizing that they no longer have the real power to defend it. Alexis de Tocqueville attributed the French revolution of 1789 to the fact that the nobility found themselves in this position, and a similar analysis can explain the violent reaction against conspicuous but powerless ethnic minorities like the Asians of Uganda or the Jews of central Europe before the Second World War.[6]

When the scene shifts from Quebec to Canada as a whole, a somewhat different picture of recent developments emerges. For a long time after Confederation the relatively high birth rate of the French Canadians enabled them to maintain their share of Canada's population with astonishing consistency, despite a near-total absence of reinforcement through immigration. As late as 1941, when the census showed a slight improvement in their position, hopes (and fears) were expressed that they might eventually comprise a majority of the Canadian population. Even in 1961, after fifteen years of heavy immigration plus the annexation of Newfoundland, their share stood at 30.4 per cent, less than 1 percentage point below its level at Confederation. Despite the failure to maintain more than a feeble French-Canadian presence in the West, and despite the losses through assimilation in Ontario, the place of French within Canada appeared reasonably secure throughout this period.

Since 1961, however, the French-Canadian birth rate has declined so sharply that it is now at, or even below, the national average. Although the federal census of 1976 did not collect information on ethnic origin, perhaps wisely in view of the increasing sensitivity of the subject, its data on language usage suggest that French is losing ground. In any event the combination of low birth rates and lack of reinforcement through immigration will inevitably expose the French Canadians to a fate that overtook the Scottish and Irish Canadians at an earlier period in our history, namely a steadily declining share of the national population.

Closely related to the declining demographic weight of French Canada, and perhaps more easily measured, is the declining political weight of Quebec within the federation. This may seem an odd suggestion to those English Canadians who are convinced that Quebec is taking over the country, but long-term socio-economic trends must be distinguished from political circumstances peculiar to Mr. Trudeau's term of office, which presumably will not last forever. Since 1951 Ontario's margin of population over Quebec has increased from 542,000 to more than two million, while the West has caught up with and surpassed Quebec in terms of population, and even more decisively in terms of economic strength. Quebec's share of Canada's population was 29 per cent as recently as 1961 but will be only 26 per cent by 1981, and probably much less by the end of the century. The revival of the federal Progressive Conservative party under John Diefenbaker's leadership drew attention to the fact that a federal election could be won with minimal support from Quebec, a feat actually achieved by the party in 1957 and 1962 and one that it came very close to achieving again in 1972. The recent redistribution of seats in the House of Commons, reducing Quebec's share to an unprecedentedly low level, will make it even easier to form a government without Quebec support than in the past; in fact the Progressive Conservatives would have won the 1972 election had it been fought under the new boundaries.

The resurgence of Quebec separatism (a term no longer favoured by its adherents) is thus motivated in part by anxieties which result from declining power, mainly in relation to Canada as a whole, and in part by self-confidence and the sense of increasing power within the narrower Quebec milieu. Both in its pessimistic, defensive aspect and in its optimistic, expansionist aspect, Quebec nationalism represents the perceived self-interest of a "new middle class" or *petite bourgeoisie,* even if it seems to have gained considerable support from members of other classes, who may not thereby be acting in their own best interests. Both the *petit-bourgeois* class base and the ability to mobilize some support elsewhere are characteristic of nationalist movements through the world. In an effort to mobilize the additional support some left-wing policies may be dangled before the masses, but the fears of some unsophisticated businessmen, and the hopes of some naive radicals, that Quebec is turning to "socialism" appear to have singularly slight foundation. A study of de Valera's Ireland is more likely to provide clues as to the nature of an independent Quebec than a study of Castro's Cuba.

Although the Parti Québécois, like other Canadian political parties, includes a wide variety of views on specific issues, and although its proposal for "sovereignty-association" may represent a compromise among divergent views, it appears to have three major objectives, all of which have roots in earlier versions of Quebec nationalism.

The first objective, which many observers have viewed as the central thrust of the so-called "Quiet Revolution" in the early sixties, is to expand the number of managerial and professional jobs in Quebec available to the French-speaking *petite bourgeoisie*.[7] The "Quiet Revolution" began when it did because the number of French-speaking Quebecers qualified for such jobs increased sharply at a time when access to the best jobs in the private sector and the federal public service appeared to be largely monopolized by English-speaking Canadians. Although both the private sector and the federal government have since taken steps to remedy this problem, the slow economic growth of Quebec and the continuing expansion of its educational system have caused the shortage of opportunities to continue. Transformation of the province into a sovereign state would inevitably increase the size of its bureaucracy and would also lead to an exodus of the English-speaking Quebecers who continue to be disproportionately represented in private-sector management and the professions.

The second objective, characteristic of many nationalist movements, is to control class conflict within Quebec and make it harmless to the *petite bourgeoisie,* who would be the only real beneficiaries of "independence". Nationalism contributes to this objective by deflecting the resentment of the French-speaking working class outwards against the convenient scapegoats of "Ottawa" and *"les anglais".* As was suggested earlier in this chapter, members of the English-speaking minority of Quebec are particularly well-suited to the role of scapegoats because they are conspicuous and apparently privileged but actually powerless to defend themselves. Because the working classes of Quebec are relatively militant and class conscious, at least by North American standards, it is important for the *petit-bourgeois* nationalists to persuade them that ethnic interests are more important than class interests, and that "independence" would benefit all French-speaking Quebecers, regardless of class. An impartial observer must view this claim with extreme scepticism.

This objective, even more than the first, has long antecedents in the history of Quebec nationalism. In fact federal-provincial conflict as a sublimation of class conflict has been practised in other provinces as well, notably in British Columbia where Premier Dufferin Pattullo during the depression and Premier W. A. C. Bennett a generation later practised it with considerable success. Maurice Duplessis, whose era spanned those of Pattullo and Bennett, was also adept at using federal-provincial conflict in this way. Duplessis, to his credit, never used internal minorities as scapegoats, but some of the more extreme Quebec nationalists among his contemporaries were more unscrupulous than he was. Since the "English" were then too powerful to be openly attacked, the Jews were a more convenient scapegoat, and anti-semitism flourished in Quebec throughout the depression and war years. Today the English can be attacked with impunity, and the need for anti-semitism has declined.

The third objective of the Parti Québécois is to compensate for Quebec's declining demographic and economic weight in the Canadian federation by, in effect, giving Quebec a power of veto over Canadian economic policies. In this respect the "sovereignty-association" of René Lévesque is directly descended from the "equality or independence" of Daniel Johnson and the "associate states" proposed by the Société Saint Jean Baptiste in the 1960s. All were acutely aware, as was Robert Bourassa, of Quebec's actual and prospective decline in relation to the rest of Canada. Although the details of the relationship proposed between Quebec and the rest of Canada vary, the common premise is that Quebec should be placed on a footing of "equality" with the rest of Canada, even though it is little more than one third as large. The joint economic policies of the two entities would be decided upon in a way that would give Quebec's interests equal weight to the combined interests of all the rest of Canada. The Parti Québécois government argues that the rest of Canada would accept "association" because of Ontario's need for Quebec markets, but this assumes both that Ontario could not find other markets and that Ontario could impose its will on the eight smaller provinces. Both are very dubious assumptions.

CENTRE AND PERIPHERY

Conflict between regions resembles conflict between ethnic groups in that it too is the product of economic stresses and strains arising from a particular division of labour or an unequal distribution of benefits.[8] Few countries, apart from the very smallest, do not experience it in some degree. Federalism is perhaps better suited to the management of regional than to the management of ethnic conflict, but no more in one case than in the other can federal institutions eliminate the roots of the problem.

From one perspective — the most common one among influential Canadians in recent years — Confederation is viewed as primarily an effort to accommodate the differences between anglophones and francophones. But from another, geopolitical, perspective Confederation was the annexation of eastern, and later western, hinterlands by the Province of Canada.[9] Economic and political power after Confederation were concentrated in the old Province, now known as Ontario and Quebec. The new Dominion, which inherited the name of Canada, was shaped in the image of the old Province by those who held political and economic power. The resentment of the hinterlands in the face of these facts has been an enduring theme of Canadian history, and has inspired some of the great classics of Canadian social science. Yet while this conflict is hardly new, it has been altered and exacerbated, just as the English–French conflict has been, by recent changes in the distribution of power.

The most striking change in the Canadian political economy during the 1970s has been the growing importance of the far West: Alberta, British Columbia, the territories, and to some extent Saskatchewan. For a variety of geographic and economic reasons, the westward shift of power has proceeded less consistently and steadily in Canada than in the United States; it was temporarily reversed for a generation after 1929. In the last quarter century, however, Alberta and British Columbia have both doubled in population. The scarcity and higher price of energy resources since 1972 has given an additional impetus to western development that is almost without precedent. Canada's reserves of coal, oil, and gas are overwhelmingly concentrated in the provinces west of Manitoba, while Saskatchewan has more than half the nation's reserves of uranium, which may well become for that province what oil has been for Alberta.

The impact of these developments and the new sense of power have been particularly conspicuous in Alberta, which has both the largest share of energy resources and the liveliest tradition of political dissent and resistance to the metropolitan domination of central Canada. Yet there has been enough real and perceived impact on the two neighbouring provinces to lend some credibility to the claim by Alberta's political, economic, and adminstrative elites that they speak on behalf of "The West" when they demand a renegotiation of the federal relationship to reflect the new realities of economic power. The notion of "The West" as a region with distinct interests has a strong appeal throughout the region, although this is stronger in Alberta than elsewhere, and serves a dual purpose; it legitimizes both the ganging up of western provincial governments against Ottawa and the new economic and political demands, by associating them with the older traditions of agrarian populism and protest in the hinterland. The concept has acquired a more concrete form with the development over the last few years of mechanisms for contact and collaboration among the four western provincial governments and the adoption of common positions on a number of issues. The recent reports of the Western Premiers' Task Force on Constitutional Trends, documenting in impressive detail what are viewed as federal "intrusions" into provincial jurisdiction or federal policies unfavourable to the region's interest, have been one outcome of this increased collaboration. It is apparent that the West will have to play a major role in any renegotiation of Confederation, and its views are not likely to have much in common with those of Quebec, despite superficial similarities, since its real interests are very different.

CANADA AND THE UNITED STATES

In Central Europe during and after the First World War there was a saying to the effect that the situation in Germany was serious but not hopeless, while the situation in Austria was hopeless but not serious. Perhaps it is no coincidence that the second part of this proverb seems an uncomfortably apt description of the mood of anglophone Canadians since November 1976. Canadians are the Austrians of North America. History decreed, contrary to what might have been expected, that we would not be a part of the larger and more dynamic national entity with which most of us share a common language, but we remain vicarious participants in its affairs, uncertain whether or not we would like to participate more fully. The weakness of our sense of a separate identity is suggested by things that most Canadians take for granted: the American content in our newspapers, the American unions to which most of our organized workers belong, the fact that most retail shops accept American currency, and even the ambiguous name of the "National" Hockey League. The vocabulary and pronunciation of Canadian English are noticeably more Americanized than they were even twenty years ago, when the impact of television was just beginning to be felt. For those who have consciously or unconsciously opted to share in the continental community, concern for the prospects of the Canadian state is not likely to be serious, even if the prospects are dismissed as hopeless.

The proximity and pervasive impact of the United States, more than anything else, explains the phenomenon noted at the opening of this chapter: the fact that the long-established Canadian federal state appears so fragile, so provisional, so much "in question". That Confederation was in 1867 the only realistic alternative to eventual annexation by the United States was recognized at the time by both its supporters and many of its opponents. The corollary to that fact was that some form of closer association with the United States remained, for each province, at least a theoretical alternative to Confederation, even after Confederation was achieved. An English journalist predicted in 1881 that Canada would collapse once Ontario realized that it could be more prosperous within the

United States than by carrying single-handed the weight of the less-developed provinces.[10] Rodrigue Tremblay, Quebec's present minister of Industry and Commerce, wrote a book before he entered political life that argued in favour of a common market between an independent Quebec and the United States. More recently, the possibility of Quebec's secession has led a group of businessmen in the Atlantic provinces to suggest a "free trade zone" comprising the United States and the Atlantic provinces. The leader of the Newfoundland Liberal party has said that Quebec's secession would lead his province to seek some form of association with the United States, an option that many Newfoundlanders preferred to Confederation in 1949.[11]

The apparent success of the Canadian federal experiment buried the American alternative in the background of our collective consciousness for most of the years after 1867, aided by the economic self-interest of some Canadians and the distaste of others for American nationalism and republicanism. Yet the alternative has never entirely disappeared. Especially in the last two decades, when the economic, social, and cultural integration of Canada into the North American melting pot has increased so sharply, the Canadian federal state has lost much of its original reason for being, and hence much of its authority and legitimacy. The basic functions usually associated with central government in the modern world are military defence, the promotion of economic growth, and the maintenance of a distinctive pattern of communications, values, and "culture". Of these three functions the first two are already performed to a large extent by the U.S. government for the whole of North America, while the third is rendered increasingly futile in a Canadian context by the pervasive American presence. It is not surprising that Canada's federal government has difficulty persuading the provincial governments or the public that its duties require it to maintain its present share of tax revenues and administrative manpower, or even that it needs to exist at all. If it suddenly disappeared tomorrow, both the military defences of North America and the existing North American patterns of trade, investment, communications, and culture would survive with relatively slight modification. This fact must make the dissolution of the federal link a less unthinkable option for any Canadian province than it could ever be for an Australian state or a Swiss canton. Canada is alone among modern federations in the fact that separatism is not considered eccentric, scandalous, or unthinkable, even though most Canadians do not favour the secession either of their own province or of any other.

Only in this continental context is it possible to understand the declining authority and effectiveness of the federal state over the last two decades, the increasing self-assertiveness of the provincial states, and the rise of separatism, in one province as a serious political option and in other provinces as at least a potential one. Only in this context can one understand the curiously muted reaction, outside of Quebec, to the very real possibility that Quebec may break its legal and political ties to the rest of Canada. The American presence has contributed to the rise of separatism. It will also be decisive in determining what follows the secession of Quebec, should that occur.

THE CHALLENGE OF SEPARATISM

What would be the consequence for the rest of Canada if Quebec became independent? Most English-speaking Canadians who have expressed views on Quebec separatism since November 1976 appear to take the position that Quebec's departure would be undesirable, but that Quebec should be allowed to depart peacefully if it so decides. On the other hand, "association" after secession seems to be generally rejected, at least among political and economic elites. There appears to be a fairly widespread view, at least in Ontario, that the remaining nine provinces would continue to form a federation after Quebec's departure.

A minority of English Canadians would welcome the secession of Quebec. Their numbers are difficult to estimate, since more people probably hold this opinion in private than would express it even in the relative anonymity of the Gallup Poll. On the right are those who simply resent bilingualism, whether on cereal boxes or in the federal public service. On the left are those who regard Quebec as an oppressed "nation" and whose attitudes towards it are a curious mixture of guilt, envy, romantic sympathy, and prurient fascination. What both groups have in common is an intense dislike of the Liberal party, and they are probably correct in assuming that that party would no longer play a major role in Canadian politics after Quebec's departure.

In addition to these two types of sympathizer with Quebec separatism, a third type consists of those Canadians who would like their own province or region to become independent. At the moment these are extremely few in number, and may be easily dismissed as a lunatic fringe, but their numbers could grow very rapidly if Quebec actually did provide them with a precedent. There are reported to be at least two separatist splinter parties in western Canada, one of them headed by a former leader of the Alberta Progressive Conservative party.[12] The potential for separatism is probably even stronger in the Atlantic provinces, where psychological attachment to the Canadian nation has always been quite weak and where Canada would become geographically remote if Quebec were no longer a part of it. It should be remembered that Newfoundland joined Canada only a generation ago, and by a very narrow margin of popular support. The other Atlantic provinces have been Canadian for a longer period of time but remain in many ways cut off from the larger Canadian community.

Even assuming that the amputation of Quebec from Canada could be arranged without violence, an assumption for which the experience of other federations offers very scant support, the consequences for both Quebec and the rest of Canada are likely to be unpleasant. The most obvious losers would be the English-speaking minority in Quebec and the French-speaking minorities in other provinces, who would almost certainly have to choose between migration and the loss of their educational and linguistic rights. For the French-speaking people of Quebec there would be at best a difficult period of transition to a smaller economy and at worst a long period of stagnation which could lead to intensified class conflict and repression by the state. To replace its disrupted links with Canada, Quebec would probably have to reinforce its economic ties with the United States, a strategy that might succeed but that would promote bitter controversy between the left and right wings of the Parti Québécois. There is no reason to doubt that Quebec would be able to maintain its formal sovereignty, but the external influences on its economy and society would remain very formidable, perhaps more so than at present.

For the rest of Canada the situation might be better in some respects, but would be worse in others. Since north-south ties have so largely replaced east-west ones the disruption would be more political and psychological than economic, but this would not lessen the severity of its impact. In fact a political crisis of authority would erupt almost immediately once the desirability, or inevitability, of negotiating Quebec's independence had been conceded. Regional interests with respect to the terms of a settlement with Quebec would vary considerably, and would be vigorously expressed by the various provincial governments. The authority of the already fragile federal state would be severely weakened by the ambiguous position of ministers, parliamentarians, and civil servants who were themselves from Quebec. If they resigned voluntarily or were forced to do so, they would severely weaken the effectiveness of the federal state, but if they remained in office they would have no credibility as spokesmen for "English Canada".

With the federal government in disarray, the resulting vacuum of authority would almost inevitably be filled by the various provincial governments, which would either negotiate directly with Quebec, and with one another, or bring divergent pressures to bear on the already weakened federal regime. Having conceded the right to independence of one province, Ottawa could scarcely argue that others had no right to defend their own interests in this fashion. As a result each province would be in practice free to make its own arrangements with Quebec, with other provinces, and with the United States. Deprived of real authority or purpose, the federal state would simply disintegrate, like the Austro-Hungarian Empire in 1918.

The subsequent fate of the newly independent provinces is difficult to foresee. Provincial identity and sense of community might be strengthened by the collapse of the federation, but would be unlikely to attain the level in any English-speaking province, with the possible exception of Newfoundland, that it has already attained in Quebec. Attempts might be made to form a new federation, or possibly more than one, but the alternative of closer association with the United States would inevitably be considered in each province. The collapse of the federal authority would have particularly awkward consequences in the Yukon and the Northwest Territories, and American military intervention there would be a real possibility, perhaps even at the request of the local white population. On the other hand the threat of such intervention might be the catalyst required to bring about a new federation of at least the four western provinces, if not others. Whether such a federation would have a good claim to the territories in international law, or could establish its authority over the native population without American assistance, are questions not easily answered.

All that can be said with certainty about the aftermath of Quebec's departure from Canada is that nothing can be said with certainty. Measured against such a prospect, even the frustrations of the status quo must appear at least relatively appealing to all but the minority of committed separatists. Can the crisis of Canadian federalism, already far advanced, be overcome before the disintegration outlined above becomes the only alternative to the use of force against secession on the American or Nigerian model? No definite answer is possible in advance of the verdict of history, which becomes "inevitable" only after it has taken place. The search for alternatives must be pursued, whatever the odds against success. At the same time we must assess the alternatives in relation to the three dimensions of the compounded crisis of Canadian federalism. The concluding section of this book attempts to do so.

PROBLEMS AND SOLUTIONS

One could summarize the Canadian quandary by observing that we have a geopolitical problem similar to that of Australia, superimposed over an ethnic problem similar to that of Belgium or Northern Ireland, combined with a problem of maintaining national identity in the face of insidious pressures from a more powerful neighbour to which Austria's relationship with Germany offers perhaps the only parallel. In the circumstances one could aptly say of Canadian federalism what Dr. Samuel Johnson said of the woman preaching: it is not done well; but you are surprised to find it done at all.

It is tempting to conclude that some simple remedy, such as "decentralization", would resolve all three sets of problems, but there is little evidence that supports this assumption. On the other hand it is a counsel of despair, and a recipe for disaster, to say that all efforts must be concentrated on resolving one of the problems to the exclusion of the others. Both Jacques Parizeau and James Richardson are saying, in their different ways, that Canada can only solve its centre-periphery problem by forgetting about its English-French problem. Both are equally unrealistic: Parizeau in assuming that Canada could survive without Quebec, and Richardson in assuming that Quebec could be made to accept what he proposes. Equally unrealistic are those Canadian nationalists who believe that Canada without Quebec would be able to concentrate on solving the problem of American domination.

Yet to attack all three problems simultaneously will be no easy task. The difficulty can be illustrated by the fact that recent and long-overdue efforts in the direction of bilingualism have been interpreted by many western Canadians as fresh evidence that the central government responds only to central-Canadian preoccupations. Bilingualism is perceived as a central-Canadian response to a central-Canadian problem. In a broader sense it is probably no coincidence that the party most successful in accommodating English–French conflict, the Liberal party, has witnessed since 1949 a drastic erosion of its electoral base in the eastern and western hinterlands, where it was once exceptionally strong. On the other hand it is a commonplace observation that the Progressive Conservative party has a strong base in the hinterlands but can make no headway in Quebec.

Quebec and the West are also divergent in their economic interests, a fact that has important implications for federal economic policy, for Canadian-American relations, and for constitutional reform. The West has a very rich resource base, a strong agricultural sector, a very weak manufacturing sector, and, by Canadian standards, a small service sector. Much of what it produces is exported to the United States, Japan, and a large number of other countries. Quebec, despite separatist propaganda to the contrary, is relatively poor in natural resources. Its agriculture is also underdeveloped. Its economy is mainly based on labour-intensive secondary manufacturing and a large service sector, both of them heavily bolstered for political reasons by federal subsidies, incentives, tariffs, equalization payments, and so forth. Its "exports" are mainly to Ontario. The Quebec government's reasons for wanting "association" after "independence", whether or not it really believes this would be possible, are understandable. On the other hand the few aspects of federal-government policy that Quebec nationalists do wish to retain are those for which the West pays the heaviest economic price and which it finds most offensive. Conversely, western demands for "decentralization" in the sense of more local control over resources, transportation, taxation, and commercial policy would weaken the federal government's ability to protect the interests of provinces such as Quebec, and are in fact intended to do so.

Measures to increase Canadian independence in relation to the United States may also be viewed differently in different parts of Canada.[13] Although it is no longer true, if it ever was, that Canadian economic nationalism is a phenomenon confined to Ontario, particular policies designed to promote Canadian independence may have a regionally discriminatory effect, intentional or otherwise. To take one example, the almost paranoid opposition to natural-resource exports expressed by many Ontario nationalists is obviously a reflection of provincial rather than national interests. They might stop to reflect that both the U.S.S.R. and China are major resource exporters. As another example, protecting the vulnerable English-language media and cultural institutions from American competition may appear somewhat irrelevant to French Canadians, and if the cure is a greater federal role in cultural matters it may seem worse than the disease. Yet a properly balanced strategy of promoting Canadian independence could form the basis for a new alliance between centre and periphery and between English and French, and in the long run could alleviate the conflicts between them. It is thus particularly regrettable that the federal government seems to have virtually abandoned its limited efforts in this direction since November 1976.

Constitutional changes of the sort that are likely to be considered over the next few years may also be counterproductive if they worsen one problem while attempting to solve another. Increasing French Canada's representation in institutions such as the Supreme Court, the Senate, or the federal public service may make it harder to represent the peripheral regions which have equally strong, if not stronger, reasons to be discontented with these institutions. Conversely, greater representation of the hinterland regions on regulatory agencies such as the Canadian Transport Commission (CTC) or the National Energy Board (NEB) could be damaging to Quebec's economic interests. The redistribution of legislative powers between the two orders of government raises similar problems. Centralizing economic powers and decentralizing "cultural" ones, as recommended by the Parliamentary Joint Committee on the Constitution in 1972, is a favourite proposal of many central Canadians (although not of their provincial governments) but would give western Canada, which has distinct economic interests but not distinct social and cultural ones, the worst of both worlds. Significantly, Premier Bill Bennett of British Columbia has suggested the opposite: more economic powers for the provincial governments and complete control over social welfare and related matters for the federal government.

This is not to suggest that any constitutional change would be either counterproductive or irrelevant, but only to suggest that proposed changes should be examined carefully in the light of all three dimensions of our "compounded crisis". It should also be recognized that the benefits of formal constitutional change are largely symbolic, which is not to say that they are unimportant. The problem is how symbolically to recognize both the westward shift of economic power and the desire of French Canada for "equality" with an anglophone society that will always be numerically much larger. These requirements present a challenge to would-be constitution makers.

To ensure the lasting survival of a truly united Canada — something which has arguably never in fact existed — far more than legal and symbolic changes will be necessary. The unequal relationships between the central-Canadian metropolis and its hinterlands, and between anglophone and francophone Canadians in Quebec and elsewhere, must be replaced by relationships that are more equal, not only in form but in fact. As part of this process, and not as a substitute for it, the unhealthy predominance of American capital in Canada, with its ability to exploit regional and cultural conflicts at the same time as it submerges the Canadian identity in a continental melting pot, must be brought to an end. These objectives will not be achieved overnight, if ever, but only when they have been achieved will national unity become an accomplished fact, and not a political slogan.

NOTES

1. See the proposal by William P. Irvine in Richard Simeon, ed., *Must Canada Fail?* (Montreal: McGill-Queen's University Press, 1977), pp. 169–76.
2. Patricia J. Appavoo, ed., "Alternatives Canada: A Conference Report", *Behind the Headlines,* XXXVI, no. 3 (1978): 12.
3. Donald V. Smiley, *Canada In Question, Federalism in the Seventies,* 1st ed. (Toronto: McGraw-Hill Ryerson, 1972), p. 172.
4. R. C. Nelson, R. H. Wagenburg, W. C. Soderlund, "The Political Thought of the Fathers of Confederation", Paper presented at the annual meeting of the Canadian Political Science Association, 1977.
5. The conflict in Northern Ireland is basically ethno-cultural, rather than religious, although one would never know this from reading the North American press. The Catholics are native Irish, while the Protestants are descended from English and Scottish settlers.
6. Alexis de Tocqueville, *The Old Regime and the French Revolution* (New York: Doubleday, 1955), p. 30.
7. For an analysis along these lines, see Hubert Guindon, "Social Unrest, Social Class, and Quebec's Bureaucratic Revolution", *Queen's Quarterly,* LXXXI (1964): 150–62.
8. An interesting discussion of the subject is Tom Nairn, *The Break-up of Britain: Crisis and Neo-Nationalism* (London: New Left Books, 1977).
9. An excellent collection of essays on this theme is David J. Bercuson, ed., *Canada and the Burden of Unity* (Toronto: Macmillan, 1977).
10. Henry Labouchere, quoted in John Murray Gibbon, *Steel of Empire: The Romantic History of the Canadian Pacific, The Northwest Passage of Today* (Toronto: McClelland and Stewart, 1935), p. 225.
11. Rodrigue Tremblay, *Indépendance et Marché Commun Québec–Etats-Unis* (Montréal: Editions du jour, 1970). For the

Atlantic proposal, see *The Globe and Mail,* November 11, 1977; and for Newfoundland see *The Globe and Mail,* December 21, 1977.

12. *The Globe and Mail,* February 8, 1977.
13. Garth Stevenson, "Foreign Direct Investment and the Provinces: A Study of Elite Attitudes", *Canadian Journal of Political Science,* VII (1974): 630–47.

Index